Working Class Boy

Jimmy Barnes

Working Class Boy

HarperCollins*Publishers*

HarperCollins_Publishers_

First published in Australia in 2016
by HarperCollins_Publishers_ Australia Pty Limited
ABN 36 009 913 517
harpercollins.com.au

HarperCollins_Publishers_
Level 13, 201 Elizabeth Street, Sydney NSW 2000, Australia
Unit D1, 63 Apollo Drive, Rosedale, Auckland 0632, New Zealand
A 53, Sector 57, Noida, UP, India
1 London Bridge Street, London, SE1 9GF, United Kingdom
2 Bloor Street East, 20th floor, Toronto, Ontario M4W 1A8, Canada
195 Broadway, New York NY 10007, USA

National Library of Australia Cataloguing-in-Publication data:

Barnes, Jimmy, author.
  Working class boy / Jimmy Barnes.
  978 1 4607 5213 5 (hardback)
  978 1 4607 0700 5 (ebook)
  Subjects: Barnes, Jimmy.
  Barnes, Jimmy – Childhood and youth.
  Rock musicians – Australia – Biography.
  Immigrants – Scotland – Biography.
  Family violence.
  Adelaide (S.A.) – Social conditions.
781.66092

Cover design by Matt Stanton, HarperCollins Design Studio
Front cover image: Jimmy Barnes aged four, in Glasgow. Barnes Family Collection
Back cover image: bridge © Jason Charlton
Author photo: © Stephanie Barnes
Picture section design by Daniel Valenzuela
Typeset in Bembo Std by Kirby Jones
Printed and bound in Australia by Griffin Press
The papers used by HarperCollins in the manufacture of this book are a natural,
recyclable product made from wood grown in sustainable plantation forests.
The fibre source and manufacturing processes meet recognised international
environmental standards, and carry certification.

This book is dedicated to my Jane.
Je t'aime, Je t'aimais, Je t'aimerai.

And to my beautiful children and grandchildren.

And to Snoop and Oliver who sat with me while I wrote it, occasionally looking at me and wagging their tails to encourage me.

CONTENTS

PREFACE

———————

Where do I start? How about this? This is my story. This is the way I saw things. It might not be completely accurate and it might not be the way others saw it. But this is how I saw it.

Scotland was my first home. Cowcaddens, a suburb close to the centre of Glasgow to be exact. One of the only places in the world you can get your heart broken and your jaw broken at the same time. More than just my birthplace. It holds a place in my heart like nowhere else in the world except for maybe Australia, where I grew up, learned about life. The lucky country. But I was lucky to make it through my childhood in one piece.

I love these places equally and I feel both have helped make me who I am and for that I am grateful. But I have to look at both of these places to really see why I am who I am.

Time and trauma have taken what I was born with and what I have experienced and brewed it all into what you see before you now. Some of what I have done has not been pretty to watch. Imagine what it was like to live through it.

But here I am. Still living and still learning. You've got to love life. You might not always get things right but there is always a chance to make things better if you work hard.

I spent most of my life running from my childhood and now it seems like my time to face it. This is the story of a lifetime spent running away. Running from fear. Running from shame but at the same time running from hope. I am not running anymore. This is the story of an imperfect childhood that has led to me becoming an imperfect adult. But life is not perfect. And it is short so make the best out of it you can, with the tools you are given.

My folks made mistakes – all parents do. Some mistakes were bigger than others but I don't blame them for anything. They came from worse poverty than I did. They had very little education, no help and very little hope in their lives. Life must have been overwhelming for them nearly all the time. I always feel I had luck on my side, someone looking over my shoulder, keeping an eye out for me. My mum had no one looking out for her but us kids, and we were too small to help her, no matter how much we loved her.

Every choice my parents made, every bit of pain or fear I have felt, has brought me to where I am today. I am far from perfect but I am here and I am me. I have a beautiful family and a great life and through writing this all down I feel I can finally let a lot of the past go. I don't need to hold on to it anymore. There is no blame. It's no one's fault.

I want to pass on what I have learned to my children. I know they will have to make their own choices and their own mistakes, but now I will be around to help them deal with them. Meanwhile, I want to thank my parents for bringing me into this world and my brothers and sisters for sharing so much with me. I apologise to all of them for any pain I have caused along the way.

Working Class Boy

PROLOGUE

———

Ah. Nothing. That's better. Nothing at all. No pain.
'Hey, pass that whisky back over here.'

From the moment I start to drink, I feel absolutely nothing.

When I first started taking drugs and drinking, I found the fear that had filled me since I was small almost disappeared. The fear of not being wanted. The fear of letting my guard down. The fear of letting anyone in. The fear of being found out. The fear of not being worthy. The fear of looking into my own eyes. It was gone. All of it. As long as I stayed smashed.

'Come on. Don't hang on to it. Give me some.' I'd drink it down and for a minute, I'd stop breathing. 'Oh yes. I needed that.'

Whoosh. The air rushed back into my lungs. I was still alive. But was this what I wanted? That minute I swallowed the whisky. The minute when the air stopped filling my lungs. That was when I felt peace.

It was like being in a trance. I drank, then I slipped away. Into the void.

The odd times that I did have to be straight I could feel fear racing back over me like a freight train. Then I'd drink, and it was gone.

'Give me a line.'

All I had to do to not think or feel was get fucked up. I might never have to feel again.

'Give me everything.'

Maybe this is why, for most of my childhood, my dad was drinking himself slowly to death. Not wanting to feel his own pain and not wanting to see the pain we were feeling. Those nights when he had drunk just enough to want to talk to us but could never really get it out. Or did he try and perhaps I was too young to listen to him? 'I'm sorry, son. I love ye. You kids deserve better than this. Better than me. I need to let you know why I'm so fucked up.'

'Don't tell me why. I don't want to hear it. I'm scared, Dad. Why is it all so hard?'

But he never talked to me. He never let me in. He just left.

Did he feel scared, like I do? Did he lie awake, afraid of anything and everything, like I do? Did he drink until he could feel nothing and pass out cold, like I do?

He said he wasn't afraid of anything. 'Don't be afraid, son. You don't be afraid of anything. You're strong like me.'

Even my big brother John told me, 'I'm afraid of no man. I'm afraid of nothing that breathes.'

Now I know John was lying. He was lying to me, to himself and to the rest of the world. John was surviving. He was so scared that he was dangerous. Dad was the same. Afraid and dangerous. Especially to those people who were closest to him.

Just like me.

I can see it now.

* * *

The Royalty Bar sits right in the middle of Cowcaddens, a very Protestant part of Glasgow. Around here you could be a Sikh or a Hindu, a Sufi or a Buddhist, a Muslim, even an atheist – so long as you weren't Catholic.

The door of the pub swung open and crashed against the wall. All heads in the bar turned towards the door and looked at the figure blocking out the light. He was big and ugly, sort of like Charles Bronson after a hard night. Maybe it was the way his knuckles dragged on the ground behind him, I'm not sure, but he looked tough. His nose was spread across his face and his teeth were like a row of condemned buildings. It seemed that in every direction in Cowcaddens, something looked condemned.

'I'm the fuckin' toughest guy in Glasgow. Does anybody here want tae argue wi' me?' he snarled.

I could feel the muscles of the old guy next to me tighten up. He wanted to take him on but decided against it.

I had just arrived in Glasgow for the first time since I'd left nearly twenty years earlier. I came from this place called Cowcaddens, one of the rougher parts of inner-city Glasgow. Now that I think about it, all of Glasgow is tough, but it's home. This is where it all started.

I came to see where I came from, to find my people, and even though I'd grown up twelve thousand miles away, in a place where the sun shines all day and there are beautiful beaches with girls in bikinis baking in the sun, and hardly anyone carries cut-throat razors for protection, something about this scene felt very familiar to me.

I was a long way from the pubs and clubs of Australia where I had got away with murder and made my living singing and chasing girls. Tonight I would not get away with anything, tonight I was out of my depth. I started to get up but my Uncle Jackie, my official guide for this homecoming tour of the bars of Glasgow, grabbed me and sat me down. As I looked at him,

I knew it would be better to say nothing. He told me later that this same guy came into the bar a week earlier and started trouble, and one of my uncle's friends hit him on the head with a hammer a few times. Apparently all it did was make him mad. Maybe.

So we sat quietly and said nothing even though I wanted to stand up and hit him. The gorilla in the door looked around the room, breathed out and spat on the floor. Then turned around and walked out into the cold night. He was going to the next bar to see if he could find someone who would take him on. That's what he did for fun. This was my welcome home.

'See you next week, Charlie,' my uncle whispered under his breath as the beast left the bar. I think he was hoping to take him down one day, but not tonight.

I knock back a wee dram of whisky while my uncle gets us a refill. He drinks fast; these really are my people. Here in Glasgow they all seem to order the same thing: a whisky with a beer chaser. I drank in this bar every night I was in Glasgow and never saw anybody drink the beer. We would order one beer chaser and have twenty-five straight whiskies. And at the end of the night the beer would still be sitting there, as warm as it was when it was first poured. It was just an excuse to have a whisky.

At this rate I'll be out on the street singing before the pub shuts but so will the rest of the bar so I'll fit right in. I feel happy to be here but I notice that as usual there is a nagging voice in the back of my head screaming, 'You don't deserve to be happy, you are no good.' I have never really been chasing a dream. I've been running from a nightmare. I still wake up in the middle of the night, short of breath and afraid. Afraid that life will catch up with me, and all the things I've done wrong will swamp me like a tidal wave and drag me down. Drag me back to where I belong.

My next drink arrives.

'Oh, fuck I needed that,' sighs my uncle, the colour slowly coming back to his cheeks.

The truth is I have felt like this and heard this voice since I was a child, long before I was capable of doing anything wrong. Long before I ran away from home, long before I escaped from life through drinking or taking drugs. Long before I made records, even before I joined a band, and a long, long time before I almost let everything important to me in this world slip through my fingers. Was I born feeling unworthy, afraid, even guilty? What happened to me?

We order another round and we sit and begin to talk, awkwardly avoiding anything too personal even though it might shed some light onto why we are sitting here drinking ourselves into oblivion. We both talk too much and say nothing at the same time. I can feel my head starting to spin but I'm used to the feeling, I've felt it for a long time now.

'Let's sing a wee song,' shouts my uncle and my first night in Glasgow has begun with a bang.

the best sparring partner in Britain

S cottish people fall in love very easily, even more so on
Saturday night. I think it is because we are all crazy. If I had
to go to war, and I had the choice, I would surround myself
with Scots. Then again, I would think twice about going to the
football or a wedding with them. We can find trouble anywhere.
A Glaswegian could start a fight at a funeral, even his own.

I vaguely remember being maybe four years old and looking
out of the window on a Saturday night and being amazed at the
scene on the street below at closing time. Singing, fighting,
kissing and hustling, and that was just one couple. My mum
and dad.

Glasgow in 1960 was like a bomb site. As a kid it looked to
me like everything was falling down. There was rubble and mess
everywhere. Well, there was around Cowcaddens where I lived.
I think it was what you'd call an inner-city slum. Years before,
they had torn down the old slums and built our slum. It was
grey and cold-looking, a lot like the people, and all the buildings
were covered in a layer of soot from the coal fires. So were the
people, come to think about it. You could smell the coal burning

everywhere. To this day, the smell of a coal fire brings back a lot of memories.

When I went back in 1980 it still looked the same. It was as if the war was still going on and the place had been bombed quite recently. I guess there were trees, art and music and beautiful parts to the city but nowhere near where we lived. The only art was written on the walls of the buildings in chalk and on the sidewalks in blood.

Glasgow was, and still is really, a place that evokes mixed emotions in me. I meet Glaswegians socially and they are warm and friendly and very funny, but then I hear a Glaswegian accent on a dark street and alarm bells immediately start ringing in my head.

But anyway, back in the sixties, most of the town still looked like the Luftwaffe had had a field day there. I always thought one day they'd knock it down and start again, nice and new, but they never did.

In those days I thought my mum and dad were the coolest people alive. Mum was a beautiful girl and Dad was the Scottish boxing champion. They must have looked something when they stepped out on the town. Mum told me later that around that time they were in all sorts of dancing competitions. In fact, they were the jitterbug champions of Western Scotland for a while, a title that they won in a big dance hall near the markets of Glasgow. A place called the Barrowland Ballroom. This same hall became famous in the late sixties for a series of murders that rocked Scotland. Bible John, as he was known, followed young girls from the dance hall and brutally murdered them. He was never caught. The Barrowlands was also one of the first big places I played with my band when I went back to Scotland. I was excited to play in the place where my parents had had so much fun. I remember it was a great show but I felt uneasy in the hall. Like a lot of Glasgow, this place gave me a sense of belonging but with that there was an underlying feeling of fear.

My dad could sing, fight, drink his weight in whisky and charm the pants off anyone – literally, but I'll get to that later. I used to think that was all I needed to learn to be a man. He was the amateur featherweight boxing champion of Britain, so I guess that made my mum the best sparring partner in Britain. I'm not sure what my dad did in Scotland after he finished boxing; he probably worked with his hands, well his fists anyway. And I'm not sure if Mum worked; she probably had to, but regardless, things were pretty tough for us, as they were for everyone who lived around us. Glasgow was, and still is, a tough town.

Dad won the title in 1956, I think. Apparently he was an amazing boxer, always fought fair and clean. He was offered money to go professional but he always said that pro-boxing was way too corrupt. He always tried to teach us that you had to be fair in sport, know how to lose graciously and win humbly. That was passed on to us as well as how to fight out of the ring. The difference was that out of the ring we learned not to be beaten at all costs. Do whatever we had to do but don't give in or lie down for anybody. These and other lessons have been backhanded down from father to son since time began in Scotland.

Dad used to tell me how he would spend time in training out of Glasgow, in a town called Auchterarder. The air would have been cleaner away from the city so it was a better place to prepare for a fight. Maybe it kept him away from his mates so he didn't drink as much too. I'm not sure, but I did hear his dad used to be his trainer. That would make sense; his dad was a very tough man and I can't imagine my dad taking orders from anybody else.

I never saw Dad without a cigarette in his hand. He started smoking at the age of five or six. His parents, like everyone else at the time, didn't know the damage that smoking would do to you.

There were posters saying how good it was for you. Then again, they did say the same about heroin, cocaine and of course whisky. So they used to send him to school with six Woodbine and a box of matches in his pocket. He never stopped until about sixty years later. That meant for sixty-odd years he smoked plain cigarettes, no filters, so he got the maximum amount of tar and nicotine.

He ran fifteen or twenty miles every day for most of his younger days so I presume the running helped counteract the smoking. My dad was a champion but I think the will to win came more from his heart than his training. Dad never wanted anybody to beat him. In the end the only person who did beat him was himself.

He always had a little cough, dry and ominous. Over the years I heard the cough get slowly worse and worse. He eventually stopped smoking because he was diagnosed with emphysema but by then it was too late. It killed him a few years later. Who knows – maybe that's why I wake up in fright, not being able to breathe.

I loved my dad, everyone did, except my mum after a while. When I was young I never saw any pain or fear in his eyes. I did see it much later as an adult when he could do nothing else but sit and reflect on his life to the sound of death banging at the door. I felt for him then; I think fear was a new thing for him. He could take pain, he was tough, but real fear was different and it only caught up to him when he could no longer outrun it or drown it in booze. I never let him know that I knew he was scared. That alone would have killed him. He died a tough guy.

Mum was different. I did see the longing in my mum's eyes; a look that said, 'There has to be a better life somewhere for me.' Anywhere had to be better than Cowcaddens. Sometimes that look might have meant, 'Why did I marry this man?' I'm not sure. There was this sense of emptiness. Looking back, perhaps it was just the need for an even break. I came to recognise that look and I saw it in her eyes for most of my childhood. Sometimes it seemed to overwhelm her and sometimes she dealt with it. But even at her lowest, I could still see the light in her heart. She was beautiful. I loved her so much, I still do. She could make me feel warm and safe anywhere. I could bury my head in her chest and the problems of the world just slipped away.

Mum was tough, too. Sometimes I think that she thought she was tougher than Dad, which might have been a mistake. When she physically fought with my dad after he came home drunk with no money to feed us, she was the one who wouldn't back down. She would throw herself at him, hitting him with anything she could get her hands on. Night after night she was the one who ended up battered and bruised on the floor, not him. But she just kept getting up.

Dad would just leave so he didn't have to face up to anything. It was strange though – she seemed fearless and yet constantly afraid all the time. Is that possible? Of course it is; all of us kids are a bit the same.

Mum is the person you want around in a catastrophe. She jumps up and says, 'Get oot ma fuckin' way, I'll sort this,' and then leaps straight into whatever is going on, no matter how dangerous it might be. If someone threatened the kids they had to face my mum, not my dad. He would have been away working or drinking, so I guess she had no other options. My mum wasn't tough by choice, she had to be. She could fight better than most of the men around us. And most of them seemed scared of her.

One time my sister Linda, who was probably five, had a fight with another kid. Linda always had a bad temper and she had bitten a chunk out of the girl's stomach. My sisters were tough even at that young age. Anyway, so justice could be done, one of the other girl's parents had to confront one of my parents. As a result, my mum and the other kid's mum had a fight out on the street, in front of everyone who lived there. Mum gave her a hiding. That way everyone knew not to mess with our family. That's how we learned to deal with problems.

Mum was the enforcer. She did the dirty work. She was the one who had to be the bad guy and stop us from running wild and being brats. Dad just turned up late and let us do what we wanted. We loved Mum and would run to her if we were hurt or afraid, but if she turned on us, it was really terrifying. Something about her facial expressions could instil fear into all of us kids. She would slowly turn to us with her lips retracting. We were in trouble again. That was the signal to run. It still happens to this day.

But let's go back to the start. My earliest memories are really quite scattered and cloudy. A bit like my later ones when I think about it. There is a room that I now know was the kitchen but there was a bed in there, built into the wall. It was probably there to make use of the heat from the stove. A family could sleep in there when the rest of the house got too cold I guess.

There's nothing colder than a Scottish winter – though the summer comes close, I must say. I have vague memories of snuggling up in that bed with my mum, which is pretty good because I must have been well under two when we lived there. That house was number 169 Duke Street in Dennistoun, one of the poor suburbs of Glasgow.

At the end of Duke Street there had been a slaughterhouse many years before, but that was gone, torn down to make way for pubs and bars that were slaughterhouses in a different way. By the way, there were a lot of poor suburbs in Glasgow. We weren't anything special; there were plenty of slums to go around.

I was born James Dixon Swan at four o'clock in the afternoon on 28 April 1956. My mum was Dorothy, they called her Dot, and my dad was James and they called him Jim. I was delivered by my grandmother, Elizabeth, they called her Betty. They called me wee Jim, after my dad. He was big Jim. I weighed fourteen pounds when I came into this world. I think if I had been born in a hospital I would have slapped the doctor.

But anyway, I was born in that very kitchen. My granny made my mum scrub the floor with a brush to take her mind off the contractions. It killed two birds with one stone. She didn't notice the pain as much and she had a very clean floor. The Scots are very house proud. I'd say we were all screaming as much as each other. Granny screaming at Mum, Mum screaming at me and me screaming at the world. But luckily for Granny, she was deaf and never heard a word.

Granny was only a little deaf but more importantly she only understood Scottish. She didn't want to hear any accent or speak with any accent that resembled English. Most Scottish people seemed to have an inherent dislike for the English. Everyone spoke about the English with a touch of venom. But the bastards weren't that bad really. Not anymore anyway.

I went back to see my granny many years later. I remember one day in the kitchen of my Aunty Maude's house. Aunty Maude was married to Uncle Jackie and they were my favourite relatives. Anyway, Granny was making tea. I was reading the newspaper when she turned to me and said, 'Wid ye like a wee cup of tea, son?'

I immediately said, 'Yes please.'

I could feel daggers flying my way. She looked at me again, and in a slightly more annoyed voice she said, 'Wid ye like a cup of tea, son?'

'Yes please, Granny,' I said as politely as I could, wanting to show her the respect any granny deserved.

To my granny this probably sounded like, 'Oh rather, that would be spiffing Grandmama.' Basically it was like I was waving a red flag in front of her.

This went back and forth for a couple of minutes with Granny getting more and more worked up. I could tell because her voice had changed so much that the paint was peeling off the walls and Aunty Maude's budgie had its wings over its ears.

Finally, she said again, this time through her teeth – she had them in at the time – 'Wid ye like a cup of tea, son?'

I turned and faced her and said in my broadest Glaswegian accent, 'Aye, I wid.'

She let out a sigh and went back to the kettle whispering under her breath, 'Why'd ye no fuckin' say so the first time?'

She proceeded to begrudgingly make the tea. This was her way of showing love, I think. I'm glad she liked me. Otherwise she would have wrapped the teapot around my head.

My mum had the five of us when she was very young. John was the eldest, followed by Dorothy, then Linda, myself and then young Alan. I've made jokes for years that I was the white sheep of the family but as you will read later, that's far from true. There were no white sheep in my family. Even as children we were all a handful to say the least.

My big brother John weighed twelve pounds and my older sisters weighed about eleven and my young brother Alan was a big boy too. I don't know why we were all so big. I've heard people say that Mum must have had gestational diabetes, but I think it was because my granny made my mum drink a pint of Guinness every day of her pregnancies.

I can just hear her saying in a thick Glaswegian accent, 'Come on hen, it's good fur ye, drink yer Guinness.' Maybe not quite that polite but something like that. Guinness would fatten anybody up.

Dad kept her company and drank a pint of whisky every day. He didn't want to see her drink alone. He never got fat though, maybe because he sacrificed his Guinness to let her have it. What a gentleman. I think the more whisky you drink the skinnier you get. But that's just a theory. I've seen a lot of really skinny Scotsmen who drank like fish. It might have something to do with the fact that they don't eat.

Dad grew up in a boxing family. His dad was a pro boxer and I think there are a few old movies of him fighting somewhere but I've never seen them. He fought in the ring and on the streets and probably at home as well. He also was a bouncer and a general hard man. The sort of person you wouldn't like to mess with or meet in a dark alley.

Mum wasn't big on boxing, as she had seen enough punches being thrown around the house I guess, but John and I, many years later in Elizabeth, used to love to sit and scream with Dad as he watched boxing on the television. We all did, even the girls. I remember being mesmerised as a young Cassius Clay rocked the world, stopping Sonny Liston in the seventh round to become world champion. Our television was as battered and broken as Sonny was by the end of the fight and only just managed to keep working until the last bell. I was chosen to hold the coat hanger in the air and act as an aerial and was even given the coveted job as the remote control for the volume while Dad and John ducked and weaved with the new champion as he floated around the ring like a ballet dancer.

Bang, bang.

'What a jab. Hold that aerial up a wee bit higher, son.'

Bang, bang, bang.

'I need a chair to get higher, Dad.'

Bang, bang.

'Watch yer mooth, son. I can reach you from here.'

Bang, bang, bang.

'I could run, Dad.'

Bang, bang.

'I could get ye before ye could even think aboot runnin'. Ya cheeky wee bastard.'

Bang, bang, bang.

'I'm quick, Dad.'

'You're no that quick, so shut it. I'm watchin' the fight. What a right hand. Surely it must be all over. Quick, get oot the way, son.'

Bang, bang.

'The picture's gone. What happened? Move back where you were.'

Shhhhhhhh. Crackle. Bang, bang.

'That's it. Keep still.'

'Sorry, Dad.'

Bang, bang

'Nae bother, son.'

Every fight we saw, Dad would be rolling with the punches, weaving and lunging with the fighters on the box. It was like he felt every punch that was thrown. It must have been exhausting for him to watch, but he loved it and he instilled a love of boxing in all of us. Boxing in those days was not like the dirty, corrupt stuff that happens now that big money is involved, but the pure sport, man against man. Dad loved pure boxing and we thought it was beautiful too. He loved Sugar Ray Robinson and Cassius Clay. He'd tell us how fast hands and a quick brain could beat brute strength any time. He was a living testament to that, as he survived fights with guys twice his size all the time. He spoke quietly, never raised his voice at all, which led people to think they could take him, but when push came to shove he was deadly. He had survived the boxing ring, fighting the best in the world. And, more impressively, he survived on the streets of Glasgow where there were no rules. So he knew about death because he had faced it on many nights along the same streets where we lived and played childish games.

John was given a floor-to-ceiling punching bag and a pair of boxing gloves the day he was born. I think I might have got them as well. The girls were probably just given the gloves; they had us to belt into.

There seemed to be a lot of dark alleys in Glasgow and there were a lot of people you wouldn't want to meet but unfortunately sometimes they lived next door. The kids in the same building as you could be as dangerous as anyone you met anywhere. Everyone was either in gangs or being tormented by gangs.

There were gangs on every street. They were all dressed the same, and it looked like the clothes had been passed down from brother to brother and sister to sister. Trousers were patched up and falling down. Shoes were scuffed until you could see the socks through the leather. Shirts were dirty with snotters wiped onto the sleeves from the kids' constantly running noses. The faces all looked the same too. Reddish hair and pale and pasty skin covered in freckles and soot, with eyes that were constantly darting left to right looking out for trouble or the police.

I was too young to understand why we had to avoid the gangs, but I knew enough to be afraid of them. We were always told not to leave the street without Mum or Dad. By the age of four I had my first encounter with one of the gangs.

Myself and another kid of about the same age made the mistake of walking out of our street into the next without an escort. That was enough to put us in big danger. A gang of young guys somewhere between the ages of five and fifteen grabbed us and took us to the spare ground, an empty block where one or more of the tenement buildings had been demolished. They put us in a little lean-to shelter that workers probably used to get out of the rain.

Then they shouted, 'Don't move or we'll fuckin' murder ye.'

Then they started to throw rocks at us. I ducked and curled up, trying to protect myself, but was smashed by a few pieces of broken brick. I could feel blood running down onto my face. My mate was frozen stiff with fear.

Then they stopped for a minute and yelled, 'You've got till we count tae five to run, then we're gonnae throw bottles at yous.'

I remember telling my mate, 'Get oot o' here quick or we're deid.'

Next thing I knew I was running as fast as I could, dodging a hail of rocks and glass, but I got away. My friend was still frozen and couldn't move at all.

They pelted him with rocks and bottles until they were bored and then they cut him up and set fire to the shelter. He ended up in hospital for a long time. His family moved away, hopefully to somewhere nice, and I never saw him again. I am still left with feelings of guilt and shame for leaving my friend behind. What could I do? He should have run away with me.

Was life so bad in Scotland that even little kids had no chance? It seemed no one had a chance. I think that years of depression, war and poverty had dragged the whole of Northern Britain into the gutter and it was a long way back up out of it. They say that war is good for the economy and the morale of a country. It pulls the people together; they can all work hard to defeat the common enemy. But when it is over most people are left looking for jobs; there is no more work after munitions factories or the shipyards close down. That's what happened in Scotland, especially in Glasgow. Shipbuilding stopped and so did work for more than half the population. They were left to scramble to make ends meet and feed their children.

When I moved to Adelaide, I had a lot of friends from all over the north of Britain. They all told the same stories and they had all brought the same problems to Australia with them. But I think no one brought more problems than the Scots.

next to nothing

Glasgow wasn't horrible for us because we didn't know any better. Everyone was the same as us. The streets around us weren't pretty but they were our playground. It was home. If we wanted to play football, we would go out to the road and take off our jumpers and use them as goalposts and play right there in the middle of the road. When you're a boy you have your favourite players but everyone in Scotland, boys and their fathers, wanted to be Denis Law. Everyone wanted to become a striker for Scotland. None of us wanted to be in goal. I would fight to be the centre forward. I wanted to stand just past the halfway line waiting on the ball to be passed through so I could strike. But there was no halfway line on the road and unless I could convince my brother John to be a defender no one would pass to me. I was just a kid.

'I want tae be striker today,' I would moan.

'You were Denis Law yesterday and the day before. It's ma turn, Jim,' John would tell me.

'But I'm too wee tae be in goal. You telt me, John.'

'You're too wee tae be playing at aw, so shut it and try tae look bigger, wid ye?'

'I'm no playin' anymore. I'm goin' hame to tell Ma.'

'You're such a wean. Go on then, get up there and I'll pass ye the ball. But ye better score or I'll murder ye.' ('Wean' is what they called kids in Scotland, by the way.)

Occasionally the game would be interrupted by a car or truck but that was fine.

The footpaths were where the girls played and were covered in strange hieroglyphics that only girls could understand; this is where they played hopscotch. The mums would walk up and down the footpaths parading their babies in these huge prams with big wheels – something like monster trucks for beginners, the kind you might see in the English movies of the time. They would talk about each other's problems and gossip about each other's husbands. Who was in jail and who had just got out and who was caught sleeping with whose wife. Pretending that they were better than each other. They would walk past the pub on the corner to see if their husbands were spending the money they needed to feed their kids, on booze. If they were, there wasn't much they could do about it, not without causing a scene, not until they got home anyway. Then there would be trouble.

Mums would be going into the corner shops, trying to get credit so they could feed their kids, promising to pay it back at the end of the week but knowing that they probably wouldn't be able to. Every day was living hand to mouth, surviving for the time being then not being able to sleep at night wondering how they would get through tomorrow. I think my mum cried herself to sleep on many a night, praying for just a little help, knowing no one was listening to her prayers. She was doubting herself and what was left of her faith. Mum was not a church-going person but like a lot of the people who lived around us she would end up on her knees, praying for any help she could get. Unfortunately, help never seemed to come. But that never stopped her lying awake in bed wishing things would change.

Dad, on the other hand, drank himself to sleep and often ended up on his knees too.

You don't get used to living permanently behind the eight ball – no matter how long you've done it, it doesn't get easier. There is a constant sense of shame that eats away at you, making you feel that you're just not good enough. Some people are so poor that they can't even afford to feel shame; they have nothing. Unfortunately for us, we had next to nothing and were just poor enough to feel ashamed of everything.

The buildings were crumbling outside but inside the mums would be scrubbing the steps and cleaning the floors in an attempt to make their homes a little bit better for their kids. It was for their neighbours' benefit too. They didn't want anybody to know how much of a hard time they were having, but they were all going through the same things. Sometimes they would put window boxes on the windowsill with flowers growing in them to try to add some colour to their otherwise black and white existence. Even the flowers had a hard time seeing the sun I think. It seemed to be grey everywhere. The sky was grey. The streets were grey. Life was monochromic and depressing. These same streets had been the home to Scots and Irish for a hundred years and they had been spilling each other's blood on them for as long as they had been there. I doubt that it ever felt safe.

We didn't have regular holidays like normal people; we couldn't afford them. But I remember going to the beach at Port Seton for a holiday one year. It might have been just for one day but I know we went. It was a big thing for us to get away from the grey oppressive filth of Glasgow and see the sea. The beaches in Scotland are not like the beaches in Australia though. When we got there I wondered where the sea was and someone said, 'There it is – that grey bit, between the grey sky and the grey sand.'

No one went swimming; it was way too cold in the water, or out of the water for that matter. What they did do was kick off their shoes and turn up the bottom of their trousers and paddle around. We were on the beach in jackets and jumpers wishing we'd brought hats and gloves with us.

Mum and Dad and whoever it was who took us, went out when the tide was low and came back with a sack of mussels and whelks. We all got to eat as many as we wanted. That day sticks in my mind as one of the great days in Scotland.

We loved mussels and didn't get them often. You could buy them at some of the barrows (the markets) and the fish shops in Glasgow. We could never afford them but for very little money you could get a cup of mussel brae. I think this was the water that they cooked the mussels in with a bit of salt. But it tasted fresh like the sea to us.

We would stand outside the fish shop in the cold, shivering and watching the guy making the chips.

'What are you kids doin'? Stop hangin' aboot ma shop. You're puttin' off the customers.'

'We're hungry, mister.'

'You'll get nothin' here, now get lost.'

But we would just stand there drooling, breathing in the smells that wafted out of the door of the shop. The smell of mussels being boiled in salt water and chips with salt and vinegar would be driving us crazy.

Sometimes, if we were lucky enough, someone would feel sorry for us as they staggered out drunk from the pub and into the fish shop, and would buy us some chips.

'You weans shouldnae be standing oot here by yersels. Take these chips and go hame tae yer ma's.'

'Thanks mister, can you get us a drink too?'

'D'ye think I'm stupit? Just take the chips and fuck off before I belt ye.'

Other times the guy running the shop would walk out and give us a wee bag of all the crunchy bits that were left in the fat when they cooked the chips. This was like a gourmet meal to us.

'You kids hungry? Here, eat this and go away.'

When Dad got really drunk he would sometimes give us enough money to buy some mussel brae. He would stick his head out of the pub door and say, 'Don't tell yer ma I gie'd you this. Go and get yersels somethin' from the fish shop.'

'Thanks, Dad.'

'Don't tell her I'm in the pub either.'

He was probably in there spending all the money that Mum was sitting home waiting for so she could feed us. But when we got to drink mussel brae we felt like kings. Small, dirty, snotty-nosed, cheeky kings. But still kings in our heads.

There were good times in Cowcaddens, too. November the fifth, Guy Fawkes Night, was a great night in Glasgow. I can remember massive bonfires on the spare grounds. It seemed like the only time kids from different streets mixed. Maybe this was because the parents were around but I don't think so; it was just a chance to forget about everything and be a kid for one night. Whatever the reason, we all loved that night and couldn't wait for it to come around.

The excitement built for days as the pile of stuff to be burned grew and grew until it was the size of a house. They should have burned a few of the houses too, come to think of it; they were shocking. Everybody brought out old furniture and beds and piled them up with bits of old wood that had come from demolishing the buildings around the area and anything else they wanted to burn. Evidence, bodies – no, I'm only kidding.

We would all stand around and watch the wood and furniture go up in smoke and light up the sky. We would stand and stare into the fires until we were dragged into the house for bed. Then the next day there would be a mound of smouldering ashes lying on the ground, which were blown around by the wind, leaving more shit that never got cleaned up. But for that night it looked spectacular and Glasgow shone – in the eyes of the children anyway.

I felt relatively safe near Mum and Dad, particularly my mum, but when they weren't around my world would collapse. It hurt to be away from my mum's side. She was my world, she was everything. My first day in preschool traumatised me. My mum and granny took me to this place filled with strange kids and very cold-looking women, and just left me there. Where were they going?

'Come back, what have I done? I'll be good!' I remember screaming at the top of my voice. But they were gone. There was a playground and a wall around the outside so I ran up a slide to see if I could stop them. But they never even looked back. I was certain that they were never coming back. I thought that I was going to have to stay there and take mid-afternoon naps forever. I don't think I ever forgave them for that. I hate naps.

But kindergarten turned into school and school turned out to be not so bad. The school I went to in Cowcaddens was called the Normal School. It was sort of clean and every day you got fed a hot meal. For us and a lot of other kids that might have been the only hot meal we got. Most of the kids looked as scared as I did so I didn't stand out. I was only four going on five, but I learned very quickly that if I made the teachers like me, life would be easier. I was the kid who always had his hand up first. The kid who was always trying to get the teacher's attention. I would try to be involved in everything the class was doing.

* * *

Around the time I started school I was faced with another challenge. It came from home and a place I least expected it to come from – my mum. She started force-feeding cod-liver oil to me and the other kids. Maybe it was one of those times when all the adults in the country decided that this would be good for their kids. And it might have been, but it was torture to me. It was like tongue kissing a salmon. Not that I've ever tried kissing one. My mum had to chase me around the house and hold me down and force the vile liquid down my throat. I would be yelling and sputtering as she force-fed me. And no sooner was it in my mouth than it was all over the floor or even my mum. But after a couple of swift smacks across the legs I soon swallowed it like it was sugar syrup. I know fish oil is supposed to be good for you but that stuff nearly put me off fish for life. It wasn't until much later that I started to like fish oil – when I discovered caviar. A much better delivery system, I think.

The fish oil probably helped in the fight with the cold too. It was an ongoing battle, especially during winter. Life was tough in the summer but it was brutal in the wintertime. The snow brought another set of challenges. It was beautiful to wake up to a blanket of clean white snow covering Glasgow's usual dull, depressing shroud of grey. We would look out the window and laugh and get ready to go out and play in it. But with holes in your shoes and not enough warm clothes the novelty would soon wear off.

Quite often the snow was so high that no one could open their front doors and we couldn't get out even if we wanted to. Sometimes Dad would have to jump out the window from one or two storeys up and dig his way to the pub.

Then the pipes would freeze and there would be no water. Waiting for deliveries of coal was always a worry. If the trucks couldn't get through a lot of people got very cold. I heard stories of old people and young kids freezing to death in winter. Living in Cowcaddens in that sort of climate was not like it would have been if you lived in a quaint mountain village somewhere. There were no fondues, marshmallows, skis or toboggans where we came from. When the weather turned bad, parents all over Scotland had to work really hard to keep their families warm, lying clothes along the bottom of the doors to stop the wind blowing through. Lighting small coal fires made the difference between freezing or not for most families. For a place that was so sooty, coal was not that easy to get. It cost money – money Mum and Dad never had.

At least we didn't have to drive in the snow, because no one could afford a car. None of my family or their friends had a car. I remember seeing them parked in the street sometimes but not for long. No one wanted to get back to a car that had no wheels or the aerial and the mirrors ripped off. The cars I did see were wrecks or they looked quite funny. There were some that looked like bubbles with one wheel in the front and two at the back, a kind of enclosed golf cart. I've never seen them anywhere else. But I'm sort of glad that no one had cars when I think about it. That would have been something else to knock people to the ground with. Driving drunk would have been the norm and in the winter it would have looked like some sort of demolition derby on ice.

When the snow thawed, the street sweepers would come through and clean up the slushy black mess it left behind. A mixture of water from the melting snow and dirt and soot, mixed up with broken glass and blood from the gutters outside the pubs. Apparently no matter how cold it got, it was still warm enough to drink yourself into oblivion in Glasgow, and if you were still conscious when you left the pub you could be punched, kicked and stabbed on the way home. That particular sport went on all year round. Glasgow – it was beautiful one minute, a bloodbath the next.

There was a lot of drinking in the house, and with that came a lot of violence and abuse; not necessarily directed at us, but every punch and threat that Mum and Dad threw around hit each of us as if we'd been thrown against the wall. The sound of bottles being opened and voices slowly getting louder always sent us into a panic. Sooner or later a fight would break out and we would hide under the beds and in cupboards, crying and praying it would all stop. Often we'd be dragged out of the house in our underwear, freezing cold, to the sound of Mum and Dad swearing at each other, using us as bargaining chips or hostages. The next day all would be forgiven and the cycle would start again.

The whole world seemed to have a drinking problem. How come the children didn't eat well or have nice clothes or nice places to live but there was always money to buy drinks? That question always baffled me as a kid. Kids would be cold and hungry but somehow all the adults were drunk and fighting. Maybe that's how they kept warm.

CHAPTER THREE

Man, that's ma hobby!

Don't get me wrong, not all my memories of Scotland are bad. Some are funny. For a start, I think it's very funny that Scots like to sing. They sing anywhere, any time and as loud as they can. We don't care who's listening. Fuck 'em, we want to sing.

I have vivid memories of people standing around drunk, singing about how much they missed Scotland. The best bit was that they hadn't gone anywhere. They were still in Glasgow. Many a night I fell asleep to the sound of someone forgetting the words to 'I Belong to Glasgow' or 'Bonnie Scotland'. Surely that must have been a sign that if they actually left, they were going to miss the place. But they left in droves and got drunk in new countries and forgot even more of the words and never once sang about wherever they were now. My folks never sang songs about Australia; they didn't know any and didn't want to know any.

One song I remember, which everybody sang at the top of their voices, was a song called, 'For We're No Awa' Tae Bide Awa'. It was sung every night in pubs and at people's homes, normally towards the end of a party. The song seemed to be about not going away from Scotland, and when you didn't go away you should celebrate the fact that you're staying by drinking as much as you could. This could only make sense in Scotland.

> *For we're no' awa' tae bide awa'*
> *For we're no' awa' tae le'e ye*
> *For we're no' awa' tae' bide awa'*
> *Well aye come back an' se ye.*
> *As I was walking doon the street one day*
> *I met wee Johnny Stobie*
> *Said he to me will ye take a dram*
> *Said I, 'Man, that's ma hobby!'*

Even as children we sang this song as loud as we could. It seemed all the songs had melodies that were written to tear at the heartstrings of a drunken Scotsman and break even the toughest man down to a crying, sobbing wreck. Or get him ready for battle. Whoever wrote them knew what happened to a man when he got drunk in Scotland and they exploited it as much as they could. As a songwriter I tip my hat to them; they nailed it.

There were other songs too. Every night at the pub or at home when they got loosened up, they would all sing. Loosened up is Scottish for shitfaced, by the way.

There weren't many radios or record players at this time and no one pushed anybody into singing. It was as if they all knew when it was time. A strange silence would come over the room and people would stop what they were doing – drinking, punching someone, chatting up somebody else's wife – and wait for the singer to start.

Someone would look up from their drink and start singing a song like 'Your Cheatin' Heart'. It would be a beautiful moment, like a lone bagpiper standing on top of a castle wall. Only this would be a bloke with drink spilled down the front of his shirt, standing alone because no one wanted to be too close to him. He would raise his voice to the heavens, baring his broken heart and slightly battered liver to the world. But after one line everyone would join in and sing with him and fuck it all up. Then someone would yell out, 'Hey, one singer, one song,' and they would all be quiet again.

This happened song after song. Everyone took a turn singing their own song. Sometimes they didn't know the words and they just made sounds like the words. There would be a lot of mumbling and groaning as the singer, with tears in his eyes, desperately tried to remember the words to this song that meant so much to him.

Then someone would yell out, 'Aye, son. Tell us all what ye mean.'

And the room would break out in laughter as the tension was released. 'Aye, that song makes me cry too.'

Everyone would clap. It might not have been perfect but it was good enough to win over the crowd. No one wanted to see a grown man crying.

If you picked the right song to sing you could have them all crying in their drinks and hugging each other. But if you picked the wrong song, like a song that was someone else's specialty for instance, then you could end up in big trouble or even hospital. 'Your Cheatin' Heart' was my granny's song, 'Heartaches by the Number' was my mum's and my dad would sing 'Mona Lisa'.

Mum had a great voice and liked to sing Ray Charles songs, maybe because they were all about leaving someone or throwing someone out. That sort of thing appealed to her for some reason. My dad had a soft sweet voice and could sing like Nat King Cole. He sang 'Around the World' and 'Walk Away'. Songs that spoke about not staying anywhere and being ready to drift away at any moment, looking for love. I think these sweet and gentle songs showed what he was really like. He didn't want to be the tough guy life had made him.

Another great time for my folks and all their friends was July the twelfth, the day of the Orange Walk. Mum and Dad and all their friends were Protestants. I know this because for many years Catholics were not allowed into our house. I know the Walk was also supposed to be about celebrating the Battle of the Boyne or something, but for Christ's sake, that was back in 1690. Let it go. But they didn't let it go. Scots can hang on to things for a long time – grudges, throats, you name it.

In those days the Orange Walk was a day when the local Protestants could walk through the streets, carrying banners and flags and wearing orange sashes with bowler hats – and get to fight the Catholics. It looked like a sport of some kind, only much more vicious. Like a sport where you were allowed to carry open razors, which seemed to be the weapon of choice in Glasgow. These players liked to leave a mark on their victims, especially on their faces, so people could always tell that someone had got to them – they couldn't hide it. You see big scars on the faces of a lot of people from Glasgow.

We had to stay indoors while the Walk was on. We would hang out the windows and watch as strangely dressed men walked down the road, acting like they were some sort of royalty. Their banners and sashes had slogans from a time when it might have mattered what religion you were or what you had to shout to the world. But these days, it just didn't matter anymore. Everyone was downtrodden by someone else and the truth was, God had failed us all. Maybe we should have been fighting the church and not each other. But that would have been no fun. Churches don't scream and bleed. As it was, men could get drunk and act like animals and next day get up and go to work as if nothing had happened, happy knowing they had fought for what they believed in, but not able to remember what that was.

They worked right next to each other too, Catholics and Protestants – working as one. You couldn't tell the difference by looking at them. They all had the same colour hair and the same skin and they all had kids to feed. They all loved Scotland and Glasgow, but when a drink was had, suddenly it was as if the same guy you worked with had murdered your family. The conversation would turn to religion or football or both and a riot would break out. The hatred was overwhelming; that same hatred that had been passed down to them from their fathers was passed down to their own kids.

I liked the music side of the whole parade. Pipe bands would march down the street and the marchers would cheer and sing along with them. The Scots always like music, any time – at parties, weddings and funerals. When we went into battle, the pipes were in the front of all the troops. The sound of bagpipes makes my heartbeat quicken and the blood surge through my veins. Even as a child I felt like this. All the people we knew would lash out and fight, party or sing when the bagpipes were played. The bagpipes made us believe we could get through anything. We could take on the world if we had to and quite often did. We didn't know when to give up. That's something that runs in our blood. It comes from years of fighting to retain your sense of self when all the while you are being stood on and pushed into the gutter.

So let's talk about football for a minute. Football was something else in Scotland. Growing up I thought there were only two football clubs in the whole world – Rangers and Celtic. To say the names alone at the wrong time has been the cause of many a violent incident. I have never seen anything like the Scottish football fans anywhere else in the world. In Scotland, football is really much more than just a sport: it is about religion, it is about repression. Football teams are all most people have to look up to. They are gods; the only light in a very dark existence.

Rangers are basically a Protestant team with the same colours as the Union Jack, whose devotees sing songs about loyalty to the crown. The chants they scream out at football matches cry out for the blood of their one true rival, Celtic.

Celtic fans fly the Irish flag, and are of course Catholic and hate anything to do with the monarchy. They too have songs and chants about standing knee deep in the blood of their sworn enemy, Rangers.

Now, I know what you're thinking here. There's nothing wrong with a bit of a laugh and taunting the other team. This sort of stuff happens all over the world. Good healthy rivalry, right? Wrong. This is way beyond healthy. This is deep-seated hatred. If you shout out a team slogan or wave the wrong flag in the wrong place, you can end up battered and bleeding. If you wear the wrong colour shirt in the wrong place, you can end up dead.

I made the mistake of going to an Old Firm game when I was much older, when I first went back to Scotland in 1980. The Old Firm game is what they call it when these two teams clash.

My cousin Joanne was dating a guy called Jim Duffy, who she has since married. Anyway, Jim was a great footballer and a great bloke. He later became one of the best footballers in Scotland. As it happened, at the time he played for Celtic, although on this day he wasn't playing. He knew I was from Australia and wasn't caught up in the brutality of the rivalry and he didn't think twice about getting me some tickets for the game when I asked him, but he gave me a little advice. He said, 'Don't wear the colours of either team, keep your head down and don't yell out too much.' But I was travelling with a good friend of mine, a girl called Jan who I was seeing at the time, and when we arrived at the game, she was wearing red boots, blue jeans and a white top – Rangers colours. And it was too late to change. Jim walked us to the game and left us outside the stadium. His last words to us were, 'Meet you here after the game. I'm not sure where your tickets have you seated, so be careful.'

I took our tickets and went to our seats, not expecting anything other than a great game of football. I was in for a shock.

As fate would have it, with me being brought up a Rangers supporter, and the colours the young lassie was wearing, guess where we were sitting. Right in the middle of the Celtic stand. I was in neutral colours as instructed but I looked at my date and I thought that I might be in trouble. I've been told that Celtic supporters can smell blue blood a mile away. Luckily for me, the stand we were in seemed to be mostly filled with older Celtic supporters – the ones who had long ago given up killing people for fun. Not only that, they immediately knew by our accents that we weren't from around there. I did bung on a bit of an Australian accent out of fear and self-preservation.

'G'day you blokes, where do you get a beer around here?' I asked loud enough to be heard all around the stand. Luckily Jan was a pretty girl and I'm sure that helped. The Scots get all charming when there's a good-looking girl around. They didn't kill us and much to my surprise we survived the game relatively unscathed. I was the target of a few jokes but all in good fun and I could take that. I was a little wounded, as Rangers lost one–nil in extra time, but I would live.

Anyway, what followed was the most frightening display of soccer hooliganism I have ever seen. Both teams' supporters took turns charging onto the field. It was like trench warfare, charging from the safety of their own end, onto the pitch and into no-man's-land. More people joined in every time.

What went on in the name of football on that field scarred me for life. People were being beaten to the ground then picked up and clubbed with lumps of wood. The police were taken by surprise by the scale of the riot and tried everything to stop the violence but they couldn't; it was out of control. In the end they had to ride through the screaming crowd on horseback, swinging big sticks, knocking people to the ground, in an attempt to break them up.

In shock, we went to meet Jim. We found him on the street outside the game, surrounded by Rangers supporters. Jim had picked this place thinking it would be safer for us than being left standing among the Celtic fans. But here he was, in the worst place he could possibly be, surrounded by thousands of rampaging lunatics, burning green shops and overturning green cars. We walked in silence back to Jim's car, heads down, none of us daring to look at anything or anyone. It was a long, long walk. As a Celtic player, Jim would have been a prize trophy for one of the marauding Rangers supporters. If they had recognised him they would have put his head on a stick and marched up and down the street. I read that this was the most violent day in Scottish sport since 1926. It certainly felt like it. This was not sport, it was war. I lost my taste for football that day, at least until I was back in Australia where being brought up on sport included being good sports.

But believe it or not there were times when Scotland would unite, when the Celtic and Rangers fans joined forces and became brothers, bloody brothers; but only when Scotland played. I often wondered how they could have hated each other so much and then become partners in crime so easily. There was only one thing that made it make sense, ever – England. We all hated the English. The Scots could put away their petty arguing and fighting to go and start petty fights with the real enemy – the English. Now I see how it all works; all that fighting with each other was just training for the real battle against England. After all, we are all brothers, we are cut from the same bloody cloth.

And of course there was a host of songs to be sung about ripping our old enemy apart and tearing out their black hearts – if they had hearts – not to mention lots and lots of songs about being away from Bonnie Scotland that always seemed to sound better when being sung on Scottish soil. Funny that.

I think that the English people knew why Hadrian's Wall was built on those days when the two national football teams met in England. I'm sure they were sitting at home wishing it was about twenty feet higher and a lot longer and didn't have a train line running through it. They had songs about the barbarians from the north that were equally as bad as the Scots' songs. But no one ever listened to them where we came from.

The Scottish fans would hit London like a pack of berserk Vikings, ready to rape and pillage and on the odd occasion watch football. If they actually won a game, the partying went on for days. I hear the English girls seemed to look cuter when we won. But we never won too often. And there was no way any nice English girl would put up with a drunken Scottish soccer hooligan chasing after her in traditional dress, waving a Scotland scarf, shouting out obscenities and lifting up his kilt at passersby. So it mostly ended with packs of lonely, drunken Scotsmen crawling around the streets of London looking for unsuspecting victims to fight until they ran out of money for booze and got the train back to Scotland. If they felt really bad they could always start a fight with each other on the way home. This was the Scottish way. Always one more battle to be won before you got home and curled up with a good bottle.

In 1977, my uncle went to England by train to see Scotland beat England at Wembley Stadium. It was such a rare victory that the Scots celebrated by taking the whole pitch home with them. My uncle tells me that on the train ride home, a particularly drunken Scotsman gave him the penalty spot from the field. They took the goalposts, the nets and most of the grass back to

Bonnie Scotland and, for a short time, drank and sang together as friends. Next day it was back to the hate and fighting.

I know, like half of Glasgow, that a lot of my relatives' ancestors came from Ireland, probably during the potato famine when thousands of half-starved, angry Irish folk fled Ireland by boat and landed in Glasgow and Liverpool and anywhere else that would have them. They brought their hatred of the English with them so they fitted right in when they landed in Scotland. As I said before, we both hated the English. It was a hate that dated back more than seven hundred years but for some reason it is still so real to this day that they can taste it. They sing about it and fight about it and cry in their drinks about it, not necessarily in that order. But it is the cause of much pain where I come from. Everyone seems to have some sort of scars; if they aren't from fighting they are emotional.

Not all my scars are emotional. I have a scar on my right wrist but not from fighting. I didn't get any of those until much later. I got this one from go-carting. I can't remember whose cart it was – we probably stole it – but I somehow ended up driving it at very high speed down a hill. It was only a small hill in a back court between a bunch of tenements. The back court was about the size of a small tennis court but we didn't have tennis courts in Cowcaddens. This was just a place behind the buildings where families put their rubbish. The water drained off the roofs and flooded the back court. Whenever it rained it looked like a stormwater drain, so it was slippery and dangerous. Just how I managed to get up any speed in there is beyond me. Anyway, high speed for a four year old is not that fast. I wasn't the best driver; I'm still not the best driver come to think of it. And I suddenly realised that I was about to hit a wall. So I jumped off while the cart seemed to be going at breakneck speed. This is another one of those patterns that keeps recurring in my life.

I didn't break my neck, but someone had thrown away a rather large mirror and there it was, right where I was about to crash. I landed straight on it. I broke my fall and I broke the mirror with my hand, so my seven years' bad luck started that day; in fact, maybe it was backdated a few years. I remember blood spurting like a fountain from my wrist as I ran home. By the time I reached my mum I had lost a lot of blood.

There was a hospital nearby so I was rushed to casualty for eight or ten stitches. It seemed that the hospitals in Glasgow were specialists at stitching up gaping wounds. Who would have thought, eh? As luck would have it the cut had just missed the main artery in my wrist by a whisper, otherwise I might have bled to death. But I didn't and I was tough, so everything was all right.

CHAPTER FOUR

a real Glasgow hard man

I don't recall spending much time with my grandparents except for my granny, my mum's mum. She lived a life that I could only speculate; it made my life look tame. The world tried to break her but failed, leaving an old woman with nothing but memories and a broken heart, but she was still standing. She lived alone until she was eighty-something. And she was as tough as nails. The women in Glasgow all seemed to be really hard.

She helped bring me into this world and for that I thank her. Life couldn't have been easy for her and even though she could sometimes get a little wild, she was always loving and funny. I have vague memories of her husband, my da, but they are not very clear. They didn't live in the same house and hadn't for as long as I was around. My granny and he were friends, but I don't remember seeing them together. Maybe they didn't talk at all, who knows. That probably worked out fine for them. Da lived alone, except for his best mate, Jackie the border collie. Dorothy, my big sister, was his favourite but I don't think he had a lot to do with us.

I have no recollection of my dad's mum. I think she died young from a drinking-related illness. My grandparents all lived hard and except for my granny, they all died quite young. In Glasgow, if someone died, you didn't bury them immediately; you would go around to their house a few days later and beat their liver to death with a stick. They drank a lot. I had an uncle who drank a bottle of varnish … he had a horrible end but a lovely finish. Sorry, I had to share that. It's an old joke but a good one.

I know I met Pop, my dad's dad. I have vague memories of him being quiet and a bit scary. Apparently he was a real Glasgow hard man. Old-school hard. He was a bare-knuckle fighter, a champion during the Depression. He would fight for about thirty rounds in the alleys of Glasgow while everyone placed bets on him. Fighting in Glasgow is an art form and he must have been a master and a nightmare rolled into one. He made his money fighting. That was his job – being beaten or beating people to a pulp. My dad told us that during the Depression, when food was really scarce, if he won his fights he would buy the whole street bacon and eggs. When he wasn't fighting I don't know what they ate but it wasn't a lot.

I tried to track down more about him but no records of illegal bare-knuckle fighting were kept. The boxing officials in Scotland said it never happened after the turn of the century. They obviously didn't live anywhere near us.

I met an old guy when I went back to Scotland in 1980. I was in a pub with my uncle and I went to the bar to get a drink. We actually went to the pub at ten in the morning and sat in there all day just drinking slowly until it shut again at night. We seemed to be there every morning. After a while I asked my uncle jokingly if he was just doing this for me because it wasn't necessary; I could live without a drink at least until after lunch.

He very seriously said no, that's just what he did. It looked to me like this was sort of a job: clock in at ten, drink all day and clock out at closing time. He was out of the house the same amount of time he would have been if he was working. We weren't alone doing it either, and after a few days I had a whole bunch of new friends. Old and young, male and female, standing around outside the pub, looking at their watches waiting for it to open. It didn't matter if it was pouring with rain, they were there the same time every day, with coats and hats on, waiting for the click of the lock and the doors to swing open. Then they would pour into the bar, excitedly rubbing their hands together, ready for the first of the day. They looked a little edgy and very thirsty and they were all a little snappy first thing in the morning until they had their first drink.

Now I like a drink as much as anybody but this was just a bar; nothing happened there, no entertainment, nothing except the odd sing-song. Then they would probably go home to their wives and eat dinner with nothing to say to each other.

'What did you dae the day?'

'Nothin', just drank.'

Anyway, I was at the bar, and I got served before this old guy and he turned on me. He was about eighty years old and five feet high and he wanted to take me outside for a fight. I was a bit shocked. Was he serious? Not knowing how to react, I laughed – not at him, but at the situation. He went nuts and I could see in his eyes that he was not kidding. Had it been a few years earlier, I'm sure I would have already been out for the count. He had the air of a man who, in his prime, no one would have fucked with.

Anyway, my uncle came to his rescue – or was it mine, I'm still not sure – and said to him, 'Hey, Jimmy' (everybody in Glasgow is called Jimmy, by the way, even if you're not called Jimmy), 'this is Pop Swan's grandson.'

The old guy's demeanour immediately changed and he even looked a little scared. He apologised to me and insisted on buying me a drink. Whether he was an old mate of Pop's or an old foe,

I'm not sure, but what I did learn from that meeting was if you accidentally caught the wrong guy at the wrong time in that town, it didn't matter if he was young or old, you could be up to your neck in it before you had a chance to back away.

Much later on, when I went back to Glasgow to do some shows, I was walking down the main street of Glasgow with Armando Hurley, a rather big black American who was singing in the band with me. Now Armando looked mean; he was built like a tank and had a mohawk haircut. Really he was a gentle soul, but you wouldn't know from looking at him. He liked to bung it on a bit and keep people away from me. Anyway, we were crossing the road and this old guy with a cane was coming towards us.

'Get the fuck oot ma way,' he snarled.

'Sorry, mate,' we both said. We were being extremely polite as he was an old guy. But the streets were crowded and for some reason he thought we were getting in his way on purpose. He turned and scowled at me, ready to fight.

Now this guy could hardly walk; he was about ninety. He glanced at Armando and turned back to me and then back to Armando quickly and said, 'Ye wouldnae be so tough if you didn't have Mister T wi' ye.'

Then he grunted and swore under his breath and kept on shuffling down the street, saying something about Armando's mother as he left. I called Armando Mister T from then on. That's the mentality of old Glaswegians. They can make me laugh or they can make me afraid very easily.

Before we moved to Australia we lived at 22 Abercorn Street, Cowcaddens, close to the city. The old tenement buildings we lived in have now been turned into trendy inner-city dwellings but back then it was scary. Each building had a common entrance, or close, and a toilet outside in the back court. The back court wasn't the nicest place. There would often be drunks asleep or up to no good in the back courts. People would be making out in them or being killed in them. They were dark and you couldn't see into them from the street. So any time we went down to the back court was a traumatic experience. Unless, of course, we were with a bunch of mates or our brothers and sisters. Then we'd be the ones up to no good.

I heard something about one of my sisters being dragged into a back court by a stranger. I don't know exactly what happened. No one spoke about it. But the story I heard was that the police caught him and locked him up in a cell with my dad for fifteen minutes before they charged him. Old-fashioned Scottish justice. Violence with violence.

I used to wonder how I got like I am but after writing this stuff down I think I'm lucky that I joined a band and didn't end up in jail or dead. The Scots we knew only had one way of solving problems and that was with their fists or a lump of wood. For years I thought that was the only way to deal with stuff and sometimes under pressure I still want to revert to that way of dealing with shit. I know it doesn't work – but for a moment, in the back of my head, I think using my fists will help. Thank God I don't behave like that anymore. I'm a pacifist now. Well, sometimes I am.

In 1980, my Glasgow cousins took me to a wedding with some of their friends. It took place in a little hall not far from where we lived. Halfway through the night there was a bit of a commotion at the next table. I looked over just in time to see a man hit a girl in the face with a glass. I was shocked and outraged by this, but my cousins told me not to say anything or get involved, as it could get dangerous for all of us. I had to stop myself from reacting. I wanted to belt him but that would have been dealing with things his way I guess.

Later on in the night, as I was walking out of the toilet, a guy walked in and proceeded to pull a baseball bat out of his trousers and break it over the head of a guy who was standing at the urinals. I shook my head and kept walking. I went back to the table and thought about the whole evening. This was a wedding, a celebration of love. What the fuck was going on? So I said to my cousin, 'I want to get out of here, this is just way too violent, even for me.'

We had a few drinks in another bar, not talking much at all. I think that even they were in shock. This couldn't have been normal, could it? I finally said to them, 'Do you guys know any peaceful people in this town – some fucking hippies who smoke pot, because after tonight I need a joint.'

I'm not a pothead but I needed something to calm me down. They said yes and took me to one of their friends' houses, a guy who'd also been at the wedding. Anyway, we get to the house of the only pothead they knew in Glasgow. He seemed like a nice enough guy and we hit it off straight away. He was a big AC/DC fan and he had heard I knew the boys, so I became his best friend for life, immediately.

After a ridiculous amount of pot, I was sitting listening to *Dirty Deeds Done Dirt Cheap* for the twenty-fifth time that night, when he turned to me and said, 'It's nearly daylight and I've got somethin' tae do.'

I wondered what it could be at that time of the morning. Maybe he had to go to his job or something? I thought I'd better get out and let the poor guy get ready for work.

Then he told me something that made me sit bolt upright in my chair.

'I was at that wedding last night and some bastard hit a friend of mine in the face wi' a glass. She's a lovely lassie and he cut her bad, so I went oot tae ma car and got the baseball bat that I carry fur emergencies. Naebody plays baseball in Glasgow.' He laughed. 'I went back in and smashed it over his heid in the toilet. I didnae want tae do it in public and ruin the celebration,' he said thoughtfully.

By this point I was starting to straighten up so fast that I was getting whiplash. Anyway, he went on to tell me that in Glasgow, if you beat someone up when they're pissed, the right thing to do is to go around when they are sober and do it again. Besides, he said, it would be fun.

'I'm goin' roon tae his hoose first thing and I'm gonnae knock on the door. When it opens, I'm gonnae burst in and beat everythin' that's breathin' tae a pulp wi' a lump o' wood.'

He asked, 'D'ye want tae come and watch? Or, if ye feel like it, ye could help me oot.'

I calmly said, 'No, you're obviously very capable and you don't need me getting under your feet, especially if you have to kick someone's head in.' I then excused myself, saying, 'I best get some sleep as I've got to get up early too and beat someone up myself.'

We both laughed but I'm not sure he didn't think I was serious. Then I went home and booked my ticket out of Scotland as quickly as I could. Scottish justice was a twisted and cruel thing and I'd had enough.

Much earlier my mum, like me, had had enough of Scotland.

There were posters saying 'Come to sunny South Australia' in the office where my parents applied for immigration. Considering the amount of rain and snow that fell in Scotland, and remembering that it was so cold that it cut right to the bone,

I'm not surprised so many people signed up to be ten-pound tourists. That's what they called us: ten-pound tourists. I wore the name as a badge of honour but a lot of people, my mum included, were ashamed of it. It cost ten pounds for the whole family to move to South Australia and start a new life in the land of opportunity. But it was a big move. My mum and dad must have been scared about picking up and going around the world to live in this last, wild frontier. They expected to see kangaroos hopping down the main street and bushrangers riding horses past the house at night. I personally think that the idea of staying in Glasgow was scarier.

I know why we were told we were leaving Scotland. In the fifties there was so much pollution in Glasgow from industry and from coal fires in the homes that you could hardly see your glass in front of your face. Consequently, there was a lot of tuberculosis and bronchitis. My sister Dorothy had bad lungs and Mum spent many freezing cold nights with Dorothy bent over a pot of hot water with a towel over her wee head, trying to help her breathe. So Mum and Dad thought it would be better for her health if we moved to a warmer climate. But, as I say, I don't think that Dorothy's or our health was the only reason. Maybe it was for my dad's health, because I often heard my mum say she was going to kill him if we stayed in Glasgow.

CHAPTER FIVE

nothing like a romantic sea cruise

Glasgow Central was where we left from in 1961. I remember looking around and wondering what was going on. Where were we going? The place was smoky and dirty, just like the rest of Glasgow, so we felt right at home. But Mum and Dad and everyone around us was crying.

Some people were just going away for a little while, normal travellers going about life, going on holidays or off to work. Not like us going across the world into the unknown. But as frightening as our future was, I still knew that we wanted to get out of there as fast as we could. We were saying goodbye but all the while our eyes were looking at the train, hoping it would take us somewhere good, to a better life – anywhere but here.

'You better get on before it leaves without ye,' one of the family said, obviously trying to get rid of us so they could go to the pub. They didn't have to tell me twice; I just wanted to get on the train and go. I got the feeling we were all looking back over our shoulders hoping no one was coming to make us stay. Granny and my aunties all wanted us to go. Not because they didn't love us but because they wanted us to have a chance at a new life. Maybe they did want to get rid of us but they never let on.

'Make sure you write,' Granny said. I don't know why because I'm not sure she could read. It didn't matter anyway; no one ever wrote to anyone in our family. Mum never wrote to them and they never wrote to us. It was like the bond between us was broken the minute the train left.

I don't remember much about the train trip, I might have slept the whole way. Trains have always had a calming effect on me. Or maybe it was such a relief to get away from our lives that we all passed out. It was sad for Mum and scary for us and probably confusing for everyone else in the family. Was life really that bad in Scotland that we had to go around the world to Australia? Yes, and if we could have gone further we probably would have. So it was a train trip to England and a six-week cruise to sunny South Australia.

SWAN James Ruthven Harvey born 5 April 1929; Dorothy (nee Dixon) born 26 March 1934; John Archibald born 15 March 1952; Dorothy Dixon born 30 April 1953; Linda Dixon born 23 July 1954; James Dixon born 28 April 1956; Alan Ruthven born 2 November 1960; travelled per STRATHNAVER departing Tilbury on 7 December 1961 under the Assisted Passage Migration Scheme. (*National Archives of Australia*)

The ship we sailed on to Australia was the SS *Strathnaver*, built at a cost of £325,000 in 1931. Our ship, like everyone and everything else that went through World War II, had seen better days by the time peace came. It was battered and beaten but it had survived. After a good coat of paint and a refit she was ready to serve her country again, this time taking immigrants to new lands far away.

When we first laid eyes on the ship we thought we had died and gone to heaven. 'This has tae be the best ship anywhere in the world, it looks like a floating palace. We'll be travelling like kings', kids,' my dad said as the ship came into view. He was always an optimist. But it was a palace to us. Remember where we'd come from. Once on board we found that it had places to watch movies on deck and places to eat. It had everything. It was a palace. This trip was going to be fun.

One thousand, two hundred and fifty-two passengers squeezed into what, when I look back at it now, looked like a large tugboat or one of those ferries you see sinking on the news.

The ship left from Tilbury on 7 December 1961. It was a rocky start, with most of the guests on board getting very seasick for the first week or two. Some were sick the whole way over, but the first week or so was hard for everyone. In fact, my only memory of the first week is the smell of vomit and the sound of whinging Scots and English people.

'They don't make the food like at home. The weather's bad. I wish we never came on this fucking ship.' And so on. They both sounded as bad as each other; whinging is whinging, I've found.

Dad's optimism soon faded. Our cabin was so small he had to step outside the door to change his mind. The seven of us were jammed into a room the size of a wardrobe for our luxury trip to the lucky country. Alan was only about one year old so, as you can imagine, no one got a lot of sleep.

'Open the window, Dot.'

'It's no a window, it's a porthole.'

'I don't give a fuck what it's called, open the fuckin' thing up. It stinks in here.'

'It stinks oot there too. Have ye walked in the hallway lately, ya lazy bastard?'

'I didnae smell anything when I came in last night.'

'Aye, but you were stinkin' too. Stinkin' fuckin' drunk.'

'Gie us a break wid ye, woman? I just went oot for a drink tae get rid o' the seasickness.'

'Aye, by the look of ye when ye got back ye couldnae feel a thing. I don't think you'll feel anything for a week.'

'Shut it. And open the window, would ye?'

'I cannae open the window, it's below the water level, ya eejit.'

'Well, I'm goin' up on deck tae get some fresh air. I hear it's good for your health. It's killin' me in here.'

'Well try the air oot on the deck this time, no in the bar.'

Life in the cabin wasn't good. Mum and Dad were at each other's throats after a short time. The ship was not what it appeared from the wharf. The cabin was small, with enough beds for us all to sleep but not enough room to walk around without tripping over one another. We felt like we were in the bowels of the ship and wherever it was, the front or the back, it rolled a lot. If any of the kids woke up the whole family woke with them.

'Get oot yer bed and help me, would ye?'

'What? What? What happened?'

'Wake up and hold one of these weans. They're no well; can ye no hear them cryin'?'

'I was sleepin'. I couldnae hear a thing. I must be gettin' deif or somethin'.'

'Drunk. Dead drunk, that's what ye are. I'd be better off if ye were deid, ya lazy pig.'

'Shut it woman, a man's got tae sleep, ye know.'

'That's all ye do. Sleep and drink. You're nae use tae anybody.'

It wasn't long before at least us kids got our sea legs and made it out of the coffin we called home. I'm glad we got out, because very soon after that the sewerage backed up. I don't know if it was just our deck or the whole ship, but it smelled like shit and there was foul-smelling water all over the floors on our deck.

'We didn't have to come on a fucking cruise ship to live like this. We could get this at home,' I heard one of the other parents saying as he walked to the bar.

But it was great to be on board the ship for us kids. The good news was there was a swimming pool. The bad news was no one could swim. You couldn't walk through the pool with your pants rolled up, so that counted out most of the adults. Most of the passengers hadn't been in a real bath never mind a pool. I think one or two people might have drowned, or come close to it, on the trip. But not us, no thanks to my dad, who decided that the best way to teach us to swim was to throw us into the deep end of the pool.

John was first, he was Dad's boy. 'Stop kicking me son. You'll thank me for this later,' said my dad as he grabbed John by the back of his trunks and hoisted him into the deep end.

'Don't do it, Dad … *Blub blub blub blub*,' was the last thing John said until he surfaced screaming for his life.

'Aye, there you go son, you've got a lovely stroke,' said Dad as John clawed his way back onto the deck.

'Thanks Dad, I'll just take a wee rest while you pass on your wisdom tae the other kids.'

Meanwhile one of Dad's mates walked past. 'I tried that with the wife, she kept making it to the side too. Ha, ha! Fancy a drink, Jim? Ye cannae train the kids aw day.'

When I got older I used to get that same feeling – that I was in the deep end and couldn't swim – only I wasn't in the pool, this was life. I called it the salmon syndrome. Always swimming upstream only to get there and die. Cheerful, don't you think? Nowadays I'm much more positive. I know how lucky I am.

Anyway, I'm not sure he'd get away with it today but it worked, and before you could say Dawn Fraser we were paddling our way across the snotty surface of the pool with equally snotty noses, impressing all the young girls on the ship. Well, I exaggerate a bit; none of the young girls even cared if we swam or drowned and we didn't care about the young girls. That would be something that would confuse us much later on.

I remember it was a big deal for Dad when our ship went through the Suez Canal. He was excited about travelling, I think he really wanted to get out of Scotland and see the world, or maybe just get out of Scotland. He dragged us up on deck to see the canal. Sand, sand, and oh yes, did I mention the sand? That wasn't the most exciting thing for a five-year-old but it stuck in my mind. Looking back, I can't help think that he was just trying to find an excuse to get away from my mum.

'Aye, I think I'll take the kids up tae see the sand ... They'll love it, all kids love sand.'

We probably ended up at the bar. By the way, there were lots of times I thought were special one-on-one times with Dad, that in reality were times when Mum forced him to take me somewhere. But it doesn't make any difference; he made them special and they were all special to me. They still are.

I think that the trip was a new beginning for my mum and dad. Once they got over the seasickness they both tried really hard to make things better. They never belted each other around on the ship as far as I could see, so that was good. Dad didn't go missing like he always used to. I guess he could only go so far. I think I saw them kissing a few times too – very romantic. There is nothing like a romantic sea cruise to fix a relationship ... but this was nothing like a romantic sea cruise.

The food wasn't great but coming from our background any food was fine. Scotland in those days wasn't known for its culinary delights; we ate mince and totties (boiled potatoes) or chips. There were so many people on board and they all wanted to be fed at once, so it got very busy in the dining rooms. I seem to remember one or two sittings for breakfast, lunch and dinner and at first not really knowing what to do or when to go, but we worked it out. After that we tried to be first in line, ready to eat every meal they offered us. There was no shortage of anything, it just wasn't good. But we were happy to be eating and we were kids; we'd eat anything really. Most things they served on board were exotic to us. Pasta was exotic, fresh fruit was exotic. Anything that wasn't made of mince or potatoes might as well have been roast wildebeest; it was all gnu – sorry, new – to us.

We ran everywhere we could around the ship. Some places were off limits and obviously they were the places we wanted to go the most – to see the engines and inside the life rafts. We wanted to go anywhere that was dangerous, I guess. But the crew always seemed to be right there every time we turned a corner and we could get away with very little.

The first stop I remember was at a little place run by the British, a port called Aden, in Yemen. We eagerly lined up and went ashore. We would have gone anywhere to get off the ship for a while. Not only that, but it also looked exotic and different from any place we had ever seen. The first thing we noticed was that it was hot. Glasgow didn't get this hot unless it was burning down. Aden is also said to be as old as history itself and the way it smelled confirmed that for my parents. They moaned and complained their way around the port, looking for mince and totties or at least a pub. But they never found either.

Later on, when we returned to the ship, Dad had bought these beautiful stuffed camels with mirrors on them to take to our new home. I remember a fight breaking out between Dad and a couple of the ship's crew after they refused to let us bring the camels back on board. There is an old Scottish proverb I believe: *Never get in the way of a drunken Scotsman and his camels.*

Dad wanted to kill them, until one guy insisted on cutting one of the camels open. A couple of guys held Dad back and a couple held Mum back, which was a good thing because by this point she wanted to belt Dad, so he was very lucky. The camels were stuffed with used blood- and pus-covered bandages.

Dad was shouting, 'When I get ma hands on that salesman, he'll need they fucking bandages.'

Mum, in the meantime, wanted to kill Dad even more when she saw this. 'You wanted tae put them on my fucking mantelpiece, ya eejit?' The romance was back on good old Glasgow terms: sex and violence. 'If you don't fuck off oot ma sight, I'm gonnae kill ye.' These were courting words where we came from.

My folks weren't the only ones wrestling with the customs guys. Everyone bought the same things. That's a lot of bandages and a lot of camels left without humps. You would think that the crew could have warned us before we left the ship. Dad was sure they were getting a cut – bad choice of words – from the crooked salesmen. They were all foreigners and couldn't be trusted. I mean, we had known so many Scottish people we could trust in our lives, hadn't we? I'm sure there were a couple of blokes on the ship saying to themselves, 'We've got a load of bandages in Glasgow, there must be some way I can start a wee business like this at home. Now where do we find camels?'

Next stop was Bombay in India. Now, no one told my dad that cows – or coos as they are known in Scotland – were sacred in India and were not to be touched. Our coos never walked around the town; well, not the ones with four legs anyway.

'What do coos do in toon anyway? Are they meetin' up wi' other coos and goin' oot tae catch a picture or somethin'?' Dad said.

Apparently they could go wherever they wanted to in India, which was nice for them but a shock for some of the tourists. It wasn't long until a rather large coo walked in front of my mum.

Dad, who had not had the chance to fight anyone or anything in days, leaped to her defence. Poor coo didn't know what was going on. I'm talking about my mum here. She wasn't used to Dad leaping to her defence for anything. He wasn't a leaper really. Dad had seen red and was swinging at the beast like some kind of drunken Celtic toreador. I think he was winning when the locals broke them up. He had the coo on the ropes, giving it a terrible beating. The locals, it seemed, didn't like people having fist fights with their cows at all and soon enough we were rushed back to the ship, before Dad was locked up in a Bombay jail. Someone had to save those poor incarcerated Indian criminals from my dad. He would surely have started trouble in there. I think Mum might have been a bit taken by Dad's acts of chivalry so the sea cruise romance looked like it was on again. So it was on with the journey to strange new lands and strange new people or animals to punch in the name of love.

Somewhere in the middle of the Indian Ocean I was up on deck when I noticed something coming out of the water. It started out as just a flash of light in the corner of my eye. Then I saw one or two fish jumping. Soon there were huge schools of flying fish leaping up into the air, flying just above the waves, like they were trying to escape a predator. Maybe they just liked to fly, who knows, but they looked great to a kid from Glasgow seeing the world for the first time. The sun would hit their scales and flash back at me like something magic out in the water. I'd never seen anything like it and I started going up to look for them every chance I got.

The flashing, flying fish were soon joined by schools of dolphins surfing on the white waves the ship was making as it cut through the dark blue waters of the ocean. They would swim alongside the ship for hours and I got the impression that they were trying to entertain us as much as they were entertaining themselves. It looked like they were showing off in front of me, riding high on the waves then diving off to the side and circling back around, before darting up at high speed alongside us again, ready for another ride. They were taking turns, one after another, just like the surfers I saw much later at the beaches in Australia. Some nights when we were up on deck I was sure I could see them night surfing next to the ship but that could have been my imagination.

The ocean seemed to pull me in and I would sit and look out to sea for hours. I liked the feeling I got when I was on deck at night, looking out into the pitch-black nothingness that seemed to go on forever. I would sit, not thinking about anything. There was nothing out there. No light, no land, not another soul; it was endless and frightening like a dream but for some strange reason I liked it. I still do; I just seem to get lost.

Even as a child there was something about staring into nothing that appealed to me. We lived in very small houses. We bathed in the lounge room. We all shared the same bedroom. So the idea of seeing nothing or no one on the horizon was beautiful but frightening because we were all used to having someone close all the time.

Then the voice of my mum would pull me back to reality. 'Hey Jim, what are you doin', son?' And I would run off to play with the other kids.

CHAPTER SIX

---

sunny South Australia

We got to sunny South Australia on 21 January 1962. It was pouring with rain and it was stinking hot. Coming from Scotland, the last thing we wanted to see was rain and what we thought was hot was never higher than seventy-five degrees Fahrenheit. If the temperature in Scotland got over seventy-five it was a heatwave. It was well over a hundred and Mum thought we'd landed in hell or back in Bombay, which was the same thing to her. Anywhere outside Glasgow was all wrong to Mum, I don't know why she left really.

We arrived at Outer Harbour and waved farewell to the *Strathnaver.* By then the stench of sewerage had disappeared and we were beginning to really like it on board. I think that ours might have been the poor old tug's last journey. I felt sorry for the ship knowing it was its final voyage. It had carried us out of Britain to this new land that was going to be our dream home. I heard she was sold to the Shun Fung Ironworks of Hong Kong and was broken up and made into razor blades. I'm sure it was not the first time that ship was involved in a close shave. In fact, it might have even ended up as open razors on the streets of Glasgow, but that would have been too poetic.

We were taken by a luxury coach – well, it had a roof – to the Finsbury Hostel, our deluxe accommodation, and after a delicious meal of powdered eggs and toast we were shown to our suites. Finsbury housed about 2300 people in small cramped conditions. We shared toilets, bathrooms and washhouses. It was not good. We had paid, not a lot mind you, to travel 1200 miles to still be scared to go out to the toilet at night for fear of some drunken bloke staggering towards us with his pants down. We could have got this every night in Glasgow for free.

Our palace was what they called a Nissen hut – a curved piece of corrugated iron with a door in it. There was no insulation at all from the heat or cold. We wouldn't have minded the cold because we were used to it but the heat was a whole new experience. The inside of the hut looked a lot like the outside – dull, grey and not very homely. Even the tenements of Scotland had personality when you got inside. Sometimes that personality wasn't good but it was there; with wallpaper and little things that each family had collected like treasure as they moved from place to place. But these Nissen huts had curved tin walls so unless you had curved paintings they wouldn't have hung very well. If I'd been a little sharper I would have started painting landscapes on curved surfaces. I would have cleaned up. The furniture was the same in every hut: uncomfortable and sterile-looking couches with bad prints that smelled of disinfectant from where they'd had everything from beer to vomit wiped from them. The toilets were as bad as the old toilets in the back courts of Glasgow. The washhouse had big industrial-looking boilers so that everything that was washed was boiled too. Probably a good thing, when I think about it. I remember that when anything got loud, as Mum and Dad's voices often did, they sounded twice as loud as usual because of the tin.

The hostel made the Scottish tenements look luxurious. Every family had the same as us and none of them were happy about it. There were open drains that smelled of sewerage, just like the ship, and the food in general turned out to be as good as the first day – terrible. Everyone was complaining but no one was listening it seemed. I think this is how the myth of the whinging Pom started, with the shocking conditions when they first arrived in their new home. But the Poms do like a good whinge, and so do the Scots, so maybe not.

The rain came down on the roof, so loud it almost drowned out the sound of my mum crying. I like the sound of rain beating on a corrugated iron roof; it covers any other sound you don't want to hear. She didn't stop crying for a long time – years, when I think about it. She was just miserable. I don't remember a day going by without my mum saying, 'I hate this fuckin' place, I want tae go back hame tae Scotland.'

She would sob to herself, 'It's too hot, the food's nae good and I don't like these people. We're too different to live here wi' them.'

Nothing was what my mum and dad had hoped for. I doubt it was ever going to be what they had hoped for, no matter how good it was. We could have been put up at the Hilton and my mum would have complained.

But besides the huts, for us kids it was heaven. We would be outside running around all day. I'd never seen so many trees in my life and there were animals running around too – the only animals I'd seen before drank with my dad. I don't think I'd ever kicked a football on grass before then. It felt completely different. We could play without ripping our knees to bits and go home without gravel rash all over us. This was great. I'd get up before Mum and Dad and wake my sisters and say, 'Let's go kick the football or chase the birds. Come on, before Mum makes us do something else.'

We wanted to be outside all day, doing nothing and everything.

It wasn't long before we were running around barefoot and getting swooped by magpies just like the Australian kids. At first the magpies terrified me. In Glasgow if something came flying at your head it was normally attached to someone's hand. But after a short time I would be running and laughing at the same time, which was hard to do, and I would end up falling over as they swooped over my head like dive bombers. It became a game to try to get from one shelter to the next without being attacked, a good test of my speed and ability to change direction. I don't think I ever really got it over the magpies, they were always the winners. I realised then that I didn't have a good turn of speed or a side step but I was still convinced I would be the greatest football player ever. As long as I could run in a straight line, very slowly, that is.

Another thing I liked was that kids in Australia could get their gear off and run through a sprinkler any time they wanted. In fact, as a child I spent a lot of time chasing mates through the water as it sprayed up into the air making rainbows for us to crash through. There were colours everywhere; it wasn't dull and grey like the Glasgow I remembered. It was a new world and we loved it. The dirty stone walls of the tenements seemed like they were from another lifetime. I almost forgot about them completely although they popped up in the odd nightmare. I was too busy climbing trees and running on the soft green grass, never having to worry if someone was going to hurt me. This was the lucky country and we were the lucky kids.

All the parents just seemed miserable. Just like they did at home really. Nothing was ever right for any of them. The same old problems seemed to raise their ugly heads only now in a different location. All the shit that was happening in Scotland was going on in Australia, only my mum had no one to run to for help. She was alone. There was only my dad, who was always drunk or gone, the other kids or me. Us kids were the only ones in the world who could see what was left of that burning light in her heart I told you about earlier. The light that was being dimmed by all the shit that life threw at her.

My clearest memories are of being out all day playing football. That game saved my life I think. I'd be away from the house all day and I'd get home at night, too tired to hear the folks fighting. Because I was not home for most of the day I didn't see first-hand how unhappy my mum was. And sometimes Dad didn't come home until we were either in bed or getting ready to go to bed. He was often tired and all he wanted to do was drink and not hear any nagging. So he didn't really speak to any of us unless he was drunk. Then he was happy and made jokes at Mum's expense, telling us, 'You know yer mother's a pain in the arse – no all the time, but definitely when she's awake.'

She wasn't a pain in the arse as far as we could see, but we would laugh along with him, pretending we knew what he was talking about. The only time Mum was a pain in the arse was when she wouldn't let us do what we wanted to do, which was probably the same for him when I think about it.

There always seemed to be someone in the house, friends of Dad's or friends of Mum's. We never had a good time together with just the family. I think Mum and Dad were avoiding each other and maybe they were both avoiding us. It wasn't long until we were avoiding them too. This arrangement seemed to work for us all.

By this time Dad was working for an Italian builder somewhere nearby. He seemed to like his job and got on well with his boss although that would change later on. Both Mum and Dad always told me how hard he worked. The story was different depending who was speaking.

'Yer father never misses a day's work. No matter what he's been doin', he gets up and goes tae work. If the bastard would just bring the money hame, we'd be aw right.'

'I work like a dog all day and I get home and your mother nags me to death. "I need mair money, I want ye tae get a better job." This goes on aw night, so I cannae wait tae get up and get oot in the mornin', just to get her oot of ma sight.'

Dad seemed to avoid us most on Thursdays, when, coincidentally, he got paid. He never missed work; I've got to say he had a good work ethic. But come Thursday he would finish work, pick up his pay packet and then none of us would see him until it was all gone. He had a bad pay packet ethic. We'd be hungry and Mum would be crying a lot and telling us, 'Yer father's a pig, always was, always will be.'

That seemed to be the pattern when we were kids. In the meantime, Mum tried her best to feed us on next to nothing.

There were a number of big events in the first few years in Australia. We moved from Finsbury Hostel to Seaton Park for a short while. Dad was still working for the builder and we got to stay in one of his houses. When I say 'his houses' I mean something he was probably going to get my dad to help him knock down as soon as he could. It wasn't great. We had moved from a tin shed to a hovel but Mum seemed happier and that made it easier for Dad.

My memory of that time isn't very clear but I do remember the builder had a watch dog that he kept on a chain. It was a huge Alsatian and not even the bloke who owned it could get near it. I think he must have thrown food to it because this dog would run at anyone who came near him. He kept it there so no one would go near his building site or his tools but the dog was going crazy from being tied up all day and all night. The poor thing had no contact with anyone who cared about it.

My dad loved animals, dogs in particular. And they loved him. He walked straight up to this dog, looked it in the eye and sat down next to it and said, 'You'll be alright wee pal. Don't worry, I'm here tae look after ye.'

I'm sure he said the same thing to me but I could be wrong.

He then proceeded to show the poor beast some love. The dog didn't know how to react and just dropped its guard and fell in love with him immediately. As I said before, my dad was a charmer. Dogs weren't the only things that fell under his spell. People were the same. Everybody liked him. And he had time for everyone – everyone except Mum and us kids. I could never work out why he was like that. We idolised him. We sat around and waited for any attention he was willing to show us. A lot like that dog actually, only our chains weren't quite as obvious.

Dad always moved close, said things softly and looked you in the eyes when he spoke to you. His eyes were deep, dark and soft. His voice was slightly husky, maybe from fighting or more likely from smoking so many cigarettes. But it had a warmth that people found attractive. There was a sense of him being wounded that seemed to come out whenever he wanted to move someone. He could turn it on and off like a tap. Those same eyes looked cold and menacing when he needed them to. I've seen him look at someone and say nothing and have them cowering like a scared dog. It would happen in a second. He used to do that to Mum early on but she became more defiant over the years. I'm sure that when his mannerisms didn't scare her anymore he turned to more violent methods. He had a way with words too. He could make you feel like you were the only person in the room but that too could change in a second. Even when he lost his temper he never raised his voice that much. The tone hardened and then it felt like you didn't exist.

Anyway, the dog became really attached to Dad and every day Dad spent time with that dog. He fed him and brushed him and for a little while I think the dog thought his life had finally turned a corner. Things were looking up for him. They were as good as they could get for an Alsatian on a chain at a building site. But it didn't last. I'd seen this happen before; in fact, it happened to us all the time. Dad got caught up in some other stuff with the builder and stopped spending time with the dog and within a few days it turned back into the Hound of the Baskervilles. The poor guy. Dogs don't understand why people change.

One day the dog got off the chain and terrorised the neighbourhood. I think he might have bitten a few people. He chased us down the road, through the house and over the fences until finally someone got hold of him. They took him away and we never saw him again. I think we were told he'd gone on holidays to a nice farm where dogs ran free and had fun with other lost dogs.

We then moved to Tea Tree Gully for a while but our stay there didn't last long. We never stayed anywhere for very long, I don't know why. Mum and Dad were fighting again, we were all on edge and as usual things were going from bad to unbearable. This time we were off to Gepps Cross.

Gepps Cross hostel was about five miles down the road from our first hostel and it looked very similar. Same corrugated iron huts, same sort of people living in them. Basically we moved from one tin shed to another tin shed. But our new shed came with a lot of fringe benefits, at least for the kids.

This hostel was also surrounded by trees, and in one corner there was a pine forest, which meant there were a lot of animals and birds living there. Well, it really wasn't a forest, more a grove of pine trees, but after Cowcaddens, where there were no trees at all, this place could have been the Black Forest of Bavaria for all we knew. We used to climb trees and look for old birds' nests and of course we hid from each other out in the trees. It was great fun. Last time I drove out that way, the forest was still where we left it, and it doesn't look very big at all. But I remember it being huge and dark and if I was alone it could be very scary. Then again, any time I was alone was scary.

My older brother John said to me one day, 'Come on Jim, you're coming wi' me and we're gonnae play cowboys.'

I was happy to be included in anything John was doing; he was my big brother and I worshipped him.

'Where are we going, John?' I asked him, hoping I wasn't going to end up getting tied up or something.

But John was the head cowboy – he always was and still is – so I would go wherever he wanted to go. I don't think we had guns or cowboy hats or anything like that. We were just going to be cowboys I guess. I thought we would run around and pretend we had horses but no, John had a better idea.

'Just shut it and follow me,' he said as he ran across the paddock.

Over the other side of the black forest, across the Main North Road, was the abattoir. It seemed like we walked for miles to get there, but once again I have driven past there recently and it's not that far. I guess with smaller legs we had to take more steps. There were acres and acres of fenced-off paddocks full of animals standing around eating. I didn't really understand what an abattoir was, so I didn't realise they were waiting to be killed.

We didn't know a lot about anything really. Being cowboys was new to us, so we did things a little differently. Instead of jumping on the backs of horses or bulls, which were way too big for kids our size, we rode on the back of sheep. We were only small and the sheep still looked huge to us. We would get thrown into fences and trampled by the stampeding flock, which doesn't sound that scary now but then it was terrifying. So in our minds, we thought we were daredevils, risking our lives every time we stepped into the ring to take on one of these monsters.

It was only once I looked more carefully at the place that I worked out what happened there. Maybe I knew all along but never really wanted to think about it. You could smell death and fear in the air around there. But I had smelled fear everywhere I had been in my life and learned to ignore it unless it was affecting me. We stopped going to play at the abattoir, at least I did anyway.

When we worked out what the abattoir was, and what happened there, we realised why the area smelled so bad. Up until then we thought that when it got hot, the Australian bush smelled bad.

Music seems to add markers to my life and certain songs remind me of particular times. The song I remember most from those days was 'The Lion Sleeps Tonight' by The Tokens. I used to walk around singing something I'd made up that sounded remotely African, pretending I was in the jungle hunting wild, dangerous animals. I loved Tarzan as well so I would be yelling out at the top of my voice doing my best Tarzan impersonation, calling out, 'Ah ah ah ah ah ah ah,' to all the wild beasts in the paddocks around the hostel to come to me. Luckily they never heard me.

One day there was a lot of excitement among all the kids at the hostel. A circus had come to our town and set up in the paddocks near the hostel, probably thinking they would clean up with all the immigrant families living there. I'd never seen a circus before; I don't think they came to Cowcaddens. I had seen a few clowns walking around after closing time, but no circus. Anyway, unfortunately for the circus owners, no one had any money to spend on circuses; they had drinking habits they had to support.

But we kids would walk to the circus site and ask, 'Can we look at the animals, mister? We just want to see what goes on when there's no show. Please, mister, we'll be good.'

I think most of us secretly thought about running away and joining them but that changed when we saw how life in the circus really was. For a very short while they were nice to us but as soon as the carnie folk realised we had no money one of them yelled, 'Piss off, you brats, or we'll set the dogs on you!' So we ran as fast as we could. The evil carnie side had come out. They can be very nasty when they want to be, those carnies. One minute they're playing violins and reading your Tarot cards, next minute they're taking your passport and drinking your blood. Or is that vampires? I get them confused sometimes. Anyway, when they got nasty we all decided we hated them and their circus and wanted nothing to do with them.

After a few days we sort of forgot that they were there and were back to playing in the paddocks, doing whatever kids do in paddocks. I remember looking up one day and seeing people waving frantically at us. We thought they were just giving us the usual message to get home, and we ignored them. Next thing I knew there were police with guns running through the paddocks yelling, 'Stand perfectly still. Do not move. I repeat: stand perfectly still.'

Now this was exciting. What could be going on? Was it a man-hunt like I'd seen on television? Before I knew it, I was being bundled into a car and taken back to our hut. I thought that we must have done something really wrong. It was possible – my mum said we were always doing things wrong. So it seemed this time we got caught doing whatever it was we couldn't remember.

But we weren't in trouble at all. We were being rescued from wild beasts. The lions had escaped from the circus. Now I've heard since that the trainer didn't treat the lions very well; in fact, he beat them. All the poor animals in this circus were badly treated and malnourished. I found this out many years later when my band Cold Chisel did some *Circus Animal* shows. The circus working on the shows with us was the very circus that had set up in our paddock thirty-odd years earlier. I asked them about the lions escaping and they told me the truth about it.

It appears that the lion trainer was a bit of a drunk and to stop anyone else from getting to his booze, he had taken to hiding his bottle in the lions' cage. You would have to be really desperate to try to get it out of there. Well, he was really desperate it seems. One day, after a particularly heavy few days drinking, he went to get his secret bottle from the cage.

So the lions not only escaped; they seized the opportunity to rip him apart and eat him. Then they escaped and were, for the first time in many years, running free, through the paddock. It wasn't Africa but they were free. It must have felt great for them to stretch their legs after being caged up in those appalling conditions. Having the wind blow through their manes not to mention getting a bit of revenge on the man who beat them every day. But all good things come to an end. The police shot them dead. At least they were free again, even if just for a short time, and they died like lions, with a full stomach and with the blood of their tormentor on their lips. They were, for a moment, happy again.

I started school in Australia and had to repeat a year because I hadn't finished the year in Scotland, which meant I was a little bit older than the other kids in my year. Not a lot older, just half a year, but it was enough to help me later on. At the time, though,

I wanted to be in the class above and I was worried about being the oldest in my class for years after that. Like most kids, I wanted school to finish as soon as possible.

I heard all Australian kids were Vegemite kids and I wanted to be an Australian kid so bad. One day when Mum went shopping I asked her to buy some of this stuff, which really was a super food before super foods were even thought of. Mum was worried but got it anyway and put it high in the cupboard where her Scottish friends would not spot it. Then, one day while she was busy visiting one of the other families who were caged up in the hostel, I snuck in and grabbed the Vegemite and a spoon. All the kids who went to school seemed to love this stuff so I wanted to find out why. I didn't know you were supposed to spread this treat thinly onto freshly buttered, toasted bread. We didn't have bread or butter and we certainly didn't have a toaster.

So I ran out into the paddock and began to eat it by the spoonful straight out of the jar. Well, it tasted great and I was hungry, really hungry. So I kept on eating it. By the time I had nearly finished the jar, I had started to turn green. Just a little at first but very soon I was blending in with the grass; I was really green. Then I started vomiting. One of the kids who lived nearby ran and got my mum in case I was going to die.

She found me lying next to our hut with the empty jar beside me. 'That's what ye get for being a greedy little pig,' she said. Realising I wasn't going to die she left me to get over it, hoping I would learn a lesson.

I think the lesson was that too much of anything is not good for you. Well, as you probably know, it took about another forty-five years before I even started to learn that lesson.

* * *

Dad went from job to job and we went from school to school, Mum went from sad to sadder and we all went from hungry to hungrier. I can understand why my folks were unhappy – where we were living was atrocious. We had no privacy and the whole hostel knew when Mum and Dad had a fight. Well, we knew when any of our neighbours were fighting so I presume they could hear us. And like I said earlier, everybody seemed to have brought their problems from Britain to Australia, so there were a lot of arguments around the hostel. I would hear the sound of raised voices coming from the house next door; then there would be a crash and it would all go silent. That silence was the most frightening sound of all. I heard that same crash and silence many times as I lay in bed. It appeared that everybody was fighting with each other and waiting for the government to tell us all where we would be living on a more permanent basis. The longer that took, the more strained the relationships became. Tempers were frayed, a lot like the clothes we were wearing, and like our clothes, Mum and Dad's relationship was in tatters.

We thought that every couple fought like they did and that they all had the same problems. Maybe some of them did, but it became clearer and clearer to us that Mum was getting more unhappy. Not just when they fought but all of the time. She would sit at the table and tell us, 'That's it, I'm leaving yer bastard of a father. I cannae take any more o' this.'

We would be crying and begging her, 'No, don't go Mum. Don't leave us. We want tae stay wi' you.'

'Don't worry, I'd never leave you kids with this pig. You're ma babies and no one is ever gonnae separate us. Remember: I love you more than life and I'll never leave yous.'

Something went horribly wrong while we were in Seaton Park or Tea Tree Gully. I'm not sure what or where. There was something horribly wrong from the start but this was a new, more life-changing kind of wrong that I have never worked out.

Dad stopped working for the Italian builder. He never said why. All I know is that he and Mum were going through even more shit than they were before. Something had happened between them. Something drastic.

No one wanted to talk about it; it was just pushed under the rug, which would have been fine except we didn't have a rug. It was always there in front of us, along with all the skeletons that should have been in the closet we couldn't afford.

My little sister Lisa came along on 12 December 1962 and she was beautiful. She had dark olive skin and thick black hair. Dad called her his little pizza pie. The rest of us kids loved Lisa and carried her around whenever we could. She was an angel and we all thought that having a baby as lovely as this would fix the problems Mum and Dad were having, but it didn't. Life for the two of them could no longer be sorted out by Mum giving birth to a beautiful baby. Looking back, I can see it had never helped before.

In the meantime, Mum and Dad were waiting to find out where we would be living. For all we kids knew this hostel might have been permanent but obviously Mum and Dad were being told something by someone. We started to hear about this place out of Adelaide called Elizabeth, we heard that it was a satellite city, which sounded pretty impressive – we had no idea what a satellite city was but it sounded good. It turned out to be about twenty-odd miles to the north of Adelaide and it was a place that would shape the person I would grow up to be, for good and for bad.

the city of tomorrow

As kids, you adjust quickly to your surroundings, so I had settled into life in the hostel and the thought of moving again didn't appeal to me at all. I had friends here and a place to live. It wasn't great, but we were dry, and most importantly, I liked all the trees and open space around me. What if we moved into another dirty city or a tenement building?

We'd been in Australia for nearly two years when the big news came. Mum couldn't wait to break it to us so finally, after chasing us all over the hostel, she got us all together, sat us down and said, 'We're moving into our own hoose. This will be our hame and you kids will be going tae a new school. There'll be no more moving from place to place. This is where we'll stay forever. I promise. And it'll be clean and new.' I believed her. She had never lied to me, I could trust her.

As the day of the big move came closer, the excitement and the tension grew. There were a few more fights but there was also a bit more laughter. Could this be the answer to our problems? Mum started to plan what the house would look like. Her dream home. I hadn't seen her this excited before. She hadn't even seen it but she was happy. I think she thought she would at least get away from the nightmare the hostel had become to her.

'We'll have a garden and maybe even a dog. This'll be so great for us.' Looking back, I'm not sure who she was trying to convince – us or her.

On the day of the move the heavens opened. It could have been a sign. I hadn't seen rain like this since the day we arrived in Australia. It looked a lot like the Scottish summer. The rain was coming down sideways. Was God really going to make this harder for us than he needed to? Couldn't he just give us a break and let it stop long enough to pack up the house and finally get to a home? It seemed that he would make it as hard as he possibly could.

By the way, I'm not sure my parents even believed in God. I'd heard a lot about him at Sunday school. But I was sure Mum and Dad only sent us there to get rid of us while they got over Saturday nights. Where we came from, the only time people really prayed was when they wanted something they couldn't afford or when they had messed up so bad they needed someone to forgive them because no one at home would. 'Oh God, forgive me for what I did last night and help me get through this wi'out gettin' killed. I promise I won't fuck up again. Sorry, I didnae mean tae swear; forgive me for that too, please.'

It seemed we would have to fight against God and the elements for our home and our happiness. I was really starting to dislike this God character I kept hearing about. He didn't seem to do anything for anybody, especially the people we knew. Maybe we didn't deserve his help.

The people moving our stuff told us the roads were flooded and we probably wouldn't get through so maybe we would have to move another day. I'm not sure if it was the pleading of my mum or the thought of telling my dad they couldn't do it that made them push on through and brave the rising waters. But they did it.

Everything we owned, borrowed or were given by the government was packed in the truck. All that was left was to squeeze the family in too, and we could be off. After some tearful goodbyes to friends, it was one last look back over our shoulders at the tin can we had called home and then off, to face whatever life had to offer us. It was late 1963 and we were moving to Elizabeth.

To say it was wet was the understatement of the decade. The rain never stopped for a minute. By the time we were halfway to Elizabeth we felt like the truck was more than just a moving van, it was our life raft, and if we all held on tight it would save us from the raging torrents that threatened to wash us off the road and back to the hostel, or worse, back to Glasgow.

About five miles out of Elizabeth we had to cross a creek that was so swollen that the water had risen up to the doors of the truck. It felt like there was a good chance we would be washed away, but we drove straight through it, without a second thought. Nothing was going to stop us reaching our new home.

As the truck got closer we could see that some of the streets were not quite finished, but it looked like heaven to us. This was a place that was actually being constructed from the ground up instead of being torn down or falling down like we were used to in Scotland. It looked like there were football fields on every corner, and shops, and parks and swings for little kids. It all looked too good to be true. But it had been a long day and I was getting really tired. I was trying to keep my eyes open so I could be first to spot our house, but it was getting harder with every minute. By the time we finished the drive, the excitement and the rain had worn me out. I don't even remember getting there.

Mum must have carried me into the house and put me to sleep on the floor somewhere and covered me with a coat. That's what always happened when Mum took us out at night. I'd wake up in a corner in the middle of a party, not knowing where I was or how I got there. Not to mention whose coat I was wearing. I was normally not the only one who didn't know where they were. The adults looked the same.

Eventually our beds were put up and I slept until morning. When the sun came up, the clouds had cleared to reveal our dream home. By then I could hear Mum telling Dad, 'Move that over there. No, no there, over there. Are you deif or somethin'?'

This went on until she was happy or he'd had enough, but by then the place almost looked like home. I walked around the house and I knew straight away that this place was much better than any hostel. It was made of bricks and was solid and felt permanent. Permanent was something new to me. Not only was the house new, it was clean – and, most importantly, it was ours.

It smelled of fresh cut wood and paint. There was a bath and a shower and a toilet built into the house. The boys had a separate room from the girls. We even had a small fireplace to remind us of Scotland. Mum was happy, everything was great. Mum was busy hanging things and moving what little furniture we owned around the house for the tenth time, much to my dad's horror. He wanted to go out and find a drink somewhere. There was even food ready to eat. Life was looking up and again I felt like we were going to be all right. I felt like this most mornings, by the way, and normally that didn't change until something went wrong later in the day. How long would it take this time?

The sun was shining outside and I ran straight out to see where we were in this new world. There was a big paddock across the road from us and beyond that there was a train line. I heard a whistle blowing and spotted a train as it raced across the horizon. It was like a magnet to me. I would have to go across the paddock and check out the train lines when I got the chance.

The rain had stopped but there was water everywhere in pools. There was mud in the yard where the builders had been working until the day we arrived. They must have left just before our truck got there. I could see tracks across the front yard, deep troughs where the wheels of the truck had fought their way out of the mud that gripped onto them like quicksand.

Our street was neat and tidy in its layout, except for the mud. As I looked down the street I could see rows of houses, all nearly the same as ours. All new and waiting for families to arrive and breathe life into them. There were pale brown brick homes and red brick homes, in no certain order, some were bigger than ours and a couple seemed smaller. But they all looked roughly the same to me.

A few of the houses were already occupied. There were cars parked on the street and some of the houses had lawns fighting to push their way up through the mud. I could see signs of other children living nearby: the odd bike leaning against a fence and a ball or two that had been left out in the rain overnight. I knew I would be fine here.

Forty-five Heytesbury Road, Elizabeth West, was my home for the next few years. They would be some of the best and some of the worst years of my life so far. In those years life twisted and turned like none of us could have expected.

Time passed, and Mum and Dad didn't find their dream; in fact, things went from worse to much worse. The life lessons that they were supposed to hand down to us, didn't come as they should have. Those lessons – like every other lesson – got lost in fear and violence and drunkenness. We never learned about hope or the chance of finding our dreams. That didn't happen to families like ours. Dad drank more and gambled more, Mum tried harder until she had nothing left to give.

* * *

Elizabeth looked like such a great idea on paper. They called it the City of Tomorrow. Bring out a hungry workforce ready to seize an opportunity to start fresh new lives and put them in a place where there were factories for employment, schools for their kids and homes for them to live in happily ever after. What could go wrong? But everything seemed to go wrong, right from the start. The factories paid just enough to feed the families and if they were frugal enough, and if they didn't drink at all, they might just scratch out a life. But when you throw in alcoholism and ignorance along with all the other problems that people brought with them from Britain, life fell apart for most of them pretty quickly.

The families we knew had trouble making ends meet, mainly because of the drinking problems they all seemed to have. The ones who didn't drink were doing a little better. The families whose parents were sober seemed to keep away from our type of people and even looked down on us. I can see why now. Don't get me wrong. It was hard for all the families, even the sober ones. But somehow if the parents weren't drinking all the money, things went a little smoother. Funny that, don't you think?

When I walked home with the kids from school who seemed to be doing better than us, it sometimes got uncomfortable.

'Can I come into your place for a while and play? I'd like to see inside your house.'

'My mum doesn't want you … er … anybody to come in tonight. Sorry Jim, you'd better just go home.'

'That's okay, I've got things to do anyway.'

And I would walk away feeling ashamed of myself and embarrassed that they didn't like me.

Some families drank more than others. My dad drank as much as any and we were struggling because of it. Dad would work hard trying to keep his drinking under control until pay day, then he would be gone. At the start of every week, Mum would work out a budget that might just feed us and clothe us, and then would have to scramble to make ends meet when Dad drank the budget. Many a time we would have gone hungry if Mum hadn't whipped up something from nothing. Mums seem to be able to do that.

Mum tried her best to make Elizabeth our home. She got out in the garden and planted a lawn and fruit trees. She planted candle pines in the driveway. I know that sounds grand but the driveway wasn't that long, which didn't bother us because we didn't have a car. I'm not sure Dad knew how to drive. Later I would take little cones off the pines and use them as ninja weapons to throw at my sisters. They were hard and spiky and I could throw them from a distance and still have time to make a getaway – most of the time.

Even Dad got involved in the planting. I remember one of the trees he planted was called a million-dollar peach. I can still hear him saying, 'Aye, million-dollar peaches, kids. These are the best peaches you can get. It won't be long till you're eating them every day. You'll be almost sick of them.'

We stood listening to him with watering mouths. We would have been happy with any peaches. Two-dollar peaches, fifty-cent nectarines would have done. It didn't matter what they were worth. We just wanted them, right now. But these did sound like something really special. Unfortunately, it took quite a few years for the trees to fruit and when they did, Dad had lost interest in them. The birds and bugs seemed to be the only ones who got to eat this glorious, expensive-sounding fruit. And by the time they were ripe enough for human consumption the best were already gone and all that was left had been half eaten.

The other thing Mum and Dad wanted to plant was corn and after a few months the backyard looked like a farm. Well, a really small farm if you shut one eye. We hadn't eaten corn that much before and it didn't take long until we all got sick of it. I think it was all we were eating.

Later on, Mum tried to grow other vegetables besides corn, so that we would have something to eat when the wages didn't arrive but they died pretty quickly. You need to look after the plants and water them. If you don't they won't grow to be any good, a lot like kids when I think about it. The pumpkins thrived; they took over the backyard for a while. We ate a lot of pumpkin for a little while there.

Before long any interest in gardening was gone. Mum and Dad were back to only being interested in indoor pastimes again, like drinking and fighting.

The house seemed to me to be quite big even though I know it wasn't. There were four bedrooms, and a lounge and a kitchen of course. I remember Mum cooking in that kitchen. She had bought a pressure cooker and everything seemed to be cooked in it. Potatoes, cabbage, anything.

The sound of the pressure building up was *Tsh Tsh Tsh Tsh*. It reminded me of the sprinkler on the football ovals at night.

Tsh Tsh Tsh ...

'What's for dinner the night?' Dad would ask.

Tsh Tsh Tsh ...

The noise of the pressure cooker was speeding up.

'Cabbage and mince and totties.'

'Again,' he'd moan.

Tsh Tsh Tsh ...

'You've always said ye loved it.'

Tsh Tsh Tsh ...

'I do, but no every fuckin' night.'

Tsh Tsh Tsh ...

'And shut that pot up, it's drivin' me nuts.'

Tsh Tsh Tsh ...

It seemed to get faster and faster.

'I need it tae cook for the kids. I'm cookin' for them, no for you.'

Tsh Tsh Tsh ...

'I don't want yer food. I'm goin' oot for a wee while.' He was almost exploding himself, and would walk out.

Bang the door would slam.

Tsh Tsh Tsh ...

The pressure cooker seemed to be the soundtrack to their tempers, building and building until it was like a bomb waiting to blow. And then Mum would take off the lid from the top of the pressure valve and then,

SHHHHHHHHHH.

It was like the whole house had let out a big breath and we were finally ready to sit down and eat. John and I would line up fighting over who got to drink the juice from the cooking cabbage. It tasted like soup to us, salty and filling, and we were hungry.

'You got it last night. It's my turn,' he'd shout.

'No I didn't, you did.'

'Mum, he drank it last night, it's my turn.'

'Stop fightin' and I'll share it between the two o' ye.'

Mum would be pouring the hot water from the pot into the cups. With all the steam coming up from the cups you could hardly notice the tears in her eyes, but I could see them.

We had no garage but that was fine because, as I said, we never had a car. Not one that actually ran anyway. For a while there was some old wreck sitting in the driveway that us kids would sit in and pretend we were driving around the country. I'm sure Dad always had grand ideas about fixing it up for the family, but the only thing handy about Dad was that he lived with us. He really wasn't very good at fixing, hanging, painting, changing or growing anything. I'm not sure what he was good at but fighting and smooth talking. But damn he was good at both of those. When I think about it, I don't think it would have been a good idea to get in a car with him anyway.

Many years later I was doing *Sixty Minutes* for television and I went back to Elizabeth to stand outside and film the house we grew up in. The woman who lived there saw me and asked if I wanted to come in and look around. I said straight away, 'I used to live here when I was really young.'

She smiled at me and said, 'I already knew that before I rented it.'

When I walked in I couldn't believe how small it was. This house was tiny. For us to have lived there with six kids and parents who couldn't stand to be in the same room as each other was amazing. No wonder we all went crazy. The house looked a lot better than when we lived there and felt like a happier place.

I told her that I felt glad to see that the place finally had a loving family living there. A house needs a family that loves to make it a home. She gave me a cuddle and I left.

The house was a semi-detached and another family lived there, right next to us. The walls were thin and didn't stand a chance of blocking the noise that went from house to house. We knew what they were eating; in fact, the walls were that thin we almost knew what they were thinking.

I felt sorry for the neighbours not only because of the fights Mum and Dad had, but because of us kids. We were wild, always running in and out, slamming doors or stomping up and down the hallway shouting at each other.

'Get lost, you're a scab. Mum, he's hitting me.'

And so on. Maybe we weren't that polite either. We would regularly climb onto the roof and run around up there. Especially me; I used to think that I was in the television show *The Samurai* and I'd climb up to the roof and jump off all the time. Sometimes onto my sisters; other times, if I was escaping some imaginary enemy, I would jump into the poor neighbours' yard and scare the hell out of them.

I thought I was a ninja and would throw things at people and hide up trees, waiting in ambush to spring onto an unsuspecting foe. I even made my own throwing stars out of cardboard. They weren't very dangerous and they didn't go very fast or far. Some of my friends made them out of the top of tin cans. I think they cut themselves up more just making them than they cut anyone else throwing them. But they were dangerous and they didn't mind throwing them at anybody.

I would run around and hide in the paddock opposite our house. I thought I was really good at hiding like a ninja, until I realised that no one was looking for me. That's why they never found me. That sort of took the shine off things, but I kept on playing regardless.

One of the neighbours at the back of the house was a singer and had a hit on Adelaide radio covering something like 'I Remember You', the Frank Ifield song. Me and the other kids would sing it over the fence of his house as loud as we could. As soon as the back door opened we would be gone, not a trace of us anywhere. We thought it was cool for about five minutes to have a pop star living nearby and then we forgot all about it. I never heard his name again so I don't think he had another hit. How fleeting was stardom in those days; not much has changed really.

Of all the neighbours, the ones I seemed to get on with the best was a Dutch family three doors down. Billy was my friend and we played football and anything else we could think of together. I seemed to spend a lot of time at his house. I would even go in and sit with his parents when he and his sister weren't there and they treated me just like one of their own. I remember even learning a little of the language from the dad. I can still count to ten in Dutch.

They were a nice family and always made me feel welcome. I think that they were appalled by the behaviour of some of the other families in the street, including mine. They were very quiet and had a very neat, tidy house and neat and tidy lives, just like most of the Dutch people I know now. They had little windmills and clogs on their shelves to remind them of home. But they moved away, I hope to a better street with better neighbours.

Dad got a cheap wooden shed from somewhere and he stuck it in the backyard for us to use as a cubbyhouse. This was not a tree house like you might see on *Leave it to Beaver* or any other American TV show, come to think of it. This was a shed that he nailed together with six-inch nails, so it had nails sticking out of the walls. If you weren't careful you could rip a big hole in yourself. It was a Glaswegian cubbyhouse; you took your life in your hands just by standing in it. I don't know where he got it; maybe it fell off the back of a truck. Lots of things seemed to fall off trucks in those days.

There were no windows at all, just one door. It wasn't very nice. My sisters tried to make it better but they could only do so much. They took over the shed completely and told me in no uncertain terms, 'You're not allowed in here at all. This is our house.'

I wasn't happy about this. So one day I decided I would get them back. There was a little hole I found on the roof while I was being a ninja and climbing on it when they weren't there. I blocked the door so it was hard to get out in a hurry and then I climbed onto the roof as quietly as I could and threw stink bombs into it. They never expected me to do something as clever as that, so there was a lot of screaming and swearing and crying but eventually they fought their way out of the shed. Of course I was well gone by then, running down the road zig-zagging, with my knees bent just like the ninjas I had seen on television.

I was not planning on returning until much later, when they had forgotten it had ever happened. My big mistake was that sisters never forget. This, it seemed, was the hard lesson I had to learn. And to make things worse, like I said, my sisters were much tougher than I was. I would pay for my shenanigans. I would pay a huge price. I got beaten up by them and their friends and then I had to be their slave for days, until they didn't need or want me around. Then I was off the hook and could become a ninja again and return to jumping off roofs.

As I mentioned before, the meal of choice for most Scottish families was mince and totties, which was basically boiled or mashed potato and mincemeat cooked with onions and carrots. Never mind haggis, I think this is the Scottish national dish. We ate it every day we could afford it, occasionally broken up by chips, baked beans and eggs, another Scottish staple. Mum made it particularly well but you know how it is, your mum's food is always the best. I think it has to do with the love they pour into it. But it got harder and harder for Mum to find the money to feed us or the love to put into it and some nights we would get chips and not much more than that.

In fact, the plates were normally covered in chips – not the ones you could eat, unfortunately. Mum tried her best to keep the table nice but slowly the setting got sparser and sparser. The knives and forks no longer matched. Pieces were lost, thrown into the bin accidentally, or Mum and Dad had thrown them at each other as they stormed out of the house. We always drank out of cups. Mum and Dad saved the glasses for adults and booze. Cups were fine for water.

Then there was the time my dad got chickens from someone at the pub. He probably won them in a bet. How you win chickens in a bet, I don't know. What was he betting if he lost, the kids? But he decided that we were going to have the best eggs to eat in the street.

'Okay kids, these wee feathery bastards will gie us fresh eggs every day,' he told us.

It reminded me of the peaches but I didn't say anything. Mum and Dad always seemed to have these plans that they never followed through. Well, as I now know, in order to get eggs you have to feed the chickens. This is the basic principle of raising animals: you've got to feed them or they will die. If you don't feed them chicken food, then you need to give them lots of scraps. Well, we didn't have chicken food, we couldn't afford it, and the only scraps we had, we ate ourselves.

Over the few months that the poor chickens lived with us Dad would get drunk and go outside and talk to them. 'Evening ladies. What a lovely night it is,' he would say. 'You're all looking very nice tonight. Are you wearing your feathers differently? How's the scratching in the yard going for you?' I think it was easier than talking to any of us inside the house.

Anyway, it was only a matter of time before the sad day came that the chickens had to go. We couldn't feed them and we didn't have anything to eat ourselves so Mum said to Dad, 'Jim, ya lazy bastard. You're goin' to have tae go oot there and kill a chicken or two to feed the weans.'

Now Dad hated any cruelty to animals. He didn't seem to mind cruelty to humans; but they could speak up for themselves, animals couldn't. He had names for them all and the thought of having to kill them broke his heart. Dad preferred the company of animals to humans. You only had to look at his friends to see that.

I remember that fateful day. He went out to the backyard with a hatchet and called out to the girls, 'Harriet, Gertrude, Dot. Come here, girls.'

They had names like that. How one got named after my mum I don't know; maybe they both had thin legs. Only Dad could answer that question. I sat and watched my dad sit down and cry as he told them what he had to do. 'I'm sorry, ladies. This is not my idea. The battleaxe inside says the kids have tae eat. So please forgive me.'

Obviously Dad hadn't done anything like this before. In Glasgow you only killed things that were trying to kill you first. And normally they had axes too.

Well, he chopped the head off one of his chickens. Funny, Dot was chosen first. She ran around the yard headless and bleeding to the sound of my dad screaming like he'd killed one of the kids. It was all too much for him. He wiped the blood from his face and hands and walked out of the yard and down to the pub. We didn't see him again for days.

Mum had to finish the job off; she had been ready to kill something or someone for years. Thank God Dad was gone. And after a few tears and protests from us kids, not to mention the chickens, we sat down to a meal of Mum's boiled chicken. That's what we ate for about a week. Chicken, followed by more chicken, until they were all gone. We hated chicken by the end but after a few weeks we would have done anything for another chicken to eat.

I didn't like chicken for a while after that. Just like corn and pumpkin. But not for long. Beggars can't be choosy. And we were obviously beggars.

CHAPTER EIGHT

cardboard inside our shoes

There were days we would be kept home from school waiting for Mum's children's allowance cheque to come in the mail. It was too wet to go without the right clothes or shoes to wear. Mum would be waiting on the only money that Dad couldn't get his hands on, so she could count on that at least. Fourteen dollars a fortnight was all it was, but it meant we could eat or she could buy a pair of shoes for one of us; we all needed them.

We would go to school in the rain with bits of cardboard stuck inside our shoes, covering the holes in the bottom, hoping it would stop the water coming in and wetting our already frozen feet. The cardboard never really worked. It seemed fine at home but once you left the house water just oozed in. I used to sit in school with cold, wet feet. I'd be hungry and uncomfortable and I just couldn't concentrate on what was going on in front of me. I think the teachers knew because they would reach out and try to help me get through the work.

Sometimes school was great because we could forget what was going on at home for a while, but other times the water inside your shoes or the dirty clothes you were wearing just made it too hard to forget what was happening. There were a lot of other kids who looked like they were escaping something or someone, or maybe both.

The kids at the school all looked the same. Mostly immigrant kids who came from lower working-class families that were struggling to get by. Most of us wore clothes that were either second-hand or looked second-hand; some were cleaner or newer than others. We were all wearing coats that our big brothers or sisters had been wearing the year before, well past their prime by the time we got our hands on them. Shirts with odd buttons sewn on them. Pants with patches on them covering holes that had been made the year before. Each patch like a reminder of a winter past full of sliding, playing football on grass and mud and gravel.

Everybody wore shoes that were scuffed and dirty. I wondered how many of the kids were like me and had pieces of cardboard box stuffed into the soles of their shoes. My socks always seemed to have holes in them too. Sitting in class with your toes sticking through a huge hole in your sock could be so distracting. A lot of things were missed in class as I tried to concentrate on wriggling my toes into a position where the hole would stay covered.

'Do you know the answer, Jim?'

'Ah, no miss, I wasn't listening. I dropped my pencil. Sorry.'

'Pay attention, Jim, and try to keep your feet still please.'

The teacher always seemed to smile as if she knew what was going on.

'Yes, miss, I'll try.'

And I would return to my magician's trick of getting my toes back into the socks that were not capable of holding them anymore without anyone noticing.

If my feet were too wet, I would try to slip my shoes off under my desk to let them dry. But when the socks were in too bad a condition my feet had to stay hidden in my shoes. It was the only way. I didn't need something else to be embarrassed about.

* * *

My brother John was so proud to be a Scot that he would wear a kilt to school. He said it was because he was proud of where he came from but I thought it was so he could swing at anybody who commented on his clothes. Maybe that was the best thing he had to wear, I can't remember. He looked very smart. Even the teachers commented on how good he looked. But, of all the Scots that were in the school, I know that John was the only one who wore a kilt. I never inherited the kilt so I didn't have to fight as much as John, thank God.

John also played snare drum for the whole school to march in time to when we were called to assembly. He was always standing still and straight with his sticks at the ready. Waiting for a nod from the teacher or the headmaster. Then he would press the sticks to the skin and begin to play. If you had seen him, you would have thought he was playing at the Edinburgh Tattoo. Head up, eyes straight ahead. Perfect posture. He learned all this from the pipe band, where he was a member, which was another reason he gave for wearing his kilt.

'I need to wear this if I'm going to play the drums properly.'

'Can I play your drum, John?'

'No you can't.'

Whenever John left his drum lying around I would give it a bashing but he never caught me.

Later on, after John left the primary school, I became the drummer too. I tried to be as good as John, but my posture was never like his. Still, I thought I was just like my big brother, which made me very happy.

John was dabbling in rock music between his time playing football and playing with the pipe band. His band would come to the house to practise when Mum and Dad weren't there, which was more and more by then, so it's little wonder that the neighbours never talked to us. I think they might have been afraid of us. I don't know why really. They wouldn't even nod hello if I passed them on the street. Maybe it was because I jumped from the roof into their garden sometimes. But I think it was probably because Mum would scowl at them and say stuff like, 'What the fuck are you looking at, stupit?' or 'Take a fuckin' photo, it lasts longer,' whenever she stormed out of the house after fighting.

I'm sure our neighbours had their own problems, but not like ours. To me, no one did.

At school I made up for all the things we didn't have by trying really hard. I became top of my class. I was smart but I also tried harder than everyone else because I wanted to feel as good as the rest of the kids. I didn't want anybody to know what was going on at home.

In my first class in Elizabeth West Primary School all the kids loved our teacher. She was so calm and caring and seemed to have time for every one of us. She was never too busy to help you draw or try to write. It was her job, I know, but she made us all feel good as she did it. At the end of every day we would all line up at her desk to say goodbye, as if each one of us was the only one she cared about. We wouldn't want to go to our homes and face whatever was going on. I remember seeing my teacher crying after giving one of the kids a cuddle one day. The teachers seemed to know that the kids needed a little more care than normal and they all gave it to us. We were lucky.

For some reason I was singled out as a singer in my class. The teachers would make me sing any song that we had learned. I would be chosen to go around the other classes and show them what we were doing. Some of the songs were traditional school songs, others were Australian folk songs. They were always trying to remind us that we lived in the lucky country. It didn't always feel that lucky but it wasn't snowing on us and the sun did seem to shine a lot more here than in Scotland.

At Christmas time we sang carols. Not simple everyday Christmas carols, but songs about goannas and brolgas. I remember standing in front of one class singing 'Orana Orana to Christmas Day'. I sang it with so much heart and love. I didn't have a clue what Orana meant. Still don't. But I knew the birds were singing too and if cockatoos were singing it, it was good enough for me.

I guess I couldn't have been too shy or I could never have done this. I was pretty happy to get out in front of the other students and belt out a song. I think I liked the attention; it made me feel special, or just good about myself. I didn't have a lot to be proud of as a child. I was always feeling not good enough on some level, and singing was the one thing that made me different from the other kids. I could sing; it was my gift. The teachers thought it was a good thing too. I worked out that singing made me look better than I thought I actually was. This is another one of those things I learned at an early age and have used all my life to make myself feel good.

My first good mate at school was a guy called Rob and he and I were inseparable. We hung out all day at school and played football until dark after school. We both came from poor families but for some reason I always felt that Rob's family was a little more stable than mine. He and I wouldn't talk much about what went on at home or anywhere else come to think of it; we lived in our own world. He was always a little nervous around people and I got the impression he was like me, always a little scared. I think he might have started hanging out with me because I wasn't afraid to fight anyone who bullied us. Rob and I would sit together in class and hang out at lunch break. We both had no money so we quite often shared whatever we had to eat; sometimes that wasn't very much. We were best mates and what I had was his and what he had was mine. Unfortunately, I didn't have a lot.

'Are you hungry, Jim?' he'd ask as he pulled out his lunch. He could tell by the way I was looking at it that I needed something. It wasn't a lot but he was happy to give me half.

Some days I would feel so bad because I knew he was hungry too. So I would pretend. 'No thanks, mate. Not hungry. You eat it.'

But we were mates and if Rob felt bad, I felt bad too. A year or so later, I noticed things weren't going as well for Rob at home as they had been. He seemed to be a bit withdrawn and he started to look paler than usual, like he wasn't getting enough sleep. I thought he might have been sick or something.

'Are you all right mate?' I asked. But he couldn't talk about whatever it was.

'Yeah. Mum and Dad are fighting a lot.'

'So are mine. They always do. It'll be all right.'

'Yeah, suppose you're right. Let's go.'

We still laughed and ran around wild all day. Then one day after school he said to me that he couldn't play, he had to go straight home.

'Why? Stay and play football with me at the shops.'

'Na. Dad's not good and I best get home.'

'What – is he sick or something?'

'Na. Not really. I gotta go.'

We both laughed, but inside we knew it was no laughing matter. We walked together as far as the corner.

'See you tomorrow, mate.'

'Yeah, see you then.'

And I headed to my place and Rob went to his.

He got home, walked in the front door and found there was no one in the house. He went through the lounge room into the kitchen and still he couldn't find his parents. So he walked towards the back door and saw his dad, sitting on the step of the back porch looking out onto the red dusty backyard. That's when he noticed the shotgun in his mouth. He quickly opened the door but before he could shout stop, his dad pulled the trigger, spraying blood and brains all over him. I'm sure his dad wasn't expecting him home. But Rob was never the same from that day on. We stayed friends until he and what was left of his family moved away. They couldn't take living in that house anymore.

I caught up with Rob many years later at a pub and we had a few drinks. He and a few friends came back to my place for a party. I knew he had changed a lot, but after what he'd been through, I thought that was fair enough. I wanted to reconnect with him, even if it was just for a night, but it never happened. Of course we'd had a lot to drink, but I noticed earlier in the night that his eyes were all glazed over. Then later on he grabbed me to one side and asked me to have a shot of heroin with him. I was just drunk enough that he nearly talked me into it too. I even let him tie a belt around my arm and get the needle ready before my survival instincts kicked in and I said no. This was not the same guy I had run around the oval with at school. This wasn't the guy who shared what little food he had with me when we were kids. He was gone; he died that day on the back porch of a dusty, cheap, housing trust house with his dad.

I never really saw him again after that, maybe once, but we didn't have a lot to say. I hope he's still alive and has found some happiness. Rob was my best mate and I loved him. I died a little for him that day too.

* * *

When I was seven or so, Dad decided to get us a dog. I think it was for himself actually. It was a beautiful collie that looked like Lassie. We all loved him and wanted to walk him and brush him all the time. But we weren't allowed to walk him unless Mum or Dad told us we could.

One afternoon when I finished school, I went into the backyard and decided to take the dog for a walk without a leash. I knew if I asked my folks for the leash they would say no, so it was a bit sneaky.

The dog was very clever and followed me everywhere. I was having the best time. I was on my way home and I was running so I would get there before Mum or Dad knew the dog was missing. I was about two streets from our house when I looked behind me to see the dog running across the road just as a car came speeding by. The car hit the dog and never even stopped. I ran out onto the road and I held the dog in my arms. I pulled him close to me, sobbing and telling him how sorry I was, as he slowly stopped breathing.

By the time anybody came to help, I was covered in blood and the poor little dog had died. I just wanted to sit and hold him until he was okay again. Someone went to get my mum and I just sat and cried. I cried for days and even to this day I wish I hadn't taken the dog out.

I wanted to play music. Any music. I started playing the coronet which was basically the same as a trumpet. It was shiny and loud and that was all I needed. I was learning from the Salvos, but this meant I had to do Sunday school and have people preaching at me. So I didn't last too long. Long enough to drive the neighbours completely nuts though. I would practise in the room right next to their wall. At night when Mum and Dad weren't there I would play even more, just to drive the rest of the kids nuts too. I wasn't playing Miles Davis or anything cool, just Salvos songs. Eventually I drove myself nuts. So the coronet had to go.

I was keen to join up to the pipe band with John. So off I went to the Caledonian Society Pipes and Drums. John played the military snare and I moved on to the bagpipes. Now there was a musical instrument that made a lot of noise. Like I told you, I had grown up listening to bagpipes. I knew what they meant to Scots everywhere. When I heard them, my heart beat faster, I loved it. But to learn to play bagpipes you have to learn the basics on an instrument called the chanter. A scrawnier-sounding musical instrument has never existed. I think that cobras would throw themselves in front of passing cars rather than have to climb out of a basket and dance to a chanter. It peeled paint off the walls. It takes many years to master the chanter, and even when mastered I don't think anyone plays it for enjoyment. But it is the only way to the bagpipes and I wanted to play bagpipes so much.

On joining the band, I learned that discipline was a big part of being in a pipe band. You worked as a unit to play and to march in military formation while doing it. It seemed to be like lessons in being truly Scottish. There was no one but Scots in the society; it was a new place I had found where Scottish people could congregate and celebrate being Scottish. Up until that time I thought the only place this happened was in the pub.

There were members of the band who drank but this was not a drinking club. This was important business and the other members took the music, the marching and the culture very seriously. I felt a new sense of pride about being Scottish. Before then I was proud to come from Scotland because that was what every drunken Scotsman I had ever encountered had asked of me. This was a different sort of pride – pride based on doing something great together.

I remember the man who taught me the chanter was a very straight Scotsman. A lot of Scotsmen seem to be either drunks or really straight. There's not too many in the middle. We tend to be a tad extreme, us Scots. This one was a really nice man but I knew he didn't like my mum and dad which put me off him a bit. But he would give me extra lessons for free at his house. I think he felt sorry for me.

He was a stern-looking man who didn't smile at all even if I got things right. 'Aye that's good, now just stand up straight and get on wi' it. You'll never make a piper wi' posture like that,' he would bark at me like we were marching in the band already. His accent was very broad, though I knew he had been in Australia a long time. It seemed to me he was one of those people who weren't really happy to have left Scotland. Just like the windmills and clogs in my Dutch friend's house, he had little bagpipers in full tartan regalia and a small Edinburgh Castle standing proudly on his mantelpiece. He was holding on to everything Scottish he could, including his accent. He rolled his r's and broke into broad Scots whenever he could.

'It's a braw nicht the nicht – ya ken whit I mean, laddie?' he'd say as I walked through the door.

'Aye, it is. It's a bonnie night oot there,' I'd say and he'd almost smile at me but never did.

I would think of funny things to say on the way to my lesson, to try to make him laugh, and have them ready to go as I walked in the door.

'That's a bonnie pair o' pyjamas yer pipes are wearin' the night,' I'd say. Nothing. He never once reacted.

He also refused to say anything that was remotely Australian. I sort of liked it. He couldn't afford to go home so he kept home in his heart. He would probably die whispering 'Scotland' with his last breath.

His family sat down at the table and ate together. He spoke civilly with his wife and they even appeared to care for each other's feelings. This was all new to me. He didn't drink at all whenever I was at his place, in fact; I didn't see signs of alcohol anywhere in the house. Everything seemed to be orderly and in its place. Nothing was broken or falling apart and the house was clean and tidy. I wanted our place to be like this but it wasn't.

I liked him a lot and was sorry he had to stop teaching me. I never actually made it to the full set of pipes or into the band, as things got too rough at home and I had to quit.

We all loved music. My sisters and I would pretend to be in bands like The Beatles and stand on the porch and mime songs along to the radio. Like the music my parents listened to, the music we listened to reflected how we felt. Songs about wanting to hold someone's hand were like cries for love coming from the radio. We were crying out just like that. Songs where the singer was begging for help – I'm not even going to go there.

One day while John was playing music in his room, I saw an album cover and whoever it was, was playing a square guitar. This really caught my eye because the girls and I had been trying to cut guitars out of cardboard for a while. But we found it way too hard. Bo Diddley, the guy playing a square guitar on that cover, changed everything. That was it – we only made square guitars from then on.

The girls were all good singers and we worked out a few routines we could do at parties to make all the adults think we were cute. We would sing something about having fun in the car with Fred. I always had to be Fred. I hated it. I wanted to sing the main vocals.

* * *

I was sitting watching an old black and white movie called *Imitation of Life* with my dad one day. I was not that interested. It was a good movie but I was only about seven and I would rather have been watching a cowboy movie or a cartoon if the truth be known. But I was with Dad so I was happy.

The movie was basically about a young black girl who had very fair skin and when she grew up she left her family and pretended that she was white. She, like me later on in my life, was running away from her real life. This worked out for her for a while but she had problems, especially when her mother died. At the end of the movie she attends her mother's funeral. I can't remember that much except for the end of the film, when she was in the church at the funeral. There was a woman singing and I remember being stunned by this woman's voice. I sat straight upright and was immediately glued to the screen. Even as a kid I could hear that there was something exceptional about this voice.

The movie finished and I waited for the credits to roll to find out who this woman was. Her name was Mahalia Jackson and I made a mental note to myself that when I had a child, I was going to name the baby after this singer. Luckily for me, my wife Jane and I had a baby girl first and I named her Mahalia. If she had been a boy he would have had to learn to fight at a very young age.

Mahalia Jackson singing in the church in this movie made me think for a minute that there might be a God after all. No one sang with that much power without a little help from somewhere. If he was up there he should've looked down on us a little more often; things might have been better. Now it's too late; I don't need him.

The paddock across the road was the scene of many of life's lessons for us. We would run and hide there when we were in trouble, which was often. And we would run and hide there when home got too much for us. Unfortunately, that was more often. I spent many a night hiding there as the sun went down, scared because it was getting dark but too scared to go home. Afraid Mum and Dad would be fighting or drinking or both. Not wanting to see the state the family was in. We were falling apart and every day things got worse. There were more fights. If there was no fighting it normally meant that Dad had not made it home and Mum would be angry and frustrated and once again we would be scratching for something to eat. Mum would end up crying in her room and we would all be left looking at each other, wondering what was going to happen next. I was afraid of everything in those days.

I also had big fights with other kids in that paddock and I laughed and cried in that paddock. That paddock was a huge part of my life. I spent more time there than in our house.

The first naked girl I ever saw, not in a bathtub with me, was in that paddock. A friend of one of my sisters took off her clothes in front of me when I was about seven. She was a lot older than me and I didn't know why she did it but I knew it was taboo. It scared me too.

There were all sorts of things to do. There were ants' nests to disturb and hills to run up and down and even the odd animal to hunt. One day I caught a blue-tongue lizard and decided to keep him as a pet. He would be my friend and I would teach him amazing tricks to impress the family. I found an old cardboard box and put some grass in there so he would be comfortable. I wasn't even sure if lizards worried about comfort, but I wanted my lizard to have all mod cons. I decided that he had to be a guy because he was so ugly. I never saw any good-looking ones so I could have been wrong. I took him home and snuck him into my room. My sisters found him, while they were looking for something else they said, but I know they were just snooping through my stuff.

'Mum, he's got a filthy wild animal in his bedroom and it smells really bad!' They exaggerated a lot. He looked clean to me and he hardly stank at all.

Mum was her usual calm self. She shrieked, 'Get that scabby lizard oot ma hoose before I kill the both o' ye,' in a voice that even scared the lizard. He probably still has nightmares about it.

That meant he had to live outside. I was very disappointed. I made up my mind that if he wasn't going to live in my room he was better off in the paddock where he came from.

So in a scene reminiscent of *Born Free* I said my teary goodbyes to my scaly, slightly smelly little friend. 'You'll forget about me soon, Bruce.' He looked Australian and needed an Australian name. 'Don't worry about me. Just run and be free with all your other wild friends.'

Then I took him back to the paddock to let him run free with his mates. He didn't really run at all by the way, so I was going to let him walk very slowly to freedom.

I reached into the box to pick up my dear insect-eating friend as gently as I could when suddenly, 'Ahhhhhh, ahhhhhhhhh!' He bit me, grabbing onto my finger like a vice. 'Ahhhhhhh! Somebody help me!' I screamed again, sounding like a little girl. And I ran around the paddock waving my hand, with the lizard attached, in the air. He wouldn't let go.

'Oh God, get him off me.' Suddenly I believed in God again. If I wasn't in so much pain, I would have prayed. But this was no time for kneeling. Panic was setting in.

'Ahhhhhh, ahhhhhhh,' I screamed again. It must have sounded a lot like my Tarzan impersonation but still no one seemed to be coming to help me.

'Jesus Christ almighty,' I screamed at the top of my voice but he didn't hear me either it seemed.

I had read about Gila monsters in a book at school and how their jaws locked and could take off a finger and I thought my time was up. A budding career as a piano player was disappearing out the window. Hang on, I never played piano. Oh well. I ran up to a tree and proceeded to bash my dear old friend, who was now my mortal enemy, against the tree as hard as I could. He let go, and then, without so much as a glance back at me, he very slowly walked away into the bush. Friends can be so fickle.

The main department store in the Elizabeth shopping centre was a place called John Martin's. As kids we would see the John Martin's Christmas parade rolling through the streets of town. It would be on the news and in the papers. Every Christmas, kids and parents would line up to go into Santa's magic cave. Not us though. It wasn't just that we weren't taken there. We didn't want to go. It seemed stupid to me. Some big fat guy in a red suit promising things that never arrived. But the shop did hold a place in the hearts of most of the community, especially the ones who could afford to buy things there.

In the shopping centre there were small gift stores and a hardware store. Various clothes shops and a coffee shop. The coffee shop would end up being a meeting place for the youth of Elizabeth. Gang members sat and drank coffee in there along with mums and dads and kids just out of school.

The shopping centre also housed a pool hall. This was a place where we would all congregate as we got older. But as little kids we weren't allowed even to stand too close to it. We used to walk by it or stand outside watching the older guys going in and out of the place, with girls on their arms, acting cool. Then the guy running it would tell us to piss off. We wanted to be in there too, playing pool and banging pinball machines. Just like the big guys.

* * *

My friends were all stealing what they could from the centre shops and they all thought that they were really tough. Most of the time they never stole anything they really needed. I couldn't work out why. Why would you risk getting caught for something you could live without? I had pinched the odd thing from the local shops in Elizabeth West when I was hungry but what my friends were doing seemed stupid to me. But they kept doing it and teased me for being a coward because I didn't steal. Eventually I buckled under the pressure and four or five of us went into one of the big shops at the centre with the intention of taking something – anything would do.

We must have looked suspicious: four or five skinny kids with no shoes and dirty clothes walking around pretending we were deciding what we were going to buy.

'Yes, this looks good. Maybe I could purchase one of these?'

We spoke this way because we looked guilty, and the way we acted or spoke just confirmed our guilt. No one spoke like that in Elizabeth unless you were stealing something or in the back of a police car. I have heard adults speaking this way as they are being led to the back of a paddy wagon, drunk, after belting their wives.

The fact that we walked in together and then split up made us all the more guilty-looking. I was walking down the aisles looking at nothing in particular. What do you steal when you are trying to be cool in front of your friends? There was nothing to eat in this shop; that was all I wanted. Every time someone came towards me I would panic and look to the floor. I don't think I looked anyone in the eye from the time I walked into the shop. I must have looked like I had a big sign over my head saying, 'I'm a thief. Grab me and lock me up, quickly.'

Every now and then one of my friends would pass me in the aisle, walking the other way. I could see things bulging under their shirts or down their trousers. Surely someone in the shop had spotted these guys? They looked guiltier than I did but they didn't seem to care. They would look at me and snigger a little and nod their heads, sort of motioning me to get on with it.

After a couple more laps of the clothing section, I selected my target. I was going to take a T-shirt. I had seen one that I might wear if I had to; it was a plain-looking T-shirt that I could wear underneath something else so no one would ever see it. I thought that anyone seeing me wearing such a thing would know it was stolen. I couldn't have bought it and I had no other new clothes. So I looked around quickly; my head turned nearly a full circle in one move. I grabbed it, and stuck it under my shirt then walked on casually, trying to look like I hadn't seen anything I wanted. Everything was going well. Then I realised that none of my friends were left in the shop; they had all bolted.

As I walked to the door I could see out of the corner of my eye a man sort of tracking me from the other side of the shop, closing in on me with every step. I picked up the pace as I was approaching the door. I had already made up my mind I was going to get out and run as far from the shopping centre as I could, as fast as I could. As I reached the door and was just starting to feel that I'd got away with it, I felt a hand on my shoulder.

'I think you'd better come with me, son.' He turned me around. There, staring right into my eyes, was the man I had spotted tracking me from across the shop – the shop's security guard.

He took me into the office at the back of the shop and sat me down. My heart was pounding. I could see it all: I would be sent to reform school and wouldn't get to see my family ever again. It would be the first step into a life of crime that would see me in and out of reform school until I was old enough to do hard time. Then I'd be breaking rocks for the rest of my life. I was terrified. Then suddenly I had a much worse thought – my mum was going to kill me.

I was alone. My mates got away and I was the only one caught. 'Please, mister, don't tell the cops. My mum will kill me,' I pleaded.

'You should have thought of that before, son,' he said, frowning over his glasses as he scribbled something down onto a piece of paper.

'I didn't mean to steal it. Honestly. I was going to put it back when you caught me.' I was desperate.

'That's why you were headed out the door, eh?'

I was guilty too.

'If you let me go I'll go and get some money and pay for it, I promise.'

The guy had heard it all before. He had probably read the book. I could tell by the look of disbelief on his slightly red and irritated face. He had obviously caught many kids just like me and I was a goner. 'Just sit where you are and be quiet.'

He just kept writing away. I was trying to see what was being written but he kept covering it with his arm. This was surely a note for the police. Some sort of report. Then he left the room.

He made me sit there for an hour. I went through a million scenarios why I needed that T-shirt and why I should go free. 'I was stealing it for my sick brother. My mum was cold.' No, that wouldn't work, it was a hundred degrees outside. Finally I just sat, resigned to the fact that I was going to the big house.

After what seemed a lifetime, he came back and said, 'Today's your lucky day, boy.' I don't know why. Maybe the major crime squad were tied up and couldn't come to get me. 'I'm going to let you go this time.'

I looked at him and swore, 'I promise I will never do this again, mister.'

The colour must have been slowly coming back to my cheeks because he took his time looking at the paper before he dropped the bomb. 'I'll need your address because I'm going to come over and tell your parents about the incident. They can deal with you.'

'Please don't do that. I promise I won't do it again. Please. I'll tell them if you want. I know I've done the wrong thing.'

He lifted up his hand and stopped me talking and said in a voice that chilled me to the bone, 'It's not a problem for me to do it, son. That's my job.'

I got the feeling he liked visiting kids' parents and telling them how bad their children were and ruining their lives forever.

My world came crashing down again. I would rather have to share a cell with a serial killer than face my mum. Maybe he would reconsider. I was sure the cops weren't that busy, but no, he had made up his mind and my fate was sealed. It was a fate worse than death – the wrath of my mum.

He let me go and I walked from the shop with my shoulders slouched. My bottom lip must have been dragging on the ground by this point and I headed for home and certain death. Halfway home, as I crossed the paddock by the railway line, I considered jumping onto a train and running away but they were going too fast. Then I thought I could chuck myself under one. That would have to be better than facing Mum. No, too painful. I sat down in the red dirt in the middle of the paddock and cried. I stayed until dark, hoping to see if he turned up, but he didn't come that night.

Next day I got up early and escaped to the relative safety of the paddock again and waited for him to come. Still no one showed up. He was dragging it out, I was sure, just to make me suffer even more. I would sit out there in the snake- and spider-infested paddock until he showed. After a week I realised he wasn't coming. He had already punished me more than even he expected, I had suffered enough. I went back to my life knowing that there was an axe hanging over my head. I would just have to wait and see. I had learned my lesson, for now anyway.

* * *

Linda's two best friends lived down the street and round the corner and to say they were wild would be an understatement. That's why they got on so well with Linda, I think. They were close to the same age as her. The brother was a year or so older than the girls. But they were all crazy. The brother had a strange collection of things in his room including odd books and magazines and a pile of dead animals. There were bits of cats and possums and anything else he could hunt or find lying dead on the road. They were all in various stages of being skinned or drying out under his bed. This was very creepy to me. It is what I would imagine to be the early stages of becoming a serial killer.

Walking into his room was like walking into a tannery. It smelled very bad, and I wondered how he got away with it. Didn't his parents care or were they potential killers too? I don't think he let his mum into his room but he was young and you would think she had to go in there at some point. If she didn't know what he was doing she would have got a big shock when she found out, I would imagine. They were a very strange mob.

Linda would take me into the room to scare me. The brother would roll over his mattress to reveal his stash of horror toys. He said he cut them up to see how they worked. He was only eleven or twelve years old at this point so who knows what happened to him. Maybe he became a doctor, I hope, or maybe he's in jail; I don't know. But I was always more than a little scared by the whole idea of his collection. I didn't go over to their house very often and never at all without Linda. I was too scared of them. The sister was Linda's best mate. She wasn't a collector like him but she was wild in different ways. I think she and Linda terrorised young boys their own age. They were tomboys. In fact, they were tougher than most of the boys of their age around our area. They knew how to control them too. Linda wasn't afraid of getting into trouble. She had problems with anyone who tried to have authority over her – school, the teachers, and especially Mum and Dad. If you told Linda she couldn't do something that was the first thing she did. The guys in the area weren't quite as prepared to be punished as she was. The guys avoided getting caught at all costs but Linda didn't care.

Linda and her mates would drag me along as they jumped fences into the back of shops and factories, anywhere they weren't allowed to go. They would sneak into the swimming pool or con their way into the skating rink by batting their innocent-looking eyelids at some poor old guy who felt sorry for them. They could find trouble anywhere.

One hot summer's day Linda, me and a few other kids from the street decided to walk a few miles from home to a creek near the Edinburgh Air Force base in Elizabeth, next to the Weapons Research Establishment. I had heard there was a deep hole there that was perfect for swimming, so we wagged school. We jumped the fence like commandos on some sort of raid and crawled across the paddock so we wouldn't be seen. There were signs on the fence saying 'No Entry' but no one caught us; in fact, we never saw anyone on patrol. For what we thought would be a high-security place it was very easy to break into. Maybe the weapons they were researching weren't that good and not worth protecting.

I remember sitting down on the ground in my underwear, getting myself mentally ready to swim, when I felt the worst pain I had ever felt, and in a place where I had never expected it. Unbeknown to me I had sat on top of a bull ants' nest and I was covered in them. They're not the nicest insects and they don't like it if you sit on their front doors so they attacked me. I ran screaming to the swimming hole with ants biting my balls and anywhere else they could sink their teeth. Do ants have teeth? Never mind, whatever they had, they were sinking them into me. When I dived into the water it was the happiest I had ever been to be underwater in my life. I went home and I didn't wag school again for a long, long time.

To escape the house there was another place us kids used to go to swim. This place was a little more difficult to get to. My mates and I would break up into groups and hitchhike, if we could get a ride. It was between Smithfield and Gawler. About two or three miles out of Smithfield there was a farm, and on that farm was an old quarry. The quarry hadn't been used for years and underground water had filled it, turning it into the perfect swimming hole. It even had small cliffs to dive off.

There were just a few things that made it less inviting than it sounds. If you didn't get a lift from a passing car, the walk along the Main North Road was long. And in the summer – the time you wanted to swim – it was extremely hot. It was so hot that we had to wear shoes as the sun melted the tar on the road and it would burn bare feet. I know this because I walked it in bare feet a few times. Even if you wore shoes they would sometimes stick to the road, making it an unpleasant walk to say the least.

That was just the first hurdle. Next we had to climb over a barbed-wire fence and walk a mile or so through a paddock covered in prickles. Now prickles weren't new to us; all over Elizabeth there were millions of prickles. For young kids who liked to go barefoot or wear plastic sandals like a lot of us did, it could be like walking through a field of land mines, one wrong step sending agonising pain shooting through your legs.

There were two main types of prickles. The first and the ones most commonly found were burrs, and they just inflicted a little pain, but they got caught in your socks and were generally a pain in the arse. Especially if you got them on your arse somehow. The other type, though, were lethal. They were small but deadly. We called them three corner jacks and if you stood on one you normally leaped into the air in pain and, unfortunately, that meant you landed on more of them. Because there was never only one. These prickles were designed by nature to use their spikes and the fact was they always attacked in numbers.

The next big stumbling block you had to face on this pilgrimage to the quarry was by far the scariest. Scattered throughout the paddocks, between the road and the quarry, there were always cows, but sometimes, if you were unlucky, there would be bulls. On more than one occasion I was chased by a bull while walking happily through the fields for a swim, only just escaping by jumping through the fence and tearing my clothes. Granted we did tease the bulls, but they were much bigger than us and could have killed us if they got to us.

If you managed to conquer all of these challenges you could enjoy a fantastic swim in the cool, clear, fresh water of this fabulous pond, provided the farmer didn't come by and chase you off. A few of my friends were shot with salt pellets by the farmer while they were on their way to the pond but I was always lucky.

We would lie flat on our backs in the long grass with our eyes closed and bake in the hot summer sun, dreaming of food and girls and anything else that came to our minds. Then we would swim to our hearts' content in the quarry, which we considered our own secret club. We never told anyone we didn't like about this place. It was all ours.

At the end of the day we would drag ourselves back to the road, so tired we would be pulling towels and whatever behind us, hardly having the strength to talk, praying that someone would take pity on us and pick us up when we got to the highway. Otherwise, we would have to walk home, which meant we wouldn't get back until after dark and might miss any dinner that was to be had. Mostly, even if I didn't eat I would sleep like a baby. I might be hungry but I'd be happy.

the sound of breaking glass

Christmas was a hard time at our house. Like most kids we wanted everything we saw, but unfortunately Mum and Dad had no money, so we never got that much. But that wasn't the problem. The real problem stemmed from my folks feeling guilty about not having a lot to give us and that would lead to Dad drinking more to make himself feel better.

He was born an alcoholic, just like me, only he never addressed it. He just let everything that happened in his life give him one more reason to drink. I think even his drinking problem depressed him and made him drink more. It was never going to end well.

Like on any other day of the year, a fight could break out between Mum and Dad, especially once they started drinking. We would all get scared. We didn't want all the toys in the world. All we wanted was for them to love us and make us feel safe. They tried their best, I guess, and every year they would scrimp and save to get us something so that Christmas morning there would be at least one thing for us when we woke up.

I remember not being able to sleep one Christmas Eve and sneaking out and seeing one of them painting some broken old bike they'd bought, trying to make it look new for me. Next day I was out riding in the street getting paint all over my hands because it hadn't dried. But it looked new to me and I loved it.

Dad would tell us, 'The old ones are much better than the new ones.' I think he was trying to convince himself.

Parties usually happen on special occasions, like Saturday nights. But a party could spring up on any day in our house. Thursday was a good one because a lot of people got paid on Thursdays.

But when there was a special occasion, a birthday or the like, Mum and Dad's friends would turn up in their good clothes. Mum and Dad liked to look their best and most party nights they looked pretty good. Mum scrubbed up well considering she didn't have a lot of money to spend on clothes. Her hair would be in rollers all the day before and come the night it would spring into action exactly as she had planned. She looked beautiful, she wore high heels and her make-up would be perfect. Dad wore a good shirt and tie and for really special occasions he wore a suit. Dad had a way of always looking well-groomed and handsome.

Some of their mates were not quite so stylish. They looked like they'd got off work twenty minutes before. They probably had. You could see the odd bit of grease and mud behind their ears or on their necks that they'd missed as they hurriedly washed to get to the party on time. Dad's mates didn't seem to have the same sense of style that he did. And a few of them looked like they'd been dressed by their mothers – shirts tucked in unevenly and hair pushed back as if their mum had licked her hand and stuck it down.

The women who came to the parties always thought that they were dressed up to the nines, swaying like streetwalkers as they walked in the front door. Some wore tight blouses and skirts, and had shiny earrings that reminded me of fishing lures.

Others wore loud patterned dresses with plunging necklines that looked like they might have been in fashion when they left Scotland many years before, but not anymore. They weren't like my mum. I thought that she always looked perfect but I might have been biased. I don't think so. They seemed to wear a lot of make-up too and were smothered in perfume, maybe too much. By the end of the night they looked a little worse for wear – eyes glazed and lipstick smeared across their faces. Often, the perfume mixed with the sweat from dancing and the booze coming from their pores made them smell a lot less attractive than when they arrived. It was overpowering for a young guy but Dad's mates seemed to like them as they groped and grabbed at the women who cooed and smiled at them towards the end of the night.

Booze was the main thing on the menu. They all seemed to like a good liquid meal. I don't think some of their friends ever ate anything in all the years I saw them at our house. So there wasn't a lot of food at the parties unless it was New Year. Potato chips, poured carefully into bowls and placed around the room before anyone arrived, quite often lay there at the end of the night, soggy and sharing their space with cigarette butts and beer bottle tops. There always seemed to be one bloke who'd drunk too much to notice, who would be eating them by the handful as the party wound up, chips flying out of his mouth as he told bad jokes and staggered towards the door.

The big celebration for us and all the other Scots we knew seemed to be New Year, or Hogmanay as it was called in Scotland.

Every year Mum would clean and cook to get the house ready for a big party on New Years' Eve. They would fill the bathtub with drinks and the fridge with food. Where the money came from suddenly, I just didn't know.

Sometimes we would watch the Royal Edinburgh Military Tattoo on television. They quite often replayed it on New Year's Eve, probably for all the Scots in Adelaide. Keep them inside and off the streets; it would be safer for everyone in the town that way. Even if it wasn't on, there was always lots of Scottish music playing in the house. Singing those same old songs about Scotland and wanting to be home that they always sang when they were drunk, whether they were in Australia, Scotland or anywhere else. But because it was New Year they seemed to sing with even more conviction, as if they were trying to let the folks back home hear them. They would be singing the exact same songs in Glasgow and in every other Scottish community around the world. It was like they were one, connected with each other through the songs of their fathers.

If you came to a party at our house, or any of my parents' friends' places, there was always a chance that someone would bring a record player and their favourite records, mainly pipe bands and the odd Andy Stewart album. We'd hear the same records wherever we went. Maybe they all had the same albums.

The night would always start well, with eating and singing and everyone waiting until midnight, then the party would really take off. At five minutes to midnight we would all gather around. The music would be turned off, except for maybe the radio, so we could all count down to the New Year.

Dad would quieten down everybody who wasn't ready to count. 'Shut it, come on, shut it, everybody. I cannae hear the wireless.'

And then everyone in the house would stand by with a glass of whisky, even us kids. And we would all count down the last ten seconds to midnight together.

'Ten – nine – eight – seven – six – five – four – three – two – one!'

A roar would go up and everyone would kiss and hug each other and we would all sing 'Auld Lang Syne' at the top of our voices. I never really knew what I was singing about but it sounded important so I acted like I meant it. Mumbling any bits I didn't know the words to, just like all the other Scots I'd seen singing at parties, hoping no one noticed.

I always remember the feeling in the house was that all the bad stuff that had happened throughout the last year was gone, washed away by whisky and drunken tears of joy, and as if by magic all our lives were going to be all right. Mum and Dad even seemed to love each other.

'I love you, Jim,' my mum would say with a sound of hope in her voice.

'I love you too, Dot,' Dad would reply.

And we would feel safe. That was, until later.

There is a Scottish tradition called first-footing, where after midnight, someone tall, with dark hair, will enter the house bringing gifts of whisky and coal. It usually ended up being one of my folks' friends or Dad himself. But whoever was chosen to first-foot had to leave the house before midnight and then re-enter straight after the clock struck twelve, bringing good luck to the family.

The coal was to bring warmth into the house, and the whisky was to toast a Happy New Year and bring good cheer. The coal was normally thrown away quite quickly, but the whisky always seemed to get things heated anyway. Quite often the first-footer in our house ended up getting thrown out later on for getting too drunk, especially if it was Dad.

Not long after midnight all the kids would be sent to bed. Mum's mates' kids would be stuck into bed with us so the older people could drink more, which was a bit strange because they were already drinking like fish anyway. How much more could they drink without us around?

We would lie in bed and hear the voices getting louder. Someone would mention football or look the wrong way at someone else's wife or even spill another man's drink. Then there would be arguments, verbal at first, but sooner or later there would be a crash and someone would fall to the ground.

'Don't you hit ma man, ya bastard.'

'Shut yer fuckin' mooth ya hoor or I'll belt ye tae. I'm sick tae death o' that drunken pig.'

'Leave him alone.'

'Come on now, everybody, calm doon. It's Hogmanay. Let's aw just get another drink and have a wee sing.'

Smash. It was beyond calming down. Punches were being thrown and blood was starting to flow. The party had come to a screaming halt.

'Get oot ma hoose. Now!'

'You lot cannae hold yer liquor. I'm goin' hame.'

'Good, go. Just fuck off.'

Bang. The door would slam and out would walk one of Mum's mates, taking with her a small splinter group of glassy-eyed song-singing desperados, heading to another house and another party and eventually another fight. Singing and annoying the neighbours as they went.

'I belong tae Glasgow ...' The sounds of Scottish drinking songs fading into the next street as they staggered to another house, stopping to piss on people's flowers along the way.

We would be in our rooms crying, not knowing what had gone wrong. Dot would sing to us to try to cover up the screams and shouts of the responsible adults in the other rooms.

In the morning we would go out to see what was left of the party, hoping for some food but normally there was just broken glass, empty bottles and cigarette butts everywhere. As I got a little older I remember sneaking out and finding half-finished whiskies that I would drink before anyone woke up. The spiral had already started, it seemed.

Outside in the yard there would always be one or two of Dad's mates passed out in the garden with the burning sun beating mercilessly down on them. I would just step over them and head out to play. It was just another year, the same as the one before and the one before that.

Dad's drinking got worse, and life got harder and harder for Mum, and things started to disintegrate around us. The fights at the house started to happen more frequently.

Mum and Dad seemed to be too caught up in their own stuff to worry much about us and we were able to run around without any supervision. We sort of always did really when I think about it, but it happened even more now. I would come home with cuts and bruises and they wouldn't notice. Before, Mum would have noticed when she bathed me but now we had to look after ourselves so she didn't see them.

Like any kids, we wanted warm beds, food on the table and a chance not to be afraid. For a long time, Mum tried to make that happen. She knew that all our friends had television so she worked out how to get one for us. She found a place where you could rent a television very cheaply. Before then, we had TVs that worked then broke or were given away or even pawned. But this was a TV that Dad hadn't organised. It was a rental and by all rights no one could pawn it.

Only one catch, though: you had to feed money into the back of the thing to keep it turned on. We had very little money so that meant very little television. If it wasn't for the lack of coins to feed into it, it was because the electricity had been turned off because we couldn't pay the bills. Sometimes it was the gas and Mum would scratch and save to get the service returned as soon as she could. But until then we would sit around with Mum in the dark, cold and afraid.

My little brother Alan was always really quiet. He played happily unless there were fights around the house, and as those fights became more frequent, Alan's days of playing happily were taken from him. He became a very nervous young boy and would sit quietly and suck his thumb and curl his hair around his finger and pull it away, removing big chunks of hair. He had a big bald patch in the front of his head. Mum tried to stop him doing it; she hit him, she tried to shame him out of it, but that only made it worse. She even started painting his thumb with foul-tasting concoctions but she could not make him stop doing it. It didn't work; he just kept sucking his thumb.

He was afraid of something. We didn't know it then, but like all of us he was afraid of everything. The fighting in the house, and God knows what else, was systematically shutting all of us down. I think that was Alan's way of escaping into his own head, where he couldn't be hurt. He was four years younger than me and had no other way of dealing with life.

Because he was that little bit younger than us he had no voice at all; he was invisible. We could at least escape or rebel. Not that anyone really cared. While all the mayhem was going on around him no one stopped for a minute to really look after him. Mum and Dad should have done that, but they were too self-absorbed. Too trapped in their own shit to think about us. He was a good boy and deserved a better childhood, as did all of us.

By this time Dorothy, my sister, had taken over the role of mum to all of us, including Lisa, the youngest. Dot tried to feed us and wash the little ones. It was all too much for her and for us. I don't know how we survived.

Dad worked at the British Tube Mills factory during the day and drank most nights at the pub. Mum worked nights as a nurse's aide in Hillcrest Mental Hospital and was tired most days. She told us stories of the cruelty and pain that she saw at the hospital. She had taken a shine to a kid they called the spider. Apparently this kid was always naked and climbed the walls, hence the name. She cried when she spoke about him. She said that she was reaching out to him and he was warming to her. Until one day she came home with a busted arm and a black eye. Old spider wasn't that keen on her after all it seemed. He had reached out to her and eventually he caught her. Threw her across the room a few times and bashed her off the walls.

When Dad found out he said that he'd always liked spiders. Most of the time now, Mum and Dad tried to avoid each other and so we were left pretty well alone.

One night, Dad was in the pub and he had John with him. John was only young and shouldn't have been in there in the first place, but that's another story. So he was sitting drinking lemonade in the corner, when in walks a guy who goes up to the bar and has a few drinks.

Well, the booze must have made him talk a little too much and he started saying or slurring to the barman, 'I'm a black belt in judo and I reckon I could beat up any bloke in this pub.'

If you hadn't noticed, this seems to be a common form of entertainment in the pubs we go to.

The barman turned to my dad and said, 'This is Jim Swan, he's a boxer and I reckon he could take you.'

The guy jumped up and said, 'I'll put you down before you can even get your hands up.'

Dad got up slowly, put out his cigarette, pushed his glasses up the bridge of his nose and looked at him. When my dad did this he meant business and someone was going to get hurt. I saw my dad push his glasses up the bridge of his nose many times and normally that was enough to make me do whatever I was supposed to be doing.

Anyway, Dad says to him, 'Leave ten quid behind the bar and we'll go outside. The first man back takes the money.'

The guy quickly agrees and leaves his money with the barman next to Dad's. He does a quick stretch and heads to the door where Dad is waiting patiently, wanting to get back to his drink. Dad was always a gentleman and he opened the door for him.

'After you,' he said and let the guy walk through.

As the judo expert got halfway through the door my dad slammed the door really hard on the back of his head and knocked him out cold.

Dad shuffled back to the bar, hardly lifting his feet off the ground; it's safer to walk that way when you drink as much as he did. Then he lit up a cigarette, smiled to himself and picked up the money. Dad didn't like to gloat but sometimes he couldn't help it. He then bought drinks for his friends as if nothing had happened.

That was my dad – always calm, but always dangerous.

When the guy came around he left the bar embarrassed, with his tail between his legs and a very sore head.

Dad used to spend a lot of time with some mates of his across the paddock in Broadmeadows. Shuggy was a skinny Glaswegian, a pool hustler who drank way too much, and he was married to

Betty who also drank way too much. Dad got on very well with them, as he also drank way too much.

Like our family, this family had major issues. They might have had even worse problems than we had, who knows. They had a lot of kids – I never really counted them – but those poor kids looked skinnier than us. Their house looked like ours: holes in the doors, with the flyscreens lying on the ground from where people had jumped in and out of the windows, and there always seemed to be rubbish lying everywhere. The front door was always wide open with anybody who wanted to walking in and out of the place, day and night. I look back now and can see that our place was the same, only then I thought it was better.

Their kids were in constant danger, just like us, and like us they spent a lot of time running around the streets getting into trouble. I often saw the boys hiding in the paddock the same as I did. They looked like they were escaping from something. These kids were escaping from reality. From life. From pain. From the past. From the future. Everything. I could tell because that's what I was doing too.

They lived in a house that had revolving doors. Anyone who wanted to could walk straight in and walk straight out without anyone checking on them. The doors that weren't ripped off their hinges had holes punched in them. The damage mostly looked like it was done by someone trying to get away from the house; the sort of place you would break out of, not into.

Kids like them and us were just scared. Scared of what might happen or scared that the same shit might happen again. It was like being in a loop. You'd think things were getting better then they'd fall apart and get worse.

I never liked these kids much, probably because of their parents. Mum hated them and instilled the same sort of hate in us. To us, they looked feral. Snotty noses and bad clothes and worse habits. Looking back, they probably had the same problem with us. We didn't look any better.

Mum had a problem with the parents; she thought they encouraged my dad to drink more. Believe me, Dad didn't need any encouragement; he was doing just fine by himself. But if he went missing she started to work out where to find him – he would be with Shuggy at the pub or with Betty at their house. Either way he was up to no good. I used to see her looking out across the paddock swearing to herself and calling Betty every bad name under the sun.

'That Shuggy is a drunken pig and don't get me started on that fuckin' hoor wife o' his.' The words spat from her mouth like venom. It might have been true but it was cruel to talk like that in front of us. 'If your father likes her so much he can fuckin' have her. I don't want him here. He's nothing but a drunken bastard.'

I guess if Dad was spending that much time with her, they both deserved all they got. But it only added to our misery.

Dad would come home with his tail between his legs. 'Sorry, Dot, I must've drank too much. You know I love you.'

He had no money left, nothing to give to Mum so she could feed us. His only solution was to send one of the kids down the street to borrow money for food.

For some reason, I was normally chosen. I would walk down the street to these other friends of my parents and knock at the door. I would ask as quietly as possible so no one else could hear me. 'Can my dad borrow some money from you until payday because we have nothing to eat and we're starving? He said he'll pay you back on Thursday when he gets his pay.'

The woman who lived there always wanted to give it to me but I could hear the voice of her husband yelling and swearing at her. 'Tell those bastard kids to fuck off away from our house and don't come back. And if I see their father around here I'll kill him.'

There was no chance he could have hurt my dad but I do think something was going on between my dad and his wife. Her husband had every right to be mad but he hated us because of it. We had nothing to do with anything; all we were trying to do was not be hungry.

She always found something to give me and would say, 'Tell your father it's from me, not him,' pointing towards her husband, 'and he can pay me back the usual way any time he wants.'

Then she would kiss me on the cheek with her red lipstick and cigarette and whisky breath and send me on my way.

It was a downhill slide from there on in: more drinking, fighting and gambling. That was just the kids. No really, I shouldn't joke but laughing is the only way I have got through most of my life.

Dad was more out of control and that meant Mum had to work harder to make ends meet so therefore we were left alone much more often. Mum seemed to work a lot at night. She said that she always took the night shift because the pay was much better and it wasn't as busy at work, so she could get a wee lie-down sometimes. But when she got home in the morning she was exhausted and had no time for any of us.

When our parents weren't there we ran riot. There were also more and more dodgy people hanging around the house. I've learned from being an addict myself that when you're caught up in the middle of your addiction you hang around with people who you wouldn't normally spit on if they were on fire. Well, Mum and Dad were the same. There were people, so-called friends of theirs, who were allowed to get close to us. People who should have been locked up, never mind hanging around young children.

CHAPTER TEN

messing with the kids

Near the school there was an old train; the council had put it there for the local kids to play on and we all loved it. We would climb all over it, pretending we were driving it at high speed.

The train sat next to the shops. A road through the car park ran right next to it. Cars would snake their way through there, avoiding kids as they ran from the train to the grass verge where we played football. It seemed that everyone knew the kids played there and seemed to drive a little slower. Occasionally the football would crash into the windscreen of a passing car and someone would roll down a window and hurl abuse at us but we didn't care.

'You shouldn't be playing there. Someone will get killed if you're not careful. You stupid kids. Where are your parents? Don't you have homes to go to?'

'Fuck off, you whining old bastard, and leave us alone.'

If they wanted to get to us they had to park their car and come after us and by then we would have grabbed our shirts from the grass and be gone down the street or up into the train, hiding.

On the other side of the train were the shops. They weren't that big or nice to look at and from the top of the train you could look down into the area behind the shops where the shopkeepers put their rubbish. I used to see the guy from the hamburger place smoking cigarettes and picking his nose back there. I never wanted to eat his hamburgers, no matter how hungry I felt.

Every day after school we would all rush to the train and play. But if someone arrived with a football we would jump off the train and take off our shirts and use them as goalposts and start a match. These games were very serious. Every night we played our own version of the World Cup finals right there at the shops. The idea was to pick the best team you could before the other guy got all the good players. But you had to pick your mates too or they would be upset with you and go home. Slowly the squads would be put together. The last two or three picks were always made out of desperation. There were some people no one wanted but we had to make up the numbers.

'Okay, I'll take Stevie.'

'Yes. Woo!'

Stevie was the worst player of all the boys and was always happy that anyone picked him. I always seemed to get stuck with him.

'But you better do what I tell you. I'm the captain and I tell people what position to play.'

'I want to be centre forward.'

I would sometimes have to revert to the tricks that my brother John had used on me.

'Come here. I need to talk to you alone.'

'Yeah, okay.'

'Listen, Stevie. The others don't know it but you're the best fullback out of all of these guys. I can't win this game without you. Do you understand?'

'If you really need me to be, I'll be fullback.'

'Great, Stevie. They don't know how good you are.'

John had been using these tactics on me for years, to get me to do anything from making him toast to cleaning the mud off his soccer boots.

'Listen, Jim, no one can clean a pair of boots like you. It's a skill that very few people can master and you're great at it. Please do it for me.'

'Okay, John. Then can I play football with you?'

'Not tonight, Jim, but you're the best. When you finish just put them under my bed. I'm going out.'

I fell for it every time and now I was using the same tricks on my little mates.

We took football very seriously. Everyone I knew wanted to be Pelé or Eusébio or George Best. But we didn't want to be famous just for the sake of it, we wanted to play football in the World Cup. That was it, that was what we were training for, to represent our country at the World Cup. I wanted to play for Scotland, like Denis Law. I imagined myself scoring the winning goal against England in the World Cup final at Wembley Stadium. I daydreamed about it all the time. I would be a Scottish hero, just like I thought my dad was. Even though I lived in Australia my folks never let me forget that I was Scottish. Dad would tell me how lucky I was to be from such a great country. I wondered why they left. But it was Scotland I wanted to play for.

We practised every day waiting for our big break to come along. How it was going to come along I'll never know. We were in Elizabeth West playing football at the shops. I don't think this was the number one place that big football club talent scouts headed for when looking for the next Bobby Charlton but stranger things have happened. We thought if we tried hard enough they would find us.

We weren't the only ones who hung around the train. All sorts of things were going on there after dark too. And it wasn't long before the train was covered in broken beer bottles and stank like piss. The smell of rotting garbage, wafting up from behind the shops, mixed with the smell of stale piss and spilled booze that oozed from every corner of the train. We didn't even notice it after a while. The train was fine as long as you didn't go into the driver's compartment. There, the smell became overbearing and the floor was littered with all sorts of filth and blood. Who knows what went on in there when we weren't around?

The council never cleaned it up so it just stayed that way, which was a shame for us kids. But even that never stopped us playing there. We just had to hold our breath in some parts of the train or until we got onto the top of it. Then we could breathe freely.

There were always shady characters hanging around the shops at night too. What they were after, I had no idea. Maybe they wanted to break into them or something. But if they did, they looked way too drunk to even think about it. I couldn't work it out.

Often there was some bloke lying in the shadows, out cold, having pissed his pants, moaning and shouting obscenities at no one in particular. These were grown men. How could they be so disgusting? Didn't they have homes to go to where they could piss their pants? Why did we have to put up with them? Why do people get so smashed? What are they thinking?

'Oh, I got so hammered last night that I pissed my pants. What a great night. Did you see me? I can't wait to do it again tonight.'

The older guys who hung around with us would sometimes kick them and tell them, 'Fuck off, you dirty old bastard.'

But it never really did any good. There always seemed to be another one ready to take his place. Sometimes the bigger kids would give these guys a real beating just for fun. But that was only when they were really bored or things weren't going well at home. We all had our own problems to deal with. Maybe they couldn't go home either or didn't have homes to go to.

If we knew the guy who was out cold, that was worse. It might have been a friend's dad or one of the gang's parents. Then we all just pretended we didn't see them.

I was out one night, I think that there was a fight going on at home, and I wanted to keep away from it. So I was wandering around the shops looking for something to do. I couldn't find anyone to hang out with. It seemed I couldn't even find trouble if I wanted to. So I went to sit on the train. From the front of the train on the smokestack I could see most of the front side of the shops. So I would see any of my friends if they walked past. I was just sitting there bored, doing nothing, looking at the moon.

Then I heard a noise coming from behind one of the shops. Sitting where I was, I had a view straight into the back, where they kept the rubbish bins. I could see something or someone moving back there in among the trash. So without thinking, I sat and stared. My eyes took a minute to focus in the bad light. But it didn't take long to work out what was happening.

There in the shadows was a group of young guys, grabbing at a young girl who had no clothes on. They looked like animals to me, snarling and baring their teeth at one another and pushing each other out of the way to get at the girl. She wasn't fighting them off. She just lay there saying nothing, staring straight up at the sky. I couldn't work out if this was supposed to be fun or not but I knew I didn't want to keep watching. And I definitely didn't want to get spotted by the bigger boys. They would turn on me. So I ran away. But I had seen enough to make me question whether what was going on was right or wrong. It couldn't have been right. She wasn't fighting them or screaming or anything. She just lay there and looked sad. I was confused.

I saw them all later walking down the road, smoking cigarettes and laughing. The young girl was with them; she was still not talking and she still wasn't laughing at all. But she was with them so it must have been okay. But what I saw disturbed me for a long time and I kept away from the train at night from then on.

This was my introduction to sex – cold, violent and animalistic. I didn't want to know about it. Why would anyone want to do that?

But it didn't put me off girls. In fact, soon after I developed a crush on a girl in my class. She had beautiful long blonde hair and she looked like a doll. I used to follow her around like a dog, hoping she would notice me.

I would offer to do things for her. 'Do you need me to open the gate for you?'

But she just ignored me. She would flick her hair around and walk away as if I wasn't there.

I tried to walk with her after school. 'Can I carry your bag for you?'

She still ignored me. For a little while I walked behind her, back about fifty yards or so, hoping she would warm to me. But she didn't.

She turned around and cried out, 'Go away, or I'll tell my mum on you.' Then she picked up a rock and threw it at me.

That should have been enough to put me off but it didn't. I was just hurt and didn't understand why she would have nothing to do with me. But I had the feeling her parents had warned her about kids like me. I came from one of those bad families.

I pretended I got over her but I didn't really. I still remember her like it was yesterday.

Dad seemed to prefer drinking in the pub to hanging around with us. I remember looking into his eyes on those nights he did come home drunk, and seeing tears welling up when he spoke to me. It was as if every night might be his last chance to tell us how much he loved us. Every night I caught a glimpse of him leaving in his eyes.

It was only a matter of time until it happened. I had felt this for as long as I can remember. Each night at home normally started with Dad coming home drunk and Mum waiting for him.

'Where have you been, ya bastard? Call yersel a man? You don't even bring home enough money tae feed yer kids.'

'God, woman. Let me just sit doon and rest. Just gie us peace a minute.' He always looked worn out.

'Why don't you just get the fuck oot o' here and go back tae yer pals?'

As things got louder and louder, my sister Dot would grab Lisa, Alan and myself and hide us away from them. 'Come on, kids, let's go play in here where it's nice and quiet,' she would say as she led us little ones to the other room to hide in the cupboard. We knew Dot was as scared as we were but she tried to hide it.

The cupboard wasn't that big. It was just an old second-hand wardrobe. But it was our only shelter. We spent a lot of time in there. I remember it was dark and with the door shut it was hard to hear a lot of what was going on outside. Dot would sing to us, trying to drown out the words they were screaming at each other, words that we shouldn't have heard. But I always heard them, every word punctuated by the sound of breaking glass. Mum's screaming always seemed to cut through no matter how hard Dot tried to cover it.

Mum never let up on him. She would have been waiting for hours for something to feed us and it never arrived. She had a lifetime of waiting for something that never came. She wanted to kill him.

'I hate you. Why did I marry you?' she would cry, half sobbing and half cursing.

Then, nothing. There would be silence. When it was quiet we didn't know what was going on but we knew that was when it was most dangerous.

Some nights we would fall asleep in there, waiting for the all clear to sound. Then Dot would cover us up with Mum's or Dad's overcoat. I remember almost feeling safe then because I was able to smell them on the fabrics. The slight scent of Mum's perfume mixed with Dad's cigarette smoke made me feel a little calmer as if I was closer to them both.

Some nights I felt nothing at all. It was as if my senses would shut down to stop me from being scared. At those times the darkness of the cupboard swallowed me up.

After the shouting had stopped, Dot would slowly open the door. Just a little at first as if she didn't want to see what had happened. The light would shine through the half-open door, blinding us, and we'd cover our eyes as she poked her head out. Then we would follow her as she walked out of the bedroom and into the kitchen to see what damage had been done this time. Broken glass and smashed furniture was all that was left of our lives. That and the sound of Mum crying in the bedroom again.

Sometimes, if he hadn't already left the house, Dad would bundle us out of the wardrobe.

'Come on kids. Everything's gonnae be aw right. Yer dad loves you.' That same look on his face every time. 'I'm sorry,' he would whisper.

Dad didn't know how to love us. His dad never showed him.

* * *

The fights were getting more intense, more extreme, and we were in more danger. Sometimes physically, but more and more of the time, we were in emotional danger. Some nights we were in the cupboard for hours waiting for the battle to subside, other nights we couldn't leave the cupboard at all. The police never came to stop all the fighting. They must have had bigger fights to stop or families who were in bigger trouble to save, but all I know is they were never there to save us.

We would have to get up for school early and leave the house – walking over broken glass and blood, with nothing to eat, no clean clothes. Dot would say, 'Just keep moving, I'll find something for you to eat at school.'

She never really did. She had no money just like the rest of us.

On one occasion Mum locked Dad out of the house because he came home too drunk. I remember Dad calling out to be let in. 'Come on Dot, I meant to come hame but it was Shuggy's birthday. I had to have a wee drink wi' him.' He wasn't angry sounding, just unhappy.

But Mum just screamed from the safety she thought she had behind the locked door, 'I've had enough of you. You're no comin' in here.'

Dad suddenly went quiet ... and then *bang!* He punched a hole in the front door. This was a heavy fire door so I don't know how he did it. Then he put his hand through the hole he had just made, opened the door, came in and sat down, and began to calmly watch television as if nothing had happened. He never said a word.

The silence was frightening. Mum ran to the bedroom and came out with a stiletto-heeled shoe and started screaming, 'I'm sick of you!', hitting him on the back of the head with the heel.

Blood spurted out everywhere. I know one of them ended up on the floor. You can guess who. Dad passed out in the chair.

Dad didn't hit us, as far as I remember. Mum was the enforcer of the family. I don't remember seeing Dad hit Mum either, but I know he did. It was probably so fast and deadly that we looked away and missed it, thank God. But some mornings I would get up and there would be Mum with a black eye or a fat lip, sitting alone in the kitchen crying while Dad was unconscious, snoring on the bed in their room, sleeping it off.

It seemed that in those days it was normal for husbands to hit their wives. All Mum and Dad's friends seemed to do it at some time. Their wives would turn up on our doorstep with black eyes, crying to Mum, saying, 'That's it. This is the last time. I'm never goin' back. He'll never lay a hand on me again, I swear to God.' They always went back and the violence never stopped.

It wasn't right. We always knew it was wrong and sometimes we wanted to hurt Dad for hitting her. We were learning that lashing out was the way to solve problems and we were hitting each other and kids at school. This was all wrong.

Someone was messing with the kids. There was a family who were friends of Mum and Dad's who were around all the time. If they weren't at our house we were at theirs. Mum worked nights with the wife, wherever they worked, and they spent a lot of time together.

We used to go over to their house and swim in their aboveground pool. In the summer it was really hot so we loved this. We would swim in the pool with these kids and I remember the girls, who were my age, not much older, would swim underwater and touch me and when no one was around they would take off their swimmers and want me to look at them. I thought this was just normal. Maybe it wasn't normal, but it was where we came from.

Something weird was going on with our parents too. I'm not sure what it was; we didn't know anything about anything. Was Dad having an affair with the wife? That was more than likely. Maybe Mum was the one playing up, who knows?

They had a son who was a few years older than John and he was a fucking deviant. It seems he was messing around with all the kids. We have never talked about this with anyone; in fact, we have never spoken about it with each other, so this is hard to write about. I am writing from what I feel; I don't really know any facts. But what I feel has driven me to the brink of insanity for many years.

I have spent most of my life ashamed of something that I didn't understand. I have been subconsciously trying to kill myself. I've tried to drink myself to death for a start, but I tried anything that would keep me from facing things in my life that were too hard to look at. And there were lots of things that I didn't want to face. This period in my life seems to be the key to the whole mess.

I always used to say to Jane, my wife, that I thought my childhood was just normal. And sadly, in some ways it was. By that, I mean that there are a lot of kids who have gone through the same horrors that I have. But that doesn't make it right. I have been afraid all my life and for good reason, not only because of this one person but because of many. The things I went through then and since have scarred me almost beyond help.

I don't remember him touching me but I'm sure he did touch some of the other kids so why should I be any different? I wonder if my mind has blocked this time out of my memory. But it will come back to me sooner or later. Then, if I have to, I'll find him.

* * *

I can still feel the touch of drunken strangers grabbing me as I walked through the living room. The smell of booze and cigarettes on their breath as they tried to touch or kiss me. I wanted to be as far away as I could get from our home.

I used to go and stay at a friend's house because I felt safer. Until one night my friend's brother came home. He had been away for a long time in jail. In the middle of the night he came into the room where we were sleeping and told us that he was going to show us how men practised sex.

We knew nothing, we were too young to know what was going on, but by that time I could recognise danger when it was near me and I knew it was near me at that moment. I remember this man trying to fuck me. I was terrified. I screamed and kicked until I got away and I left the house as quickly as I could. As I jumped out the window I looked back and I remember not liking what was happening to my friend. His own big brother was trying to fuck him. But I couldn't help him. It reinforced to me that nowhere in the world was safe and I was on my own.

Sitting on the smokestack on top of the train, I started to shiver as I watched the sun setting again. I seemed to sit there a lot. I should really have gone home but I had nothing to go home for. So here I was, staring at people who didn't even have the time to look up, never mind to see me as they hurried past. Grabbing last-minute things to feed their families on a cold winter's night. Another day was gone and another long night was on the way. I wondered what it was like to feel warm and safe and happy. I hadn't felt that for a long time. I wasn't sure I had ever really felt it. If I had, I had forgotten when. Rain clouds were rolling in and the wind cut right through my clothes and chilled me to the bone. I kept my feet constantly moving on the cold dark metal of the train, trying to keep blood circulating as another gust howled through the shops and down the street. Mums were calling their kids in for dinner. Warm lights were starting to glow inside the houses all along the streets of Elizabeth West.

From up here everything looked nice. Just like it did when we first moved here. The streets were all neat and the houses were all in perfect rows with concrete paths and small iron fences in between each house. You wouldn't know what went on in those houses unless you were inside. I'd been inside, I knew what went on. But from the top of the train it looked perfect. So I shut my eyes and tried to imagine for a minute what it should really be like for kids like me. Then the smell of piss wafted up from inside the train and I suddenly remembered where I was and why I was sitting there.

My house was not safe. It wasn't warm. There was no one there to look out for me. I was safer outside in the rain than I was in my own bed. Out here I could see the predators as they staggered drunk and menacing towards me, and I could run away. But at home, they were invited in, even allowed to get so close they could do whatever they wanted. No one seemed to care.

Sitting on the smokestack on the top of the train, the wind bit as it touched my face but I felt safe up there. At least for the time being.

CHAPTER ELEVEN

the last bit of light

It was around the summer of 1965–66 that things really changed for us. One morning, I woke up and Mum wasn't there. I didn't wake up expecting to find her gone. I didn't hear any fighting in the middle of the night. There was no breaking glass. No swearing or cries for help. There wasn't even any shouting. She was just gone. The last bit of light in our lives was put out that day.

I went to school and when I got home she still wasn't there. We had to feed ourselves and then we waited for her to come back. She always came back. She'd told us wouldn't leave us. She loved us too much.

It took a few days to realise that she was not coming back. I think it really hit home when we kids were all alone and my sister Dot was crying, looking through the kitchen cupboards, trying to find something for us to eat.

We never heard from Mum, and Dad didn't want to talk about it, except to say, 'Yer ma left ye. She deserted ye. I'm the only one who cares for you lot.'

If he cared so much, he showed it in a funny way. We hardly saw him at all except for when he'd run out of money or needed to get clothes or a bed to sleep it off. Otherwise he was gone too. He was lying too. He didn't care, no one did. From then on it was a matter of just trying to survive. It was us kids against the world and we had to stick together if we were going to have a chance.

Dot would get ten dollars or so from Dad when he was drunk and hide it so she could buy a sack of potatoes, and that was pretty well all we had to eat.

We would go to the shops and buy this big bag of potatoes that we would drag home because it was too heavy for us to carry. Then we'd keep them in the laundry. At least now we would have something to eat for the week.

The house fell apart without Mum to maintain some sort of order. Dot tried to do it but she was dealing with too much for any young girl her age. She was taking over all Mum's duties – cooking, cleaning, trying to keep us all from falling apart. Even trying to make sure Dad was all right. But Mum couldn't do that so Dot didn't stand a chance. Dad wouldn't eat and hardly slept unless he passed out.

On top of this, Dot was still at school and struggling with normal things girls had to deal with. But she was not a normal girl. She was all we had. And these were not normal days. Even her best wasn't enough to help the four younger ones she was trying to raise. I'm sure I heard her cry at night in her bed. She didn't cry in front of us, though; she put on a brave front. But I knew inside she was just like me – afraid. We all were.

At that time Linda brought some stray cats to the house. She must have learned this from Mum because Mum always brought strays to the house. Dogs, cats, people, you name it. I remember coming home from school starving and there was nothing to eat in the house. The sack of potatoes that Dot had bought was just about empty and I had to dig around the bottom of the hessian sack to get the last of them. Unfortunately for us, the cats had shit in the sack. I was too hungry to not eat the spuds but I was gagging at the sink as I washed the shit off the potatoes before we could cook them. I had to try not to think about it when I ate or I would have been sick.

The cats, by the way, were as neglected as we were. They had been running loose on the street, trying to survive, and eating anything they could find. They were skinny, mangy and had not been taught how to live in a house. I think the cats reminded Linda of how badly life had treated her. I felt sorry for them too, we all did, but when they insisted on shitting on the only thing we had to eat – the potatoes – I wanted them out of the house.

The cats decided that this was where they would go to the toilet from then on. I was beginning to dislike them even more. I learned from it though; I learned that sometimes in life you had to do whatever it took to survive. This was a big help to me later in life. The music industry was full of shit and we would have to wade our way through that. So it came in handy.

In a matter of months there were holes punched in the walls and all the furniture had been smashed; the house was dirty and the yard overgrown. Springs were poking out of the couch and out of the dirty mattresses we had to sleep on. We had no sheets or blankets except for what we got from the Salvation Army – hard woollen blankets, covered in stains. At night I couldn't sleep from the constant itching. I was breaking out in rashes and was covered in bites. I would lie in bed thinking this was as bad as it could be and then the next day would come and I would realise I'd been wrong.

I had by this time come to the conclusion that there was no God. I knew it wasn't anything like they told me in Sunday school.

There was no one looking down on us from above and there was no heaven and no hell. Or if there really was a hell I was surely living in it. The church never helped us except with the odd pair of trousers or other pieces of clothing. I still have issues with the concept of an all-seeing, omnipresent God looking out for everyone. I grew out of that at about four years old. Maybe I'm bitter and jaded but I don't think so. I liked the Salvation Army because they had looked out for us a few times but that was about it.

Some days I would wake up and not have shoes or clean clothes to wear to school. I was once again ashamed of who we were and how little we had.

Even friends of Mum and Dad's who had been part of the problem before, drinking and fighting with them, were worried about us. They would bring over food for us to eat or something clean to wear. But Dad never noticed how bad things were and if he did he was so fucked up he couldn't do anything about it. Life was beyond him.

I tried to keep away from our house as much as I could, staying at friends' houses and even friends of Mum's. I stayed with an older couple who seemed to take a liking to me. Aunty Mary and Uncle Eddie were a sweet old Scottish couple who lived in Broadmeadows, across the paddock from us in Elizabeth Field. I would go over to their house when I was hungry or alone. It was as if they knew what we were going through and wanted to give me a break. I was happy to have a little bit of normality in my life.

My brother John was my hero in those days. He could play football, he was a boxer and he was a musician. Anything he put his mind to he could do. He was responsible for me hearing most of the good music that was around at that time. He was in bands with lots of other young immigrant kids so new music was always being played around the house.

But he was always in trouble. In his first year of high school, he didn't like the way a teacher tried to reprimand him so he knocked him out. Obviously he was expelled from school and he never went back. He didn't care. His friends all thought it was a great thing to do. I thought that no one, except maybe Dad, was tougher than John.

John was a wild boy and hard as nails, but home was too wild and frightening even for him. So at the age of thirteen, John ran away from home and joined a band in Melbourne. Not much was said about it, I don't even remember Dad being worried about him. Now I had no one to look up to.

In Melbourne John played with some of the top musicians in the country. For a while he forgot about Elizabeth and what he'd escaped from. I don't think anyone else would have been capable of that after all he'd been through and at such a young age. But something went wrong in Melbourne too. Bad people seemed to follow us wherever we went and he ended up back with us in Elizabeth. We always seemed to end up back there no matter where we ran to.

My dad tried to make things work out for himself and for John by doing what he did best. He started training him to box. John was ready to fight anyone at any time. He was fast and he was angry. Within a few months John was state boxing champion. At the same time his football team, Elizabeth West Football Club, won the state championships. He was asked to go and try out for an American football scout to play gridiron. He played top-level district football as a goalkeeper. He could sing, he could play guitar, he could play piano, he could fight and everyone who knew him liked him. He was an amazing guy.

* * *

I have a problem remembering how old I was or how long this nightmare went on for. It seemed like forever and it still hurts me now like it was yesterday. Mum must have left us when I was maybe nine and didn't come back until I was eleven – and then only for a short time before she disappeared again. How could both our parents desert us? We needed them, they were supposed to be there for us and they weren't. Mum had run away from Dad but she left us in the hell she ran from. If it was that bad, why didn't she take us with her? Why didn't she even get a message to us or check on us? She couldn't have really cared that much. And Dad, well, even when he was at the house, he was gone from our lives. He was probably never there, when I think about it. We were alone.

I used to walk home from school and look into other houses and wish our house looked like theirs did. Some of my friends from school had normal houses and normal families. I wanted to be like them so badly. I thought they were really lucky. Now, looking back, I can see that their parents worked in the same factories as ours, they made the same money as ours; the only difference was their parents were responsible and cared for them.

I then started to get defensive of my dad and would get into fights at school if anybody said anything about my clothes or shoes or even lack of food. I pretended I didn't care but I was hurting inside. I became very good at fighting and that carried on for quite a few years. There were some other families in the street that were as badly off as us, in fact, there were some who I thought had it worse. But they were just crazy families, full of neglected kids with stupid parents who abused them. I woke up one day and realised that we were one of those families.

* * *

At school I was the class milk monitor, which meant that I got to go to the lunch shed and collect the milk for my class to drink every morning. The government used to supply fresh milk in nice glass bottles for all the kids at primary schools. I think it was to help strengthen our teeth and bones. The best thing about this was that on those days when I was really hungry I could drink a few bottles of milk while I was at the shed. That would be enough to help me concentrate in class and not have to sit with my stomach rumbling while the other kids ate their lunches. During summer the milk would quite often be going off in the sun. But I would drink it anyway.

I always pretended I didn't need lunch and didn't care that everyone else was eating and I wasn't. But sometimes my friends would have a little more than they needed and I would wolf it down in a second. As a rule, though, I acted tough and didn't need food. I didn't need anything or anyone.

I know that my home life was beginning to show in my schoolwork. I started to get into trouble for things I would never have done before. I had always been the most conscientious student in class and the teachers loved me. But I was getting angry. I got in fights and one afternoon I was sent to the headmaster's room.

'I'm here to see the headmaster, miss.'

'Is it to do with schoolwork or sport?'

'No, miss, teacher sent me.'

'Oh. Take a seat. The headmaster will see you soon.'

I sat in the front office, shuffling my feet nervously on the floor. The secretary looked up.

'Can you please sit still?'

The sound of the telephone constantly ringing only made me more nervous. I'd never been sent up to this office before. I'd been at the school for years and the only time the headmaster had even noticed me was when I sang at assembly.

The door swung open. 'Right. Come in then.' He didn't look as happy to see me this time.

'Yes, sir.'

'What's the trouble here?' I got the feeling he already knew but he wanted me to say it out loud.

'Teacher told me to get out of the class and come to your office, sir.'

'Why? What did you do?'

'I punched a boy during recess, sir.'

'Yes, I heard. You're the young Swan boy aren't you?'

'Yes, sir.'

'I saw your brother a lot in here but I wasn't expecting to see you. I'm very disappointed in you. This boy was bleeding a lot. I saw him in the nurse's office.'

'Yes, sir, but he was pushing my friend around. That's why I hit him, sir.'

'Yes but you hit him more than once, didn't you? You kept hitting him.'

'I don't know, sir. I just hit him.'

By this time, I was getting ready for what I knew was coming. I'd seen the kids come back from the office with welts on their hands and legs. Crying and blowing bubbles out of their noses. I wasn't going to be like that. I wasn't going to cry. They couldn't hurt me.

'Well, we can't have kids punching each other around the school whenever they like.'

'But he started it, sir.'

'Don't interrupt me, son. This is a very serious situation. You can't go around taking things into your own hands. Resorting to violence doesn't solve anything, son,' he said, rolling up his sleeves. 'You're going to have to learn that lesson the hard way it seems.'

'Yes, sir.'

'You are a good student but no one is allowed to get away with this sort of behaviour. Do you understand?'

I grunted to myself and stared at the floor.

'Do you understand, young man?'

'Yes, sir.'

I never lifted my eyes from the floor. I could feel him shuffling around behind me, getting something out of the cupboard in the corner.

'All right, son, come here and put out your hand.'

In his hand was a long piece of cane that he flexed back and forth as if he was testing how hard he could swing it. He had a look in his eye like he didn't care at all. In fact, I thought he was quite enjoying the whole process. He even seemed to be dragging it out for maximum effect.

'Put your hand out, son, and don't you dare move it.'

I put my arm out straight and bit my lip.

Whack!

He looked me in the eye. I never let out a sound.

Whack! Whack!

He hit me twice more. My eyes were watering but I still never let out a sound.

He became more agitated and swung the cane around and, *whoosh*, he hit me across the legs.

I flinched but did not make a sound.

His face was red with anger and he began stuttering. 'N-now y-you get out of here and I d-don't want to see you back in here again. Do you understand?'

I walked out saying nothing. Tears were running down my face but I just bit my lip and wiped them away. He couldn't hurt me. No one could hurt me. I headed back to class. My hands were throbbing and I had a huge welt across the back of my legs.

I walked into class with my eyes down. I couldn't look at anyone. I didn't want them to see I was hurting. The teacher said something to me as I passed his desk. I couldn't hear it. I looked up and scowled. I wasn't listening. I wouldn't listen to him anymore. How could he have sent me to get caned like that? I was his best student.

I wasn't like the bullies in the class, picking on the small kids. I always did my work and I helped other kids do theirs. The only fights I ever got in were with those kids who picked on me or hit the little ones. He knew that but he still sent me to the office. He didn't care about me. I hated school now and I hated him.

One night it got too hot to sleep in the house. We were sweating like dogs, tossing and turning. So we pulled our pillows and blankets out into the front yard and tried to sleep out there under the stars. It was better than the backyard because we could see what was happening in the world outside. It was like camping out without leaving home. But it seemed to annoy some people from our street. One woman walked by and yelled at us, 'What are you kids doing? Get inside, it's late. Do your parents know you're out here?'

She obviously didn't know our parents and she hadn't thought of escaping the heat this way.

'Get lost, missus. This is our yard. We can do what we want,' I shouted out, knowing full well that our dad was out and not likely to be back any time soon, if at all.

I could see her thinking to herself, 'What a bunch of brats ... hmm, but that's not a bad idea.'

It felt like a safe thing to do because we were out in the open and no one could hurt us without the whole neighbourhood seeing, but it probably wasn't a great idea. We must have looked like a feral family out there on the lawn but we didn't care. At least it was cooler than inside the house. We woke up to the sun burning hot and shining on our faces. The rest of the world was getting ready for work. Traffic was starting to go by the house. So we dragged everything back inside and got dressed to go to school.

On my way home from school one afternoon I went to a friend's house to play. He was from one of the families that I thought were having as hard a time as us. I knocked on the door and no one answered. I knocked again and yelled out, 'Is anybody home?'

I heard his big sister call out from the back of the house, 'Come on in.'

I walked in and stood in the lounge room expecting him to be there. Once again I heard the voice of his sister. 'Come in here, I need your help.'

I walked into the bedroom and his sister, who was about fourteen years old at the time, was standing by the bed with a towel wrapped around her. I thought she had just got out of the shower or something and didn't think twice about it.

'Come over here a minute,' she said.

As I walked towards her she dropped the towel and lay on the bed, naked. I think she wanted me to get on the bed with her. I was only nine years old at this time and didn't know what to do or where to look for that matter. Well, I knew where to look, but I couldn't without my face going red. I had never seen a girl this old naked before and she looked beautiful, but I was so scared that I turned and ran out the door.

I started to feel very funny about girls from then on and I wanted to be near them all the time. Whenever I saw her again she looked at me and smiled but I didn't know what to say to her and I would just get away as quickly as I could. Later on, when I was a little older, I wished she had been around. We could have had some fun. But they had moved away by then.

* * *

One particular day I woke with the sun. It beat mercilessly in through my window. The curtains that Mum had put up had been ripped down months before and the window was open.

As soon as my eyes were open I was out of bed. I didn't want to be in there any longer than I had to be. The bed was dirty and stained and the blankets were itchy and filthy. There were no sheets and the pillow was torn and uncomfortable. Why would I stay in bed? In fact, I didn't want to be in that house any longer than I had to. A lot of bad things had happened to me and around me there and the only reason I was still there was that I was too scared to go anywhere else.

As I walked from the house I looked back and wondered what went wrong. It used to be shiny and new. Now it looked like a condemned building.

The lawn was now red dirt, covered with rubbish and weeds. The trees Mum planted had died, just a lot like her dreams when I think about it, except for the three candle pines that lined our very short driveway. They just kept growing out of control. Getting tougher as they grew taller. They reminded me of us kids.

I walked towards the shops dressed only in my bathers. The sun was already blistering hot and I had to run from the shade of one tree to the next to stop my feet from blistering. I was hungry, I hadn't eaten in ages; there was nothing in the house that wasn't mouldy. But I couldn't think about it now. I had to walk about four miles to the centre shops.

I walked through the shopping centre. The shops were still closed and all the rubbish bins were overflowing. The whole place smelled like a rubbish tip. I carried on past the coffee shop and by the pool hall. Around here there were always broken beer bottles and cigarette butts. I quickened my pace and ran across the car park to the swimming pool, which wasn't open yet.

That's where I was going to spend my day. I got there about half past seven and walked over to find a spot to wait. In the meantime I sat against the wall outside and watched a nest of bull ants attack a beetle. They were small and violent and they tore the bug apart. His worries were well over by the time I started watching. This is where I would wait until the pool opened at nine. By then I hoped to have hustled enough money to get in.

My plan was to look as pathetic as I could, which wasn't that hard really, and ask people on their way to work for money. I'd tell them I hadn't eaten and needed to get some food. Hopefully I would get enough to get me into the pool and still have something to buy a bush biscuit. These were one of the cheapest things on the menu. They were big too. They looked like a large milk arrowroot biscuit. For a little bit of money they could fill the hole in your stomach better than any of the lollies they sold behind the counter.

By nine-thirty I was in and swimming around in the water. Not a care in the world. The pool area slowly filled up and eventually there were families and gangs of young guys and girls all settling in for a day of fun and getting out of the one hundred-degree heat.

Elizabeth was a hot and dusty place and no one had air-conditioning. The houses were like ovens by ten o'clock so I knew I had come to the right place. I was a regular at the pool and some of the people who worked there sort of knew me, which made me feel a little safer than I did at home.

I spent most of the day there, moving from spot to spot, finding shade and trying to avoid being beaten up by the bigger guys. But I had to go home sooner or later. I wanted to see my brothers and sisters. Maybe Dot had found something for us to eat. I headed back on the same road. I was tired from swimming all day so I decided to hitchhike. I stuck out my thumb and walked along the side of the road. My feet were burning again but I didn't care by then. I was tough and tired.

Cars sped by, some people paying no attention to me, others yelling obscenities as they flew past. Finally, a car pulled up. It was a little late slowing down but it stopped about fifty yards down the road. I was happy to get any ride so I ran to the car. I opened up the back door and climbed in. The minute I shut the door I knew I had done the wrong thing.

The car sped off. The driver was looking at me in the rear-view mirror. He looked like he hadn't slept in a week. Maybe he had just finished work, I told myself. Then the passenger turned around. The smell of his breath almost knocked me out. I knew they had both been drinking a lot. I tried not to panic. I'd been in bad spots before, I'd be all right.

They drove over the bridge towards my house but instead of turning right towards Elizabeth West, they turned left into the empty roads that surrounded the Weapons Research Establishment. This area was just empty paddocks and dirt roads and I knew I was in trouble.

'A kid your age shouldn't be running around alone,' slurred the passenger with a leering smile on his face. The driver laughed.

The car pulled to a halt and before they could even turn around I pushed the door open and fell out onto the ground. I knew how to survive, I was a fighter. I got that from my mum.

I ran across the paddock as fast as my feet would carry me. The two guys in the car were still trying to get out of the doors. From where they stopped to my place was about three miles as the crow flies. I knew this whole area like the back of my hand. I ran flat out. I never stopped until I got to the Elizabeth West shops. I looked at my feet and they were bleeding but I was in one piece. I walked home. No one was there so I looked in the fridge to see if any food had turned up. It hadn't. I went outside and sat on the front step. I never told my dad or my brothers and sisters about my day. They had their own problems.

CHAPTER TWELVE

———

we were damaged goods

All of the older kids started to sneak out at night. Whatever they did, I wanted to do the same. So out the window I went. I got really drunk for the first time at the age of nine or ten or some ridiculous age like that. We had a taste for it; my father was an alcoholic, so was his father and so on. It was in our genes. We had all tasted whisky many times. We tasted it at parties whenever the adults weren't looking, and every New Year's Eve Dad gave us all a nip at midnight, remember. So drinking was just what people did as far as we knew. But getting really drunk for the first time was a different thing.

My sister Linda and her mates wanted to buy some booze but obviously they were too young so they came up with a devious plan, which was why they needed me. They decided that if someone really young, with an innocent-looking face, went to the bottle shop and said they wanted to buy a present for their dad, the guy in the bottle shop might just fall for it.

'Now tell us what you have to say when you walk in,' Linda said, going over it many times so I wouldn't forget.

'It's my dad's birthday and I have stolen money from Mum's purse to get him a present because he's the best dad in the world ...'

'No, that's not right. Let's go through it one more time.'

'Only kidding, I know what to say,' I said confidently. 'It's my dad's birthday and I have saved up all my money from my paper round to get him a present because he's the best dad in the world.'

'That's it. Now don't get it wrong or we'll kill you, okay?'

'Okay Linda, I promise I'll do my best.'

Off I went to the bottle shop. I walked in with my eyes to the floor, looking as small and cute as I possibly could. I looked up at the guy working there. Blink, blink, blink went my eyelashes, to make me look even more innocent.

'It's my dad's birthday and I have saved up all my money from my paper round to get him a present because he's the best dad in the world.'

'Yes?' he said, looking at me closely to see if I was serious.

Blink, blink, blink. 'I know he likes a wee drink and I wondered if I could get him something to surprise him.' Blink, blink, blink.

'Yes,' he said. I could tell by his face he was starting to soften.

'I heard my mum say he likes whisky.' Blink, blink, blink.

He smiled at me and thought to himself for a minute. I thought I had blown it and I didn't like my chances.

'Oh what a lovely thought. Aren't you a nice little boy.' He fell for it. 'Get this one, I'm sure he'll love it and it's not too expensive.'

He was too helpful. I began to feel guilty. But not guilty enough to stop the scam.

'Thanks, mister,' I said and took the bottle and walked shyly out of the shop. I turned the corner and there were Linda and her mates, looking like a pack of hungry wolves, licking their chops.

'Give that to us and take off, you little conman,' said one of the boys.

'That's not fair, let him come and drink it with us,' shouted Linda.

Blink, blink, blink.

'And cut out the cute act, okay? I'm wise to you, Jim,' she said and walked towards the paddock across from our house.

We all drank the whisky then ran around the paddock for ten minutes acting stupid then fell over and began throwing up. It was good to be growing up to be just like the adults in our lives.

I'm not sure when or why this next thing happened but it was horrible. I remember the family had all the same problems as us. They were living below the poverty line and the parents drank and fought. They were family friends and we would go to their house all the time. I remember we were eating with them one night and things went really wrong. Lots and lots of alcohol had been consumed by everyone old enough to drink. And by some of the kids who weren't old enough. Well, things got heated between two of the brothers, who were in their late teens, and a scuffle broke out. They were separated and one stormed out to the bedroom while the other sat at the table brooding. Everyone hoped it would blow over.

But this sort of thing never did blow over until someone got hurt. We were all sitting at the table when the older son came out of the bedroom, walked up to the table then pulled out a knife and cut his brother's throat. Right at the dinner table. They had been arguing over a packet of cigarettes. Like a lot of the Scots we knew, they were no strangers to violence and often carried knives around with them. They had no hope. Who knows what else had happened to these boys at home. Whatever it was, it had taken its toll – and one of them snapped.

The brother with the knife, who was covered in blood and crying, walked out of the house and down to the local shops. He picked up a concrete block and threw it through the window of a shop. He walked inside, picked up a pack of cigarettes from behind the counter and sat down. Then he lit one up and waited for the police to arrive. His brother didn't die but he never spoke properly again. The boy went to jail for a long time. I know that no one was shocked but it has bothered me forever. How do families end up doing something like this to each other?

Many nights at our house ended in some sort of bloodbath, so we were used to it. Dad's mates would get too drunk and there would be fights. There was always a good reason. One of them would disappear with another's wife and turn up dishevelled, with lipstick all over them. They all seemed to be very promiscuous, and slept with anyone who would let them. This, mixed with copious amounts of booze, seemed to always end in violence. I think they liked the fighting as much as the fucking. If they didn't fight, someone would get so drunk that they would fall over onto a bottle or a glass – there would be blood somehow.

The child welfare people were watching what was going on and were beginning to take notice. Looking back I think it was many years too late for us; it would take a lifetime of fear to get things straight. We were scared to death of being taken away from our dad. Now I can see that it might have been a godsend. The truth is, by the time they noticed us, we were already so fucked up that nothing could have saved us from the shame and confusion that we would have to live with. The damage was already done and staying with him just added to it. We were damaged goods.

Somehow Mum had heard what was going on from one of her friends and had started to make plans to get us away from

Dad. But it would take time and in the meantime we hadn't heard a thing from her. We were angry.

Dad made a point of telling us, 'Everything would've been fine if yer fuckin' mother hadnae deserted us. She caused aw this.'

We knew that wasn't true. We were young but we weren't stupid. Things had been fucked for as long as we could remember so we knew it wasn't just her fault. But we were angry with her for leaving us.

I can look back and see that it was a matter of life and death. The violence that went on around the house had been just one step away from escalating out of control. Anyone who has been around domestic violence knows that once it gets to that level there is only one path it takes: from bad to worse. Mum had to get away to save her life. I don't blame her for that. But she left us in a place where we were not safe. She knew how toxic the environment she had to flee from was and she chose to leave us in the middle of it. Christ, we were neglected even when she was there, because of all the shit she was going through with Dad.

Life might have improved for her when she got out but it only got worse for us. We only had each other and that was not good enough. We weren't capable of dealing with Dad's problems and our own on top of that. We had been brought up watching how Mum and Dad dealt with problems and so we could only deal with them the same way – running away from anything that scared us or, if we couldn't run, we would attack. This was the way our parents dealt with things: if something was out of your hands, revert to violence.

If things hadn't changed when they did, I'm sure one of us would have died. We were malnourished and out of control. No one was there to defend us.

We knew Dad loved us, but he couldn't do anything to stop the cycle of violence we were living in. He was going through a whole pile of his own madness.

When Dad was gone we would sit and wait for him to come back. We would lock the doors and windows and sit huddled together in the lounge room covered with tattered blankets trying to keep warm, afraid and hungry. Dot would try to be brave but every noise we heard outside the house seemed like the sound of someone wanting to hurt us. We had no television by this point and probably no heating so the wind sounded like someone breaking in and we'd be sitting making noises like dogs, trying to sound ferocious to scare them away.

'Woof! Woof! Woof!'

'Lucky we've got this big dog in here,' Dot would say as convincingly as she could. 'I wouldn't like to be the guy who tried to break into this house.'

'Woof! Woof! Woof!'

We must have sounded like idiots if there ever really was someone outside.

I started stealing small amounts of money, coins mostly, from Dad's pockets when he had passed out. Not much, just enough to get away for a little while.

Get up and get as far away as the little money I had would take me. I never stole enough money to really go that far. Dad didn't have that much money, not by the time he had passed out anyway. Everything he worked for was either drunk or gambled away, leaving coins for us to survive on. By the time I started taking money from his pants he was so drunk he never noticed. I would only take enough for the train trip and that was it. I had nothing to eat and no other money to spend on anything. I was already ridden with guilt from the little that I did take so I didn't want any more. But I had to get away.

I would get up when the sun came up and tiptoe over the strangers asleep on our living room floor, leave the house and walk to the railway station. It wasn't far but early in the mornings I would see people staggering home drunk and confused, trying to avoid the other people on their way to work. Sometimes there would be arguments between them or even scuffles as the workers pushed past them in a hurry to get to wherever they were going. There would be men lying on the ground drunk and there would be others still drinking out of brown paper bags, all mingling at the train station with men in overalls who were doing their best to ignore them so they didn't think about drinking themselves. On more than one occasion some drunk would try to talk to me or even expose himself to me as I waited for the train. But I was tough by then and just moved away and caught the first train that would take me towards the town and eventually the sea.

My days running away to the beach blurred into each other. Nothing happened that changed anything. They were like gasping for air as someone was trying to push your head under the water. Each day gave me enough oxygen to survive until the next escape. Each time seemed to be the same as the time before.

Adelaide Station was always busy and dirty and I would move as quickly as I could to change trains to get out of town and head to the beach. I was only about ten by this point but I knew how to get around by myself and getting to the beach was no big deal for me. From town I could take a tram to Glenelg, or a train to Semaphore. It would take me a couple of hours to get there in all. Then I would walk out to the end of the jetty and sit down and look out to sea and dream about a better life. Local fishermen would talk to me and show me what they had caught and sometimes even give me a lesson on how to fish. Luckily most of them were nice people and I would talk to them and listen as they told me about where they came from and what they did with their lives. I would spend whole days sitting on the jetty at Glenelg, watching the sea and dreaming.

The smell of the ocean with the seaweed baking in the sun and the sound of the sea seemed to stop me worrying about anything. The constant crashing of the waves against the shore sounded like music to me; just like the clattering of the wheels of the train on the rails when I think about it, drowning out the thoughts and fears that always seemed to be present in my head these days. Home drifted off into the distance and left me alone but happy.

Sitting in the sun, alone by the sea, I would also listen to the transistor radios that fishermen were playing on the jetty and I'd sing along in my head with the songs that were playing on Adelaide AM radio. I would daydream about being in exotic places. One day, I told myself, if I could make some money, I would go and visit all the places I had imagined.

There was a show on television called *Adventures in Paradise*. That's how I wanted my life to be. Sailing around Tahiti solving crimes and hanging out with beautiful people. Never going to the same place twice. Going wherever the wind took me. But I was only on a jetty in Adelaide, and that was good enough for me, as long as I was away from Elizabeth.

If I thought too much about it I would be overwhelmed by fear, being away by myself so far from home. The news had been filled with stories about the Beaumont kids who went missing from the very beach I was sitting at. They were on the sand one minute and gone without a trace the next. The police searched for years and never found anything. They disappeared off the face of the earth. Clairvoyants and mystics came from all over the world to try to help the family but found nothing. It was as if the children had never existed. I felt like I could disappear and no one would have known that I ever existed too.

I knew that they never caught anyone for taking those children but it didn't stop me from running away by myself. I felt I was going to die if I stayed home so I had nothing to lose. I sometimes looked around the area, hoping to catch a glimpse of the kids so I could take them home to their family but they never appeared. It seemed so sad that their parents were at home waiting and praying for them and never getting them back and here I was running away and no one even noticed I was gone. It was like I was nobody. I still think about those poor children and their family to this day.

My little escapes always seemed to be to the sea. The ocean calmed me down. Sometimes I would go to Semaphore beach jetty. It didn't matter which beach I was at; I would just sit and watch the fishermen and swim.

I used to jump off the end of the jetty into the water, it was great and I thought I was really brave doing it. But there were always reports of big sharks patrolling the beaches in Adelaide. I heard there had been an attack at Glenelg jetty, the same jetty that I regularly sat on. The story was that some guy was teaching kids how to jump off the jetty one day, and as he hit the water a great white came from nowhere and took him. Only half of him was found. I'm not sure if it was true or an urban myth. But when I heard about this I stopped jumping off the jetty and confined my water activities to the shallows. It seemed I didn't really want to die after all.

The temperature would regularly reach the one hundred mark during the Adelaide summer so getting out of Elizabeth to the sea was something I did as often as I could.

I didn't know it then, but my mum was living a few streets from the jetty and she used to go and sit there just like me and look out to sea. But I wouldn't find that out until much later. Maybe we were thinking about the same things. She might have been wondering where I was and what I was doing, just like I always thought about her.

When the sun started to go down I would retrace my steps. The evening would always come too soon and I would sit on the train and stare out of the window as the clickety-clack of the train wheels replaced the crashing of the waves and the ocean disappeared from view, replaced by the red dirt of the northern suburbs of Adelaide. I would be planning my next escape. And thinking that next time I wouldn't go home. But I always did, and no one ever seemed to miss me or ask where I'd been. Which suited me just fine because it was my escape and I didn't want them to know how to find me in case I did decide to go and not come back.

In Elizabeth it was flat and hot and nothing ever seemed to change. We were still struggling to find food and Dad was still drinking way too much. I would sit on the front porch and look out across the paddock, to the horizon that was distorted by waves of heat rising off the dry ground. I watched and waited for any sign that Mum might be coming back to me.

CHAPTER THIRTEEN

please let it be her

One day a car turned up outside the house. It looked like my mum in the front seat. My heart started to beat faster. 'Please let it be her.'

Was she finally coming back to us? I didn't know the man driving. But that didn't matter.

They didn't come in. They just sat there in the car.

I couldn't wait any longer so I ran out the door to see if it was her but the car drove away before I could get to it.

'Stop, come back. It's me, it's Jim,' I yelled at the car as it drove away.

I walked back to the house, feeling like I'd been deserted all over again.

A few weeks passed before I saw the car again. This time the door opened and Mum got out. I ran out and hugged her for ages. I didn't want to let go in case she left again.

Mum didn't come into the house. We spoke out in the street next to the car.

She didn't explain where she'd been, and she didn't explain why she had left. We were just happy to see her again. She had come home to save us from the hell we were living in.

'How are ye?' she asked, as if she had only left us for the afternoon while she went shopping.

I lied and said, 'We're great, we're all great.'

I didn't want her to feel bad. Surely she must have seen the state we were in? We were all skinny, anxious and on the verge of breaking down. The house was nothing like what Mum had left behind. The lawn was dead. The windows were dirty, which was a good thing, because you couldn't see through the ripped curtains to the misery inside. The flyscreens that once hung on the window frames now lay on the ground, ripped and broken up. I think that Mum didn't want to go inside because she didn't want to see the state we were living in. The place was a mess – not a fit place to raise kids. She knew and couldn't bring herself to face it.

She had left us here. This would weigh heavy on her heart for the rest of her life I think. We were angry but we never let her know it. Not directly anyway. I think that that anger came out in our behaviour later on. We weren't just a bunch of delinquents. We were delinquents with big problems that would stay with us until the day we died.

Then, after what seemed like a very short time, she said, 'Well, I have to go now, but I'll come again in a week. If you're good, you can come and spend the night wi' me.'

She must have been talking to Dad by this point because he just sat in the house. If he didn't know she was coming over he would have run out and screamed at her and probably swung at the guy driving. But he didn't do anything so I'm sure he knew what was going on.

I watched her drive away, wondering if she really would come back. When the car was out of sight, I turned and walked back into the house.

I said to myself, 'If she doesn't come back again, I don't care. I don't want to go with her anyway. I don't need her. I can look after myself. Dot can look after us all.' But I knew, deep down inside, that I did care and Dot couldn't look after us.

Inside, Dad was sitting by the window and I couldn't tell if he had been crying or not. All he seemed to do was cry and get drunk. When he was drunk enough to forget everything he would tell us things like, 'We don't need her. We can get by just fine. We have each other and we're better off without her.'

Then he would cry some more and it would all start again. Soon after Mum left, he went out and didn't come back for a few days.

During the whole time Mum was gone, Dad still got up and went to work. It got harder for him but he still went. He was in the depths of depression by then and it must have been very hard for him to get out of bed at all, but every day up he got and out the door he went. But just like when Mum was there, he never came home until he had drunk enough to drown the demons that were haunting him more and more. He had a lot of trouble sleeping and I don't think he really slept much at all unless he passed out.

The next week was very confusing for us. We hardly saw Dad, and when we did he was angry. None of us had much to eat at all. On top of that we were wondering if Mum would really be coming back. While Dad was out, we talked about going to stay with her. I remember the bigger kids saying they didn't want to go. I think they were worried what Dad would think or do. But I knew that deep down I just wanted to be with her, no matter what she had done to us. So I prayed she would come back again like she promised.

The following weekend she turned up. It seemed like it was all organised. Dad had said to us earlier, 'Ye mother is coming again and you can go and spend the night wi' her if ye like.'

He didn't sound that happy about it. I think he wanted us all to say, 'No, Dad, we want to stay here with you. We don't need her.'

But we didn't.

When she got there I jumped in the car without a second thought. Mum was in the front seat of the car and a strange bloke we didn't know was driving. When I say strange, I mean weird. I can't remember his name or what he looked like; he wasn't important to us at this point. He didn't say a lot. So it was a very quiet drive. I got the feeling he didn't really want us around. This seemed to bother my mum so the trip wasn't the best.

'Where are we going, Mum?' I asked.

'We're goin' tae oor hoose. We live near Glenelg beach.'

I couldn't believe it. When she said we were nearly at her house I worked out that I almost walked past it on my way to the beach when I ran away from Elizabeth. I felt like I must have known where she was, but I couldn't have. If I had, I would have waited at her door until she came out.

We got to the house and it was nice enough – clean and not falling apart so it had it all over where we lived. It wasn't a family house. We were told not to touch anything. But we were kids so we started running around everywhere checking everything out and, of course, touching everything. I remember going outside. I couldn't believe what I saw. There was a whole section of the backyard that was like a little battlefield. There were tanks and soldiers all placed strategically as though they were mid battle. I immediately started playing with them but whatever his name was came out and stopped me. I was not allowed to touch them unless he was there, and he looked pissed off that I had moved things around. He carefully put every piece back exactly where it had been. Then he showed me how it all worked. It looked like little explosions had gone off and all sorts of stuff. It was great. But I did think it was very weird that a grown man played with kids' toys.

He never really spoke to us that much and Mum was not very comfortable. I'm not sure what was going on between them. They didn't seem to like each other a lot. Was that what happened to people when they lived together? Maybe. I remembered she didn't like Dad much when they were together either. But it was great to see her anyway.

The sleepover wasn't a complete success. I got the feeling that we wouldn't be going to stay again. He didn't look happy about a bunch of wild kids running around his house. Mum didn't look happy with him.

Next weekend came and Mum didn't come back; the same the next and the next. We were alone again.

Now we were just trying to keep our heads above water, week to week, as Dad went even further downhill. But then, two or three months after the sleepover, Mum turned up again. This time the guy with the soldiers was gone and in his place was the strangest-looking man we had ever seen. Being Scottish and from Glasgow, most of the men we had met were reasonably short, at least under six feet. But this guy must have been nearly seven foot tall. To us kids he looked like a giant. But he had a kind face and he spoke to us and smiled.

Dad made jokes about him when they left. 'Did ye see him? He was a big streak o' nothin',' he said. 'What aboot the size of that nose, Jesus it was big. He looked stupit.'

But something about the guy felt good. We had to agree with Dad just to make him feel better. But even Mum seemed calm around this guy, which was amazing. His name was Reginald Victor Barnes and he was to be an angel in my life.

* * *

Next time Mum came to see us she said, 'You're all comin' tae spend the weekend wi' me.'

'I'm no goin' anywhere. I'm stayin' wi' ma dad.'

'Aw, come on, John, it'll be nice for the weans tae spend a wee bit o' time wi' their mother.'

'I'm no goin' anywhere. I don't need tae spend time wi' you. You left us. We don't need you. We're doin' just fine without ye.'

'The wee ones need me, John.'

'You should've thought o' that before you walked oot on us.'

'I had tae go, son. Don't be angry wi' me.'

'Well, I don't have tae go. And no one can make me. If they want tae go that's their choice, but I'll never go anywhere wi' you again.'

She got no argument from the rest of us. We needed to get away even if it was just for a little break.

We got to their place, a little fibro three-bedroom house. It wasn't big but it looked like a palace to us. Looking back, I think that they put the whole house together in a hurry so they could save us, grabbing pieces from wherever they could get them – borrowed and bought from second-hand places. The plates weren't all matching or perfect. They had chips on the edges and a different pattern on every piece. The cutlery was the same, a mismatch of pieces thrown together to make up a set. But they were still placed on the table with love and care, which made me feel great. The rooms were small but clean and fresh smelling, like they had been scrubbed the day before we came. There were pieces of wallpaper peeling off the walls in the corners, as if they had been slapped up in a hurry to cover something up. Lino had been freshly laid in the kitchen and was cool on my feet as I walked across it. There were separate beds for each of us and they had clean sheets and nice pillows.

From the moment I got there I didn't want to have to go back to Elizabeth again. This was like being on a holiday. Everything worked, the toilet flushed and there was plenty of toilet paper. They had a television and the electricity had not been cut off. There was a refrigerator that worked and it was full of fresh food and cold milk. Soft fresh bread that we didn't have to cut the mouldy bits off, and real butter, I loved butter. I could spread it as thick as I wanted without having to worry that it would run out.

After dinner Reg cleaned up and set the table for breakfast. I couldn't believe it – we had just finished eating and here we were, all ready to eat again whenever we wanted to.

Before bed Reg took me into the kitchen and said, 'I'll show you a secret. This is my favourite meal.'

And he picked up the cereal. Reg liked Wheaties. They seemed very Australian to me. They were dry and bland but I was happy to eat whatever he offered me. He proceeded to pour out some for us both and we sat in silence and ate. Neither of us saying a word. Then he got up and he washed the dishes.

'Come on Jim,' he said. 'You've got to dry them, then it's time for bed.'

I dried the two bowls, said goodnight and went to bed. I wasn't scared like I normally was, but I left the light on just in case, and climbed into bed. The pyjamas Mum had given me to wear smelled of soap powder and sunlight and felt soft against my skin. I climbed into bed to find sheets that were almost starched feeling. Crisp and cool, they sort of crackled as I pulled them up to my neck. I had been without sheets for so long that I couldn't wipe the smile from my face as I lay wrapped in sundrenched white cotton. I played with the corners of the sheets, rubbing them against my hands just to check that they were still there as I slowly drifted off to sleep. It felt like the first time I could sleep without worrying about what would be waiting when I woke up for a long time.

I woke up in the morning feeling happy and went out to the kitchen, and there was Reg, up and dressed and ready to give us breakfast. He was right – the cereal did taste better the night before when the house was quiet and still, but it still tasted fantastic. This was how the families in those houses I used to walk past and dream about lived, I was sure. Did we really have to go back and live like we lived before? I couldn't think about it. Dad had told us he would die without us but if we went back we would die too.

Before the weekend finished, Mum said to us, 'You kids would be better off stayin' wi' us.'

I know now we were never going back from the moment we left Dad.

Mum and Reg lived in Wingfield. It was not one of the prettiest places in Adelaide but it was just far enough away from Elizabeth to make me feel safe. It was almost where we had lived when we first came to Australia. I could walk to where the old Finsbury Hostel had been. There were no housing trust houses in the street; there were none anywhere to be seen. Everywhere you looked in Elizabeth looked the same. The same colour bricks, the same houses all sitting in rows. But not around here. Every house looked different. We forgot about where we came from for a little while. Wingfield was different from Elizabeth. The gutters weren't concreted and there were no footpaths outside the house. I felt like I was out in the country. There was a strange smell in the air but I didn't really think about it. Later on I would find out what that smell was but not until the shine had come off our new lives.

Mum cleaned us up and washed our clothes and we did things that seemed to be normal. We played games and laughed. We didn't see any booze around the house at all, which was very strange to us, but it made me feel safer. Things were calm; I didn't feel any tension in the house at all. This was something that we weren't used to. It felt strange but at the same time it felt good.

Mum was still working as a nurse's aide at Hillcrest Mental Hospital. She'd been there since before she left us, which makes me realise that Dad wasn't looking for her very hard or he would have found her.

It seemed that the Child Welfare Agency had approached my mum and told her we were going to be taken as wards of the state unless she could provide a safe home for us. So she must have been checking up on us.

Mum told us later that she had been sitting in a work friend's house, crying about the situation, when Reg Barnes walked in and asked, 'What's the trouble, love?' He called everybody 'love'. His mum and dad did the same.

She told him her story. 'I need to find mysel' a husband and then I need to find a home for me and ma six kids. And I need tae dae it quick or they'll put the kids in a home.'

'Why did you leave them?'

'I had tae run away because ma husband was a bad drunk and now they're being neglected by their father.'

'No worries love,' he said, just like that. 'I'll marry you.'

'Why wid ye do that?' she asked him.

'Someone has to save those poor kids.'

He hadn't met us at this point but he didn't give it another thought. Somehow he instinctively knew we needed him and came to our rescue. Until then, we were told, he was going to become a priest. Mum told us he had given up all sorts of things including some sort of religious calling just to look after us. But Mum was always trying to make us feel guilty about something.

Reg worked hard all his life. He was a clerk at the Kelvinator factory in Keswick near Port Adelaide. His big brother was one of the bosses at Kelvinator and Reg seemed a little bit sad that he had not climbed the same ladder to success. He had been stuck as a clerk for a long time and he could see no signs of a promotion coming in the near future. But he never complained. He just got up every morning and went to his job, day after day. He started losing sleep when we came along. He wasn't used to being a father and he suddenly had to spend all night nursing sick children with colds and fevers. Or waking up at three in the morning to comfort me when I had nightmares. I used to wake up screaming and crying. But he did it every night he was needed.

'I'm here, Jim. Just shut your eyes and go back to sleep.'

'But I'm scared.'

'Nothing to be scared of anymore, lad. I'm right here with you. Now go back to sleep.'

I'd drift off, knowing he was sitting in the room with me.

I'd see him leaving for work on many a morning, bleary-eyed and yawning. He went to work every day whether he had slept or not. Then he would get home from work to find that Mum had found a million new things for him to fix around the house. He didn't get a lot of rest after we arrived.

One minute he was alone in life without a worry, the next he was married to a mad Scottish woman and had six juvenile delinquent kids. How and why he did this has always amazed me. He didn't think about himself. This was truly an act of pure, selfless love. He was a saint. I quickly grew to love him and respect him. He was a good man.

Reg, as he said we were to call him, was actually six foot six and a half inches tall. He was a very gentle man who seemed to care about my mum and even though he'd just met us, he seemed to care for us too. He didn't drink and he wanted to spend time with us. I think he even enjoyed being with us, which was very strange for us. Even our parents didn't seem to spend time with us unless they had to.

It was a little strange having an adult in our lives we called by his first name. 'Reg' always sounded very Australian and odd to us too. People from Glasgow weren't called Reginald. They were Jimmy or Bobby, not Reg. But after living with Reg for a short while we felt he was so much more than just Mum's new partner. He cared about us, he looked after us, he loved us. Slowly, over a few months, we drifted from calling him Reg to calling him Dad. It happened by accident at first.

'Here's your breakfast, son. Now sit down and eat.'

'Thanks Dad, er, Reg, er, thanks.'

'You're welcome. You can call me what you like. Jim will always be your dad. I'm not trying to replace him, son, but I'm here for you if you need me.'

'Thanks Reg, er, Dad, er, thanks.'

He became our dad. He acted like a dad should. He was a good role model. He cared, but he was tough when he had to be. Not really tough but as tough as he could be.

He rode a motor scooter and took me for rides down through Port Adelaide and showed me where he grew up. He shared his life with me from day one. Whatever he knew or had he wanted to share it with me.

What was going on? No one had been like this in my life before. I could tell he hadn't expected to be doing this in his life either but he did it anyway and eventually we both learned to relax and enjoy each other's company. We had fun together. He probably did this with all the kids but I felt different; he made me feel special. And not like my dad did – taking me out with him because Mum made him. He took me out because he wanted to know about me. This was different.

Reg and Mum tried to make us feel safe and warm and wanted, even though we could tell it wasn't always easy for them.

Dinner was always on the table at six o'clock and Reg would always go to work and would always come home with his wages. We felt like we were living in a television show.

All us kids went from being nervous wrecks to being almost relaxed. Linda settled down and for a time she was as happy as I was. We all felt safe with Reg as far as I could see. Mum still had a bad temper but she'd always had a bad temper so nothing had changed there really.

We were safe and I could finally sleep at night. But I was still scared of everything and hated being in the dark. One day, Reg went to his mum's house and came back with a light in the shape of a lighthouse. I thought it was beautiful. He brought it into my room and said to me that when he was young he was afraid of the dark and his dad had bought this for him. He said the lighthouse made it safe for ships sailing in the dark in wild seas and this one he was giving me would make it safe for me in my dreams, no matter how wild they got. It worked, but I liked to sleep with it on most nights, sometimes because I was scared, and sometimes because it reminded me that Reg was there to look after me.

John was the only one of us who was not happy about Reg coming into our lives and he made sure we all knew about it. He would insult Reg and Mum to their faces and behind their backs. He refused to do anything they said and tried his best to disrupt our lives whenever he could. John wanted us all to be back together with Mum and Dad and be happy but I think he knew that could never happen.

Dad had always been John's hero and John had always been my dad's number one son. John worshipped Dad and the ground he walked on. None of us could say a bad word about him, no one could, unless they wanted to fight John. As much as Dad could do no wrong, it seemed Reg could do no right in John's

1. Da, his favourite granddaughter Dorothy, and his 'wee dug' Jackie. This photo says so much: my Da with the only person he liked to spend time with, and the one who shared his life, his dog. The walls in this photo sum up Glasgow for me. The chalk drawings and marks were not just graffiti. The streetlights were always broken so drunks would leave a trail marked on the walls to find their way home, a bit like Hansel and Gretel. **2. Elizabeth Dixon and John Dixon.** My Da and Granny in happy times in Glasgow. I don't remember them together a lot. Granny would go around to his house and look after him but she couldn't live with him. **3. The Scottish Western Districts Championship cup, 1953.** Dad won many cups and trophies. This is the only one we have left. Mum smashed them or threw them out or at him when they fought. **4. My dad, James Ruthven Harvey Swan.** In his heyday. He wasn't that big but he could fight as good as any man, in the ring, in the house or on the street. He thought fast and punched faster. (**ALL IMAGES: BARNES FAMILY COLLECTION**)

1. The Hut, 1952. Mum and Dad by the sea with John. My mum was very young and beautiful. Dad was fit and handsome. These days didn't last too long. **2. My dad with Dorothy and John.** The van in the background looks a lot like the cars that Dad would buy to fix up. Way beyond saving.
3. On the street in Glasgow. Dorothy, young Alan, myself and John. The Royal Bar in the back was the scene of many a bloodbath. (ALL IMAGES: BARNES FAMILY COLLECTION)

1. **Aunty Maude and me.** Aunty Maude was Mum's sister. Apart from my granny, hers is the only family I ever saw again after leaving Scotland. Her son Jackie and daughter Joanne are the only cousins I know and I love them very much. We all need family. **2. John, Linda, myself and Dorothy with Mum and Aunty Maude.** I'm not sure where we are. It might be Port Seton on the only holiday I remember in Scotland. **3. Linda, John, Dorothy and me at the beach.** Scotland wasn't famous for its beaches but it looks like it was famous for very high bathers. The sky is grey and it looks fiercely cold. It must be midsummer. **4. John, myself, Dorothy and Linda in Glasgow.** John used to say that my ears were so big I looked like a taxi with the doors left open. (ALL IMAGES: BARNES FAMILY COLLECTION)

1. **Dorothy, myself, Linda and John** on board the SS *Strathnaver*, somewhere in the middle of the Indian Ocean. We had escaped the horrors of Glasgow and landed on a 'luxury' cruise. (Barnes Family Collection) 2. **Mum on board the ship.** While the boat was a luxury cruise for us kids, Mum soon realised that she had escaped from fighting on the streets of Glasgow by jumping on board the *Titanic*. Any hope of saving her marriage was sinking fast. (Barnes Family Collection) 3. **The SS *Strathnaver*.** To us, this was our ride to a new life. It would take us away from everything that was stacked up against our family and give us a break. Well, that was the plan. (© West Australian Newspapers Limited)

1. Me sitting outside our Nissen hut at the Gepps Cross Hostel. It was so hot inside. Outside the air moved occasionally. Inside the air only moved when Mum and Dad threw things at each other. (BARNES FAMILY COLLECTION) **2. That's me aged six.** There are a few photos around with me as a kid with no front teeth. (BARNES FAMILY COLLECTION) **3. Elizabeth, City of Tomorrow.** Slow down. Who were they talking to here? It could have been the trucks that rolled in from the north, carrying food to the hungry immigrants who would fill the houses yet to be built. Or were they talking to themselves? Let's think about what we are building here. Will this work? They could be talking to the families who couldn't wait to get there and get hold of their dreams. Maybe it was written for kids like me who would be running around the streets. Look at the dry prickly ground under the sign. This sort of ground cover would ambush young shoeless boys like me. My feet hurt just looking at this picture. Elizabeth, City of Tomorrow? It seems like yesterday I lived there. (CITY OF PLAYFORD HISTORY SERVICE)

1. **Twenty-odd miles from Adelaide,** somewhere on the main highway that led north to the dead heart of Australia, lay Elizabeth. It was flat, hot and dry. This was as far from Glasgow as my folks could run. It was in the middle of nowhere. But everything was laid out nice and neat. Each separate area had its own shops, its own school and its own football grounds. They all had the same problems though. (CITY OF PLAYFORD HISTORY SERVICE) **2. Me and Alan with our mum** on the front porch of 45 Heytesbury Road, Elizabeth. That is the door Mum used when she left us. The door always slammed because it was attached to a spring. When she left we didn't hear a thing. (BARNES FAMILY COLLECTION) **3. Hamming it up** in the front yard. Mum tried to grow a lawn but it didn't work. Nothing grew well at our house. (BARNES FAMILY COLLECTION)

1.

2.

Beautiful Elizabeth, S.A.

SOUVENIR OF

Elizabeth
S.A.

(1) Skating Rink.
(2) Modern Flats.
(3) G.M.H. Elizabeth Plant.
(4) Hotel Elizabeth.
(5) Town Shopping Centre.
(6) High School.
(7) Hospital, Elizabeth.
(8) Law Courts and Police Station.

3.

1. Lisa, our little pizza pie, Linda, myself and Dorothy on the back porch. I get a feeling of emptiness when I look at pictures of this house. We were always hungry and our lives were empty. It was hard to feel love in this house. (**Barnes Family Collection**) **2. The train at the Elizabeth West shops.** The things I saw from the front of this train still crash their way into my dreams and I wake up gasping for breath, hoping I never have to think about them again. (**City of Playford History Service**) **3. If I saw this postcard** I wouldn't be booking my next holiday here in a hurry. I don't know if 'beautiful' is the right way to describe Elizabeth in the early days, but the place had a lot of potential when they first built it. Some of that potential was reached; some was lost in the haze from the heat that rose from the red dirt. But what really makes a place great is the people that live there, and a lot of great people have come from Elizabeth, and still live there. (**City of Playford History Service**)

1. The Centre shops. This photo was taken near the front of the coffee shop. I walked through here on many a boiling hot day, running from one patch of shade to the next, trying desperately to stop my bare feet from being burned by the blistering heat of the concrete on the way to the swimming pool. Later on, I sprinted through the same shops at night, avoiding thugs who wanted to bash my head in, or running with a gang of my mates, trying to get away from the police. (CITY OF PLAYFORD HISTORY SERVICE)
2. John and I in the driveway at Heytesbury Road. Behind us you can see the scrawny candle pines that Mum planted. On these trees there were small spikey pine cones that I used as ninja stars to throw at my sisters. (BARNES FAMILY COLLECTION) **3. In the summer** this was the best place to be. The temperature would reach the one hundred mark and everybody in Elizabeth seemed to be on the verge of blowing a gasket. In the morning I would sit outside on the footpath, waiting for the pool to open. Then I would run in and dive to the bottom. It was cool and quiet down below the surface. But, unfortunately, I always had to come back up to the waiting world. When I'd been in so long that my skin began to wrinkle, I'd go and sit on the grass and daydream. Thinking about life. Well, food and girls anyway.
(CITY OF PLAYFORD HISTORY SERVICE)

1. Myself, Alan and Lisa sitting at the table, ready for breakfast. Reg and I would set the table the night before so we could eat as soon as we woke up. It also gave us a chance to eat cereal before we went to bed. **2. This is me in action,** playing football after moving in with Reg. I spent most of my time as a young guy playing football. I thought I was really good, but I'm not sure I was. **3. Mum and Reg.** Mum looked beautiful and happy then. But things would change. Reg looks surprised. He had a lot more surprises once we came along. (**ALL IMAGES: BARNES FAMILY COLLECTION**)

1. **Aunty Dorrie** with her nephew Reginald. She's the one who first taught Reg to play piano.
2. **Reginald Victor Barnes.** This was before we met him. He looked kind of cool, like Buddy Holly, but when we saw him the first time we all laughed. Dad called him a big streak of nothing. But there was a lot to Reg. **3. Grandma and Grandpa.** Reg's parents. These guys were real salt-of-the-earth Aussies. No airs and graces. But they probably had skeletons in their closets too. I'm sure they did because my sister saw ghosts walking around their house at night. (ALL IMAGES: BARNES FAMILY COLLECTION)

1. Reg's grandmother, Mabel Evelyn Barnes. My sister Linda met her at Grandma's house. Reg's grandmother would talk to Linda at night and tell her about life and how to deal with it. The only problem was she had been dead for a long time before we moved to Australia. **2. Uncle John and his wife Tania.** John was the rebel of the Barnes family – the black sheep until we came along. It wasn't long until we made him look good. **3. These four brothers were all decent blokes. I liked them all.** Uncle Tom, Reg's youngest brother: a great guy who was a little wild when he was young, so he had a soft spot for us. John, who took me to speedway meetings and encouraged me to drink beer. Reg, dressed in his standard outfit: a cardigan and slacks. And Edward Barnes: Uncle Ted worked with Reg and was the boss at Kelvinator. (ALL IMAGES: BARNES FAMILY COLLECTION)

1. **Reg thought he was cool** riding around on a scooter. Mum doesn't look that impressed, although I think she is showing him a bit of leg there. Reg was probably more interested in her slippers. He would have wanted a pair too. **2. Dorothy, Lisa, myself and Alan** on an outing with Reg to Mount Lofty. We weren't used to family outings, but Reg insisted that the family do things together. Normal things. That's what families do. **3. The same day out.** A normal, healthy, happy family. At this point in time we might have been, but cold winds were starting to blow even then. Things wouldn't last. Everything always fell apart. **4. I'm not sure when or where this was.** I have a feeling that it might have been at Uncle John's house. They had outside toilets but this was getting ridiculous. (**ALL IMAGES: BARNES FAMILY COLLECTION**)

1. There's that taxi with the doors open again. This is me when we moved in with Reg. I was happy. I had just started at Mansfield Park Primary School. You can see why the tougher kids at that school thought I was an easy mark. I look innocent. **2. A very happy young Alan** in very high pants and myself in a very short tie. I might have been wearing his tie and he might have been wearing my pants. Who knows? John, who was a mod and refused to wear a tie unless it was paisley, and Warren, a bloke who went out with my sister Dorothy for a while. We were all dressed up for a party. Sooner or later trouble would break out. **3. Grandpa and my sister Dorothy.** The whole family loved Dot. She was a great kid and a great sister. If it wasn't for her I think I would have died many times. **4. Reg and Mum** getting married in March 1970. In the background you can see the piano that Reg played for us. It sounded great then and it still sounds beautiful now. **5. The Barnes family with their new members, the Swan clan.** Grandma seems to be keeping away from us a bit. Probably the best thing. You could never tell when Mum would turn. (ALL IMAGES: BARNES FAMILY COLLECTION)

1. Me, Lisa and Alan. Mum never had a lot of money for clothes so I started borrowing stuff from John. This was one of his tight mod jumpers from Merivale. Cost him a fortune. I think Alan is wearing one I had stolen from John earlier. I would borrow them and then Mum would machine-wash them so they never fitted John again. Lisa is as usual happy and smiling. I love these two guys. **2. Linda and Dorothy.** My two big sisters out looking for trouble. They always seemed to find it too. Reg would say things like, 'Over my dead body will I let you go out with skirts that short' – and out the door they would go. **3. My first real band, Tarkus.** That's me at sixteen, dressed in baby blue. Michael Smith is playing bass at the back. He and I are friends to this day. Mark, who is playing guitar, died quite a few years ago. This photo might have been taken at the Elizabeth Community Centre. I think it's the only photo of this band. We weren't that great. (**ALL IMAGES: BARNES FAMILY COLLECTION**)

1. Apollo Stadium in Adelaide. This was a place where you could see overseas as well as interstate bands. My mates and I would kick the back door in and charge through before the bouncers could get a hold of us. The other thing we did was at interval, as people were coming out the front doors for a smoke. We would push back into the crowd as it flooded out and grab a pass from the unsuspecting doorman, pretending we had been in for the first half of the show. One way or another, we were getting in. (NEWSPIX) **2. Me at sixteen with too much attitude** and a bad haircut. I seem to have had a lot of those over the years. The attitude hasn't gotten any better either. (BARNES FAMILY COLLECTION) **3. John Fraser,** a mate of my brother's; John, leaning, looking like he might have had a few drinks; and me, looking like I am after a drink. John could drink more than anybody I knew. I wanted to be just like him. I got there eventually. (BARNES FAMILY COLLECTION)

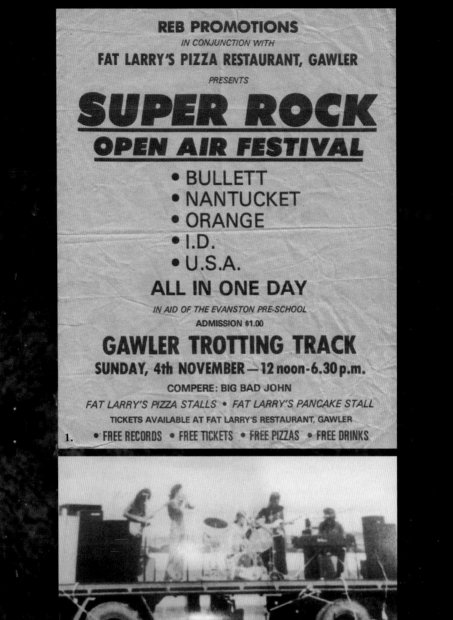

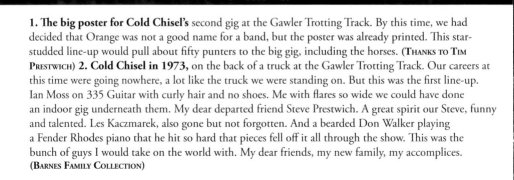

1. **The big poster for Cold Chisel's** second gig at the Gawler Trotting Track. By this time, we had decided that Orange was not a good name for a band, but the poster was already printed. This star-studded line-up would pull about fifty punters to the big gig, including the horses. (THANKS TO TIM PRESTWICH) 2. **Cold Chisel in 1973,** on the back of a truck at the Gawler Trotting Track. Our careers at this time were going nowhere, a lot like the truck we were standing on. But this was the first line-up. Ian Moss on 335 Guitar with curly hair and no shoes. Me with flares so wide we could have done an indoor gig underneath them. My dear departed friend Steve Prestwich. A great spirit our Steve, funny and talented. Les Kaczmarek, also gone but not forgotten. And a bearded Don Walker playing a Fender Rhodes piano that he hit so hard that pieces fell off it all through the show. This was the bunch of guys I would take on the world with. My dear friends, my new family, my accomplices. (BARNES FAMILY COLLECTION)

eyes. When we moved in with Reg, John went and lived with my dad not far from us in Semaphore.

They shared a little rundown one-bedroom flat that wasn't really fit for a dog. The flat was a hovel and Dad was out of control. I didn't spend much time with them at this apartment – it was cold and dirty and I would always want to leave as soon as I could. I didn't want to go back to the horror story of a life that we had been living before. Dad knew it. When I say Dad was out of control I mean he was falling apart. He was depressed and drinking huge amounts of booze and hardly eating. But John stayed right by his side, caring for him and cleaning up after he'd passed out. John loved him so much and it was killing him to watch Dad descend to new lows. But it would all change for the two of them very soon.

Dad used to bring John to see us every couple of days and leave him with us for a few hours. John would tell us, 'Things are great now. Dad and me are livin' the dream. No one to answer to. We do whatever we want.' None of us really believed him though. He was looking skinny and pale and he always seemed a bit sick. We were worried about him.

'Dad and me are best mates.' We believed him when he said that. We knew how much they loved each other. But he wasn't grown up enough to help Dad sort out his life. Dad talked him into staying with us for a few days while he found out about a job. I was out on the front lawn when Dad and John pulled up in a cab.

'See you later, Dad,' he shouted as he jumped out of the cab, as happy as could be. He walked across the grass towards me. Next thing John turned quickly around to the cab as it drove away. I could see Dad crying in the back seat, looking at John as he left. John broke down; he knew he wouldn't see his dad again and he ran down the road after the cab but it was gone.

We didn't see Dad for about fourteen years after that and that really took its toll on John. I don't think he has ever recovered.

He had to stay with us and he made life as miserable as he could for Mum and Reg. He wouldn't go to school and he wouldn't get a job, he spent his life making their lives a living hell. Of course that had a profound effect on the rest of us kids too. Our perfect new life started to unravel and slowly our hopes drained away.

Reg and Mum tried to make John lift his game and get a job but he fought them every step of the way. Mum would get him out of bed whenever she could.

'Right, up ye get. If you're gonnae stay wi' us you're gonnae have tae learn tae carry yer weight,' Mum barked at him like a sergeant major one day, but John didn't respond to that kind of encouragement.

'Come on, John lad. This is a family and we all need to do our bit to make things work. You've got to be a good example to your young brothers and sisters,' Reg pleaded, trying to appeal to John's sense of the right thing to do.

But John didn't have one. 'Leave me alone. I'm tryin' tae get some sleep.'

'If you don't get oot of that bed I'm gonnae fuckin' belt ye.' Mum would try, getting more extreme.

'Yeah. I'm really scared now. Just fuck off and shut the door.'

'Come on, John, do the right thing by your mum. She's trying really hard. Please, son.'

'I'm not your son and if you don't like it I'll move out.'

Mum pushed him and badgered him until he appeared to give up.

'Okay, shut the door and I'll get up and look for a job.'

'Good boy, I'll put the kettle on,' Reg said, thinking he had got through to him, and rushed off to make him breakfast before he left to go to work himself.

Mum went back to bed and continued shouting out orders to John. 'I cannae hear ye. You'd better be up or you're gonnae get it.'

'Yeah, yeah, yeah. I'm up.'

John was still in bed but he had his foot out from under the covers, banging it on the floor, pretending he was walking around. This worked for a while until Mum caught on. Then she burst through the door with a bucket of water and threw it all over him. Unfortunately, we shared a room so this meant I was caught in the crossfire and ended up wet too. Then she walked back to her room, cursing and crying with frustration. John laughed, found a corner of the bed that was dry, curled up and went back to sleep. Reg went to work, disappointed in him, and John got out of bed after noon and went out to see his mates.

I didn't like the way he behaved but I took note of how he got to do whatever he wanted. I didn't start to act like him straight away but I got there eventually.

The time came for us to meet the rest of Reg's family and Mum started to get nervous. Things seemed to change overnight.

Mum always had an inferiority complex. She started saying, 'They'll be toffs. They're gonnae look down on us. We're different tae them.'

She was sure that people only had to look at us and they would know we were no good. But we had to go to Reg's young brother Tom's twenty-first birthday party, no matter how weird Mum felt.

'It's what families do, love,' Reg said as nicely as he could. 'Well, they do in Australia anyway. Maybe it's different where you came from but here, we've got to support our families.'

I began to worry again. Worry it would all go wrong and we would end up back where we started. We didn't deserve a good life. We were losers, just like Mum feared, and we would end up in the gutter with the rest of the trash where we belonged.

Mum got more and more edgy as the party grew closer. She picked a few fights with Reg but he ignored her. When we were alone I asked him about it and he said, 'Don't worry love, it's just like water off a duck's back to me. Your mum has had a tough life and gets a bit stressed sometimes. She doesn't mean to start fights.'

My dad would have killed her by this point so this was a whole new world to me. How could he be so patient? Not only that, he seemed to be trying to teach me about patience and how to be a good person too. Reg took the time to explain things. It was hard to take at first, but it got easier the longer we were together – until much later, when I stopped listening.

Reg had lived with his family at 74 Wellington Street in Alberton until he met my mum. The party was at his mum's house – the house he was born in and would later want to die in. So we got dressed up in our best new clothes that Reg and Mum had bought for us so we would look good when we met the family.

Mum told us, 'Be on your best behaviour or I'll belt you. They're gonnae look doon their noses at us as soon as they meet us. So don't give them any excuses. And you John, don't you start any trouble, or else.' John was a bit of a hoodlum by this point.

Reg tried his best to reassure her that everything would be all right. But she was on guard and wasn't in a good frame of mind to go anywhere, never mind to meet the in-laws. We were worried that things would go wrong before we had even left the house. It was like she was willing something to happen. But off we went. I think things started to get strained between her and Reg on the way but we carried on regardless.

The family and the guests were an unusual group, especially to a bunch of kids from Elizabeth. We had not really socialised at all outside of our Scottish friends. Australians seemed to be a different thing altogether. Some of the men wore badly fitting suits that smelled of mothballs, like they'd been dragged out of the cupboard that morning. I got the impression that these people didn't dress up so often. These were going-out clothes and they mustn't have gone out very much: the same clothes were dragged out for all special occasions, a twenty-first or a wedding or even a funeral. Others wore jeans with white shirts tucked quickly in and ties with loose knots that were tied too short. They weren't stylish at all. These people were not like Mum and Dad's old Scottish friends, who dressed up to go out on a Saturday night. They always wanted to look good, even when they got arrested.

We walked into the house and there on the table were all kinds of cakes and biscuits. I'd never seen so many before. Lamingtons and cupcakes. Chocolate sponges and trays of sandwiches. Curried egg and ham, cheese and tomato. These were not the things that were eaten at Scottish parties. The place smelled different from the homes I had been to in the past. It smelled Australian I guess, filled with the smell of Australian food. The women all sat inside the house and the men were out the back, down near the shed where they had set up a keg. If anyone set up a keg at a Scottish party, they were begging for a fight and it wouldn't take long until our family started one.

The guests were a mix of blokes who worked at Kelvinator and bikies trying to look their best for their mate's party. The only bikies we saw in Elizabeth were animals, so the whole family was on guard, waiting for trouble to start.

The women were dressed very conservatively compared to Mum's mates. There were no plunging necklines or hip-hugging dresses. Floral patterns adorned dresses that looked like the women had made them themselves.

The language was different too. There was not another British accent to be heard anywhere. Their accents were nasal sounding and slightly coarse. The coarseness didn't bother us but the sound of the voices was like fingernails on a blackboard to my Mum. She looked like a fish out of water – not wanting to sit in the house with the women and not feeling comfortable enough to go out to the yard with the men. They all seemed to be drinking beer. Some of the women mixed it with lemonade to act a little more ladylike but most just drank it by the schooner glass full. Mum would have killed for a whisky but I'm sure she was too uncomfortable to ask.

'Can I get you a drink love?' Reg asked her, trying to break the ice.

'No, I don't drink. You know that Reg,' she said, just loud enough for the other women to hear. She sounded like she had a plum stuck in her mouth, trying to be as posh as possible.

'Come on love, it's a party. I might even have a shandy myself.'

'No, I'll be fine, thank you.'

I looked around the party and realised that we didn't fit in there. We were trouble waiting to happen.

John, my brother, was sixteen or seventeen by this time. He was a bit of a mod and was dressed in a light salmon-coloured suit and platform shoes about four inches high. He couldn't have worn anything more inappropriate for the company. The bikies wanted to kill him as soon as they saw him. I think that he wanted to kill them as soon as he arrived at the party too. So the whole thing was like a time-bomb, ticking, waiting to blow.

John was a real animal and probably could have cleaned up most of them but he had been warned to be good. So he didn't retaliate when they started making snide remarks every time he walked past. If he went to get a drink one of them would make a comment.

'Nice suit ... do they make them for men?'

He just ignored them and kept walking. It must have been hard for him but he had been told. Well, it was all going well. That is, until my mum overheard them talking about him and all hell broke loose. She walked up to this big guy in a leather jacket and stood in front of him. Her head came up to his chest and he smiled at her in a condescending sort of way.

'What's wrong, lady?'

We felt a bit sorry for the poor guy because we knew what he was in for and he didn't. Next thing she jumped up and head-butted him on the nose, knocking him to the ground in a pool of blood. Then she turned to attack his other poor bikie friends. She was in full fight or flight mode and nothing could stop her. She turned on Tom's fiancée and hit her, then went for the rest of the family.

'She's fucking crazy,' I heard someone say as the party came to a grinding halt and we left. They were whispering and pointing at us as we walked out and onto the street. One of Tom's friends, a guy named Tooley – who I will tell you more about later – helped us get out of the place. I'm still not sure if he was helping us or them. Either way it was time to leave.

Out on the street we were being dragged away with Mum screaming obscenities at Reg. 'Your fuckin' family are a pack o' pigs. How dare they talk aboot ma kids!'

My whole world just flashed back to Scotland and being dragged outside in the snow. Life was imploding around us as we walked to find a bus to get away from there.

Reg came running after us, calling out to Mum, 'Why are you blaming me? I'm on your side. Slow down. We'll sort it out. Everything will be all right.'

Mum wasn't listening. 'Just fuck off, ya big streak o' nothin'. Go back tae yer own fuckin' family.'

I had heard this term before. My dad had called Reg the same thing. Glaswegians, as I said earlier, are not known for being tall, so they don't feel comfortable around tall people. I'm sure they have lots of insults to describe anyone over five foot ten but 'a big streak o' nothin'' was the popular choice for my mum and dad. Had they used it together when, in happier times, they shouted it abusively at a tall person they both didn't like? I'm not sure but it is almost romantic to think so.

Reg would not leave; he stayed with us. We ended up back at our house thinking that life was back the way it used to be. Reg helped calm down everything, including Mum, and eventually we all got to bed.

Next day he told his parents he was disgusted with Tom's friends' behaviour and the way they treated his new family. His parents were very sorry about the whole thing and even apologised. Good thing too because Mum wasn't going to. Things settled back down to normal. I'm not sure normal is the right word to use for our family. I do know this would never have happened in a Scottish family. A good Glaswegian family would have been fighting about it for years.

CHAPTER FOURTEEN

because I love you, son

The Barnes family liked to sit around the house and drink tea and play cards. They would drink tea all day and night. If they weren't drinking it, they were making it. I remember hearing the phrase 'put the kettle on, love' all the time I lived with Reg. He said it all the time, his dad and his mum said it and his Aunty Dorrie said it.

Aunty Dorrie must have been his dad's sister. All that side of the family were well over six foot tall and very thin. Aunty Dorrie was no exception; she was six foot two inches tall and thin but she looked like in her day she would have been very beautiful. She had very high cheekbones and long limbs and was very elegant-looking. As a young girl she would have been as sleek as a gazelle. I often wondered why she wasn't married. Maybe she'd had her heart broken or had a tragic loss or was going to be a nun or something. She was just like the rest of the family, very reserved and very nice – but she had a look of sadness about her.

Grandpa and Grandma Barnes, Aunty Dorrie and Reg were great euchre players. They taught us how to play too. So we would go over to their house and drink tea and play cards. They didn't watch TV, so the house was always quiet except when someone won a game. I never saw them playing for money, just for points. They played from morning until night.

The only time the silence was broken – besides someone calling out for cards or making tea – was when Grandpa would sit down and play the piano. Now he never played that well, but it always sounded to me like what piano would have sounded like at a vaudeville show. He slapped the ivories, rather than tickled them. Looking back it reminds me a bit of Chico Marx playing the piano. Reg and Grandpa would sing along at the top of their voices to happy songs I'd never heard before. They must have been old Australian songs, I never heard anyone from Scotland sing them. The way they sang, you would think they were singing top forty songs. Reg would look at me to see if I recognised any of them. But I didn't. I don't think that they had bought a record since the 1940s, never mind anything in the top forties.

'Come on,' they'd say, 'you must know this one.' And Grandpa would tear into another song that Charlie Chaplin might have danced to in a silent movie. I would scratch my head and look blankly at them. But they were loud and funny and we always ended up laughing along with them.

Later on Reg brought the piano to our house and he used to play it every night. He played a lot better than his dad but the piano still sounded out of tune, just like it did when Grandpa played it. I'm not sure if it was the piano or his playing. The song I remember Reg playing most often was 'Für Elise'. He played it every night. I think this was his way of escaping from all the worries he had inherited when he adopted us. He could slap the keys like his dad when he wanted to. Playing the piano seemed to take him back to his home and family in Port Adelaide. I could see it on his face. He was distant but happy. It never lasted that long before he had to stop. Mum would always tell him to stop because she had something she wanted him to do. He didn't get a lot of rest, old Reg.

He always wanted to teach me the piano. 'Come on, love,' he'd say to me, 'give it a go. You'll thank me someday for this chance.'

But I wasn't interested. I wanted to play the guitar by then. Something louder. But Reg was right again – now I wish I had taken him up on the offer.

Reg's family were a caring, Australian working-class family. No airs and graces. They called a spade a spade. What you saw was what you got. But they were warm and open to us. They hardly drank as far as I could see and never had big fights. I didn't know what was going on, but in the back of my head I felt that surely this would all fall apart on me sooner or later. Everything always did.

They didn't have a lot but they kept everything clean and in its place. The toilet was outside but it was clean and neat and not like the outside toilets I had seen anywhere else. There were no spiders and it had a light – I think so Grandpa could read his paper in there.

The wallpaper had been on the walls of the house since Reg's mum and dad bought the place forty or fifty years earlier. The whole house looked like it was from another time. A museum. The same pictures were on the wall as when Reg lived there as a child; if you moved them there was darker wallpaper underneath, that's how long they'd hung there. He pointed them all out and told me who was who and what was what.

'This was Uncle Billy as a young lad.' It was like he slipped back to a time when his uncle was there with him. I could see it in his eyes and hear it in his voice. His tone softened like he wanted to be back there again.

'Life was tough back then, Jim. You know, my family had nothing but they worked hard and life was not too bad. You get nothing for nothing. You have to work hard. There's no two ways about it. Just keep your head down and your bum up and things will work out for you.'

'How long did you live here?'

'All my life. I was born here and I'll probably die here. It's not big and fancy but we had everything we needed.'

'Who's that, Reg?'

'That's Aunty Flo. She was Grandpa's sister. She was a wild one in her day, too.'

'Did they all live in the Port?'

'Every one of us. We played in the street outside and your Uncle Ted and Uncle John and I fished in the river. We knew everybody in the street. When we walked to school I'd see old Mrs Smith out in her yard. Every day she'd be out there watering the plants and looking down the street to see if she could see what the neighbours were up to. They'd yell out to her to mind her own bloody business. She knew what everyone else was doing. We all did really.'

'Were there any gangs around here?'

'No, not here. There were a few ratbags down at the wharf but they never came near us. Dad would've told them to piss off. They hung around the pubs down by the docks. There was some goings-on down there though, let me tell you. This was a working-class area, full of families, and we all watched out for each other.'

This was the opposite of my life. We had moved from place to place, as if we were running from something. Every street was more dangerous than the next. But Reg never had to move. He never had to run away. It must have been good to be able to go and sit in the room you learned to read in, and just think. To play the piano that your father had taught you to play on, thirty years earlier, would have been so good. I wanted that in my life so much, but I could never feel like that. I would never be like that. I was a gypsy and I would never have a home.

Don't get me wrong; the house would have been spooky except that the family were so nice. I wouldn't have liked to stay there alone at night. Reg's family were all members of the Spiritualist Church. His grandmother was very religious and at one time was head of the church. But they weren't practising when we met them.

Reg's family never tried to convert us to anything and I don't think their church could have dealt with us anyway. But we knew that they believed in spirits. Things like that really grabbed my sister Linda's attention. She was only thirteen or fourteen and wanted to find out all about it. Unfortunately, she went about it all the wrong way.

Linda and a few of her school friends started playing with a homemade ouija board. I'm sure they were pushing the glass around the kitchen table, answering the questions they asked with the answers they wanted.

'Does Linda have a boyfriend?'

'See, I told you she did.'

Now this was all fine, until one night when Mum and Reg were in bed. A few of her friends came over to get in touch with the other side. They asked me if I would join in, but I was way too scared. I didn't even want to get in touch with the other side of the street.

I was sitting in the lounge room, not far enough away for my liking. The lounge room and the kitchen were separated by a set of sliding doors, but I could hear them going through their usual questions.

'Are there any boy ghosts here?'

All the things you would expect them to ask. Suddenly things got very scary. Linda was asking a question when the glass flew across the room and smashed against the wall.

'Hello', I thought. 'Is this a sign?' I was already frightened, but I'm sure I turned even whiter than before.

Linda sat with her head resting on the table, talking in a voice that I knew wasn't her own. It was like watching *The Exorcist* but that movie had not come out yet.

Next thing I knew she was up and running at the wall, smashing her head against it and putting a hole in the plaster. I had seen my dad, Jim, smash the plaster on walls before, but not with his own head. He smashed other people's heads, even Mum's head, into the wall. But this was much more frightening. Before I could look away Linda ran across the room and crashed into another wall. She was obviously being possessed by an interior decorator. Then she fell into a heap on the floor and started shaking like a leaf.

Reg got up and helped her to bed and sent her friends home. Now in those days we didn't have telephones so John ran up the road to ring a doctor.

The doctor came around as quickly as he could. Linda was still a mess, shaking on the bed. The doctor took one look at her and said, 'She's having some sort of breakdown. I can give her a shot that will calm her down and make her sleep and we can see how she is tomorrow.'

Then he left. The shot did nothing at all; in fact, she started to get more violent, shaking and sweating.

By this time it was after midnight and we were all exhausted. We didn't know what we were going to do. Suddenly there was a knock at the door. Reg's mum had arrived. No one had called her; remember, we didn't live close by. She came in and said, 'Linda needs me, and she had better come home with me,' and off they went into the dark night.

194

Between Linda and all the bills that my folks couldn't pay, we stood a good chance of becoming the first family to be possessed and repossessed in the same day.

I was completely freaked out by this point as were Reg and my mum. After Linda and Reg's mum left, we all had trouble sleeping. I lay in bed with the light on in my room, and the one in the hallway on too, and jumped at every noise I heard.

We didn't hear from Reg's mum for a week or two, except to say that Linda was all right and not to worry.

When Linda came home she was calm and clear-eyed, which was strange as she had always been very wild and able to find trouble anywhere. But now she was chilled out. Of course, she was a teenage girl, so calm was not really the word for her, but for a young girl, especially one of our family, she was as calm as she could get.

She was wearing a beautiful gold cross with rubies in it around her neck. Reg was very surprised by this. The last time he had seen this cross, it had been around his grandmother's neck, the one who had been head of the Spiritualist Church. He hadn't seen it in ages – in fact, not since she had died years earlier.

He asked his mum about it and she said, 'When Linda was recovering at my house, she kept asking who was the other woman who kept coming to see her.'

This had them worried because no one else was seeing her. But Linda kept insisting, 'I talk to this other woman every night.'

Then once Linda was up and out of bed she spotted a photo on the wall and said to Grandma, 'That's her, that's the woman who's been coming into my room at night.'

The woman in the photo was Reg's grandmother, who had died a few years before we joined the family. Not only that, but Linda kept asking to go to her house, which was just down the street. They couldn't work out how she even knew about this house.

Before Reg's grandmother had died she had hidden all her jewels in her house. The jewels had never been found, even though the family searched the place high and low. Reg's parents took Linda to the house, which was in ruins by this point, and she ran straight in and pulled a panel from the wall. She obviously knew exactly where to go, which had them completely baffled. Inside was all of the grandmother's jewellery and her treasures from the church, including the gold cross with rubies that she used to wear to church. They gave this cross to Linda and told her to wear it always. They told Reg that he had to watch over her too, as some very bad spirits wanted to hurt her and the cross would help keep them at bay.

Reg's grandmother had had a daughter called Linda, who'd died in Adelaide around the time our Linda was born in Scotland. Whether these two events were connected, I'm not sure, but it was spooky.

Linda told us about seeing ghosts all over the Barnes house. She said she saw them every night and they even spoke with her. Maybe it was Aunty Dorrie, who did look like a ghost to me. If I had seen one, I would have been running down the road shrieking. I never wanted to see ghosts and I certainly never wanted to talk to them. I hoped that they didn't want to talk to me either.

Life went back to normal for the family – no more spirits and no playing with them – but we didn't forget that night. It still has me rattled now, when I think back to it. Linda always wore the cross and for the next few years her life was good.

It wasn't long before we were thinking about going to our new school. The local school where we lived was called Mansfield Park Primary School. As usual I was scared about going, just because I had always been ashamed of my home and clothes and all that. Those feelings were still the same, even though I had a nice house and new clothes.

I was in Grade 6, joining the class halfway through the year, so everyone but me knew everyone else. I sat down and the teacher said, 'Class, this is our new pupil. His name is James Swan. Let's make him feel welcome to the school. Right, let's see who's here and who's not. Davis?'

'Here, sir.'

From the back row I heard a whiny voice: 'James …'

'Panopoulos.'

'Here, sir.'

'He's a James … ooh …' The voice was getting more annoying and I looked around to see a boy in the back row smirking at me. He was bigger than the other kids. He continued to taunt me whenever there was an opportunity. I wanted to get up and belt him but I couldn't. Not on my first day.

The teacher was too busy calling the roll to really care but every time the noise got out of hand he'd look up and say, 'Right, keep it down. You're not on the oval now. McCulloch?'

'Here, sir.'

'Stevens?'

'Here.'

'Jaammees …' The boys in the back were laughing along with my tormentor.

'Right you lot. Who's laughing?'

The back row sat up straight and acted as innocent as they could. The teacher had obviously dealt with these guys before and went back to what he was doing.

'Cooper?'

'Here, sir.'

'Jaaammmes …'

I snapped, and turned around to face him. 'Right, mate. After school.'

'Ooh, I'm soo scared.'

He sneered at me. The teacher finished roll call and went on with the lessons for the day.

During the lunch break some of the nicer, gentler kids told me not to go near him as he was very vicious. He was a rocker or something like that; he wore desert boots and slicked his hair back. In my head I went through what was going to happen after school and I was a little worried.

The final bell rang and the air was electric with excitement. All the kids in the class wanted to see what the new student would do when faced with the school bully. I walked out to the school gate and he was waiting for me with his sleeves rolled up and a smug look on his face. Before he could speak I ran at him and punched him to the ground. As he curled up in a ball I stood over him, kicking him.

I looked up and all his friends were yelling at me, 'That's not right. You don't fight fair.'

I stopped and screamed back at them, 'If you want to fight fair you've come to the wrong place. So fuck off.'

And proceeded to give him a beating. No one ever picked a fight with me at that school again. It seemed that they didn't fight the same way we did in Elizabeth and that was fine by me.

Things went well at school after that. In fact, not long after that, I became captain of the soccer team; they obviously saw how well I could kick. It wasn't long until I was top of the class too. All the old patterns of survival were working for me even though my circumstances had changed. When in doubt, lash out, and I did for many years to come.

Around Wingfield where we lived, there seemed to be a lot of European immigrants – Italian, Greek and Polish and all different European people. I thought this was really cool and made friends with as many as I could. But when these kids came to school, the Australian kids would pick on them. I don't know why because the Australian kids didn't have any more than these kids had. The European families would be making salami and wine in the houses next door to working-class Australian families and this seemed to cause problems. Maybe because they wanted the wine, I don't know.

Their lunches were very different from those of the other kids at school and they were picked on because of it. The European kids' lunches looked a thousand times better than ours. I couldn't work it out. We would have Vegemite sandwiches and they would have prosciutto and provolone cheese, and olives and salami. I knew what lunch I wanted.

I thought it was great and wished my folks could make salami and grow vegetables, but they didn't. I ended up getting into fights at school again, sticking up for these little Italian and Greek kids, but I didn't mind, I was happy to fight. I started to hang with these families more and more. It seemed to me that the Australian families were the ones with the problems, not the Italians or Greeks.

The so-called normal Australian families around us seemed to have problems like we had had in Elizabeth. Not quite as extreme as we had experienced but similar. The dads were drinking too much. It might have been beer instead of whisky but they still drank too much. And there was violence in their homes too. I didn't see this with the European families; maybe it was there too but I didn't see it. They all seemed to work really hard and put all their money back into the family. That had to be good. So my world was expanding and I was beginning to realise that the world was a big place and not what it seemed to be from where I stood.

* * *

If you had told me that I would be leaning on a fence of a drive-in movie watching *The Sound of Music* even a year earlier, I would have laughed and then probably slapped you. We weren't a musical sort of family. Of course I'd heard of movies like *West Side Story* but where we came from gangs didn't dance to settle disputes unless it was on each other's heads. But there I was, leaning on the fence humming along with the songs. If my mates in Elizabeth could see me now.

'You've turned real soft, Jim. I reckon we should give you a hiding to toughen you up.' That's what they would be saying to me. No, they wouldn't even be talking to me, just kicking me to bits. But I wasn't in Elizabeth anymore. I thought that the gangs around Wingfield might have a dance-off instead of a fight. I felt safe. I felt positive. I wasn't used to this.

The voices of the people around Wingfield sounded different too. I was sure I'd heard a German accent a minute ago. Along with a Greek, and an Italian. A Russian and a Polish. I might have left the country, not just Elizabeth. They weren't whining about everything being better somewhere else. They weren't lying in the gutters, drunk. They were living life and loving their families. This was *The Sound of Music*. I must be dreaming.

I had walked about a quarter of a mile from home and I was sitting on the ground with a bunch of kids I didn't know outside the drive-in, watching a movie. And I wasn't in any danger.

Well, my musical taste might be a bit damaged but I'd live through it.

So who had saved me from the life I was leading? My mum had a lot to do with it. But I had a feeling that Reg Barnes had been my Julie Andrews. He's the reason I felt safe. He was the reason I could walk the streets and not get beaten up. He was even the reason I knew the words to these songs. But he couldn't be perfect, could he?

* * *

Around that time, I noticed the girls that were my age were beginning to change. They were getting curves and bumps and I couldn't take my eyes off them. The girls that is, not the bumps. No, you were right the first time – the bumps and the girls.

I'd always liked girls and had even fancied girls for a long time but these were the girls in my class. Not only were they changing physically but they acted differently too. They seemed to think they had some sort of mystical control over boys. And they did – when there wasn't a football around. If there was sport to be played, we managed to shake it off and leave them to themselves.

The summer came, and suddenly outside the house smelled really bad. I thought that it would go away but it didn't. The smell was there all day, every day. It smelled like dead animals and I remembered when we lived in Gepps Cross and the abattoir was across the road, through the forest, so I asked Reg what it was. He told me that an abattoir and tannery were just down the road. It seemed my life always ended up around slaughterhouses and here I was again.

I walked down the road to have a look at it and found myself gagging the closer I got to the place. It was horrible. I couldn't help thinking how bad the poor animals felt. I could sense fear in the air and being a person who had spent his life afraid, this really disturbed me. I ran home and tried not to think about what was going on up the road. But I couldn't forget it as the smell lingered around, outside and inside the house.

I knew because of the smell that our house wasn't in the best area, so I spoke to Reg and he told me that when Mum and he went to get a house, this was all they could afford. The gloss started to peel away from my dream home.

I came home one afternoon to find Reg in the backyard. He was in a hole in the lawn and he had a handkerchief over his face. There was a different horrible smell this time, one I hadn't noticed before.

I shouted out to him, 'Reg, Reg, what are you doing in there?'

And he came over to me with a bucket on a rope in his hands. 'We have no money, love, so I have to empty the septic tank by hand or we won't be able to use the toilet.'

As far as I could see this was the worst thing anyone could think of doing, especially in the one-hundred degree heat.

So I said, 'Why are you doing it, Reg? It's disgusting.'

He looked at me with tears in his eyes and said, 'Because I love you, son. That's why I'm doing it.' He pulled the handkerchief up over his nose and went on with the job.

He was a bit dramatic, our Reg, but he meant it. He sacrificed a lot for us and I knew it. Most people paid for a truck to come around and empty their tanks but we couldn't afford it.

'This is as poor as you can get,' I thought. Poor Reg.

While I was checking out the abattoir at the end of the road I came across a horse-riding school. The idea of riding horses really appealed to me. I always wanted to be a cowboy, so I started hanging around the school, trying to help out when I could.

My brother John used to hang around there sometimes too. As usual, anything John tried to do he was good at, so he very quickly became really good around horses. He started working at the riding school whenever he wanted to. The guy who ran it could see how keen I was and started giving me the odd bit of work around the place too. Cleaning up shit and even feeding the horses. In return for my hard work he let me ride the horses. I was not very good at it but I tried really hard. A few horses threw me off but it didn't stop me and I developed the liking for horses that I have to this day.

I stopped for a while after a particularly big horse, a Clydesdale, stood on my foot and nearly broke it. Being a very keen football player, I couldn't afford to have broken feet so I stayed away for a while.

The idea of changing our names came up. I'm not sure if it was Reg's idea. It may even have been Mum's, one last chance to plunge the knife into her ex-husband.

I didn't need to think twice about it. I changed my name to James Dixon Barnes. Jim Swan was my father but Reg Barnes was the man who cared for me, he was my dad, and I wanted his name.

John was the only one of the kids who wouldn't change their name to Barnes. He wanted to keep his dad's name. Which was fine by us. We loved Dad too.

I was the biggest eater out of all the kids. They nicknamed me seagull because I would hover around the table, waiting to eat anything that was put in front of me. And while the others were busy with other things, homework or watching television, I would be getting ready for bed and heading into the kitchen to have one last bite to eat with Reg. It was a moment where he could ask me about school and check that I was all right. Unfortunately, the late-night cereal he and I would eat together was gone. We couldn't afford it anymore. But Reg tried to make it all right.

'Bread with milk and sugar is better than cereal, Jim,' he assured me as we sat eating at the kitchen table. 'When it gets cold, we'll heat the milk up. And it'll taste really great, you wait.'

It didn't taste that good but I still liked it because I was sitting having it with him.

'Now let's wash these bowls and set the table. If you do it now you get a little bit more time to yourself in the morning.'

'Can't we do it in the morning? I'm tired.'

'Listen, son. In this life you can't put things off. Get up and do what you have to do. Then you can put your feet up. That's a lesson you have to learn if you want to have a good life.'

Reg had a way of making me feel sad, just by how he spoke. I think it was because he had never been a parent before and every day he was learning how much it took to bring up a family. Sometimes when he spoke to me, he was on the verge of tears, trying to hold them back. This just made me respect him more; I knew it wasn't easy for him. He would tell me that life was not always easy and sometimes you had to do things you didn't want to do because it was the right thing to do. We were one of those things. I know that if Reg had to do it all over again he would and he wouldn't even think twice about it because we needed him and he was our guardian angel.

Speaking of guardian angels, Reg told me one day that he had an angel watching over him. To a young boy from Elizabeth this sounded a bit like having fairies at the bottom of the garden. But it obviously meant a lot to him so I listened as he told me about a native American Indian who watched over him. Now there was a Red Indian hanging around the house. It was already crowded enough.

I wasn't sure I believed him but it was kind of cool to think about. I never saw the Indian myself but my sister Linda, who saw ghosts everywhere, did, and said, 'He is real. I see him when Reg is sleeping, by the bottom of the bed.'

My mum said, 'I saw an Indian near Reg's bed one day when he was in the hospital.' And she wasn't one to see ghosts. The only spirits she'd seen before then, my dad had been drinking.

We would laugh it off as politely as we could but still take the mickey out of Mum. Many years later, when Reg died, as I was leaving his funeral I started seeing photos of Indians everywhere. American Indians. There were billboards that I'd never noticed before, right in front of my eyes, with huge pictures of Indians looking down, smiling at me. I found an old lighter that Reg had given me with an Indian on it. It was very strange; they seemed to pop up everywhere. When I noticed them I felt a strange sense of calm come over me, as if Reg was there somehow looking out for me again. I know he was, and still is, my angel.

CHAPTER FIFTEEN

smoke and mirrors

Soon we had to move again as Reg couldn't afford to pay for the house. Six kids were a lot more expensive to look after than he knew or Mum remembered. But they never spoke about it in front of us. I heard them talking in bed one night and realised how hard things were getting.

We started moving from one cheap place to another, mostly within striking distance of Port Adelaide. Sometimes Mum wanted to go back to Elizabeth; Reg could never understand why. He hated the place and we had nothing but bad memories from there. After each short stay in Elizabeth we would drift back to Port Adelaide. We rented houses in Ethelton, Wingfield, Mansfield Park and Seaton. Anywhere that was cheap enough. Many battling families lived and worked in these areas and we always seemed to find another place.

I can look back now and see why we moved so much. Mum and Reg would get a house for really low rent because it was a shithole and Mum would say, 'I think this place'll be really good wi' a coat o' paint and a wee bit o' love.'

'Too right, love, it will be beautiful,' Reg would say.

Then they would work really hard to make it a home for us. Mum was usually right. Not long after we'd move into a place it would be nice to live in. They were always painting and fixing up houses and of course as soon as they fixed them up the landlord would come around and put the rent up. Then we couldn't afford to stay there so we would have to move to another dive.

We moved from one suburb to another, ending up for a little while in a place called Hindmarsh, a couple of miles out of the city. It had a large Greek community. I got on well with all the Greek kids I met. These kids were not like the kids from Britain I'd grown up with in Elizabeth. They were from working-class families but they seemed to be a lot happier. Not aggressive and dark like the kids in the west. These kids liked to go home to their mums and dads. Their houses were happy places full of laughter and the smell of great food cooking in the kitchens.

The girls were cute too. I had a crush on a girl called Sue. We went to the Hindmarsh pictures together and kissed in the back row.

The guys loved football too, which made me feel right at home. I played in a Greek football team called Hellas, one of the big clubs in Adelaide. I was in the under-12s and we were pretty good for our age. Occasionally our football team got to play at Hindmarsh Stadium, which was just around the corner from our house. This was one of the biggest football grounds in Adelaide, it had lights and a grandstand and everything. I thought I was on my way to playing in the World Cup.

'Pass the ball!'

'Hey dickhead. Pass the ball over here.'

'Skase malaka!' I heard them shout at each other.

I never knew what it meant but within days of being there I was on the football pitch, yelling at the other team. 'Get out of my way. Skase malaka. What are you an idiot or something?'

One of the boys quickly gave me some advice. 'If Mum or Dad come to the game, Jim, do me a favour would you?'

'Sure, what do you want?'

'Don't try to speak Greek. You'll get us killed.'

But I was sure I heard the same words coming from their fathers as they watched us play.

The school had a choir and luckily for me they didn't sing in Greek so I immediately joined up. Then something happened that changed my life. The choir master pulled me aside after a few days and said to me, 'Jimmy, I'm going to have to ask you to leave the choir.'

I was shattered. I loved singing and I had always been a good singer – all my teachers had told me so.

'Why do I have to leave? I love singing in the choir.'

He sat me down. 'You sing too loud and this choir is about blending in. I'm sorry, but you just don't blend in with the other kids.'

I was horrified. I didn't know what to do. Where was I going to sing now?

Luckily I was listening to a lot of radio. And a lot of the singers in the bands on the radio didn't sound like they would blend with a choir either. So that was it.

'I'm going to sing in a band,' I said to myself. Not straight away, but as soon as I worked up the courage and found out how to go about it, I would find a band to sing with.

Reg had a young brother called John, the wild one of his family. There's at least one in every family.

John had long sideburns and greasy hair and he dressed differently to anyone I had ever met. Not particularly stylish but he did have a likeable quality about him. Maybe it was because he was an outcast from the Barnes clan and he could see that we were outcasts too that I liked him. He warmed to me immediately too and told me stories about his escapades in the motorbike racing world.

'I ride sidecar in speedway race meetings. You should come to see me race. I reckon you'd love it, young fella.'

Without a second thought, I jumped at the chance. The following Friday night he took me to a big meeting at Rowley Park Speedway in Brompton, near the city.

'You'll love this place Jim,' he told me. 'It smells like petrol and you can't hear nothing but bikes and cars. No bastard can talk to you even if they wanted to.'

This was a different world. Everybody seemed to be some kind of misfit. They were all fat or had speech impediments or something. They were social cripples but I liked them and they liked me. Maybe I was one of them. They were like carnie folk. They didn't care about normal life. They didn't belong in everyday society. They were like a tribe of gypsies. They had their own friends and their own rules; it was a closed group that you could only join if you were brought to them by one of their own. This was my introduction to the entertainment business, when I think about it.

The speedway show was about man and machine. But there was a bit of smoke and mirrors too. I got the feeling they knew who was going to win long before their engines had started. But that didn't stop them from pushing themselves and each other to breaking point.

I would run around in the pits, breathing in the fumes from the roaring machines, watching men frantically fine-tuning their engines. They were also being watched by some rough-looking, slightly overweight women with tattoos. These girls gazed at the men like they were athletes or even rock stars.

'Do you need anything, darling?'

'Just a kiss from you and a fast bike sweetheart.'

'What about a drink, love?'

The men were doing men's business and the women were always running to get cold beer for their champions.

There were horrific crashes when things didn't go as planned. Some nights, Uncle John and his friends would end up drunk and in tears as close friends were battered, burned and broken. Some were driven away in ambulances to waiting emergency units. I don't know if they ever saw them again. It was life on the edge. But they got the chance to entertain people who were just like them, but were afraid to take the chances these speed freaks took. Next week they would rebuild their smashed-up bikes and cars and limp back to the track again, for one more chance to be a winner.

After a few trips with Uncle John, Reg stopped me going with him. I think he was afraid that I would want to get on the bike and have a ride myself. I didn't have the need for speed yet but I could have caught the bug if I hung around long enough. I'm sure Reg was trying to keep me sheltered for as long as he could from all the dangers that he knew I was drawn to.

The other thing I remember about those times is that my mum was always scared. Every house we lived in seemed to be cased by thieves who were about to break in at any time. Nearly every night Mum would be up crying and panicking. She obviously convinced me the villains were real because after a while I was afraid too, just like her. We all were – myself and my brother and sisters. And we would end up in one bed most nights, too scared to sleep.

These same intruders were following us from house to house too. What could they have wanted? We didn't have anything worth stealing.

In the middle of the night we would hear a noise outside the house.

Bang. Bang. Bang.

The wind was howling around the house but we could still hear it.

Bang. Bang. Bang.

Mum would hurry into our room. 'Don't worry. Go back tae sleep.'

'What's that noise, Mum?'

'It's okay, kids. Reg's just making sure the windows cannae be opened from the outside.'

'What's he doing out there?'

'He's just bangin' a few nails intae them tae be sure.'

Bang. Bang. Bang.

By the sound of the nails that we heard being hammered, the windows would never be opened again.

'Why is he nailing the windows, Mum?'

'I heard someone sneaking aroon oot there and I just wanted tae be sure you were safe. That's all, go back tae sleep.'

Bang. Bang. Bang.

'But we can't sleep, Mum, you've got all the lights on and there's too much noise.'

'I know but it's better tae be safe than sorry.'

Reg would walk in through the door, soaked to the skin from the pouring rain. 'There you go love. No one's getting in. Now can we go back to bed?'

'Go roon the hoose again, just in case they're still there.' Her eyes would be darting to the window as if she caught a glimpse of someone walking past.

'There's no one there, love. No one in their right mind would be outside on a night like this. Not even a prowler.'

'Just go roon once more, please. I'm sure I heard someone. I know someone's there.'

'Jesus love, you're going to scare the kids. No one is out there. I'm bloody telling you.'

'Aw right then, you kids come tae ma room where you'll be safe.' We'd climb out of our own beds and follow her into her room.

Bang!

'What was that? I told you someone was oot there!'

'It's the wind, love. Let's get some sleep.'

Reg didn't seem to be afraid at all and always told us, 'It'll be all right, kids, you're safe here with me. No one's going to hurt you.' He would be rundown from lack of sleep and stress and always seemed to have a cold from being outside in his dressing gown. These prowlers were killing him – very slowly, but they were killing him.

So after a short while, maybe to keep one step ahead of Mum's demons, or maybe because Mum and Reg had improved the house to the point where we couldn't afford to stay, we would have to move again. To another bad suburb and into another bad house with a new lot of burglars. I said goodbye to my friends and waited to see where we would end up next. The places seemed to go from renovator's delights to hovels.

I ended up at Ethelton Primary School up near the Port, which was fine as this was close to where Reg's folks lived. He liked the area even if our house was a bit of a dump. It was on a dead end street, which backed onto a swamp that would later become a place called West Lakes. At the time we lived there, it was nothing but swamp and the remains of an old factory that no one had been in for about fifty years. There were no lights or houses, so at night it was pitch black. Mum was frightened out of her wits. I don't know why she moved there.

Once again Mum thought someone was out to get us. One night she had John and his Scottish hoodlum friends hiding out in the empty paddocks around our house, waiting in ambush to catch, once and for all, these people who had been trying to get us. She was sure that this time we would catch them and prove she had been right all along. By then, even we didn't believe her, and we laughed about it a bit. But we never did it in front of her.

Unfortunately for Mum, the criminals were too cunning for us again. John and his mates didn't see a thing. So after hours of sitting in the dark around the house, Mum called off the ambush. 'Okay John, bring the boys inside for a cup of tea. Maybe we can have a wee drink.'

No sooner were they inside and sitting down than Mum suddenly heard the noises outside again. The prowlers must have been watching, waiting for the boys to come inside.

So out they went and sat there for another few hours. I think that at least one of them brought a gun with him so we were lucky no one came anywhere near the house even by accident. They would have been killed. But no one was coming anywhere near our house, by accident or on purpose. We wouldn't have gone anywhere near it if we didn't live there.

John's friends stopped coming around much after that. I think they lost their sense of humour and had better things to do. It was back to just Mum and us again, cuddling her in a corner of the house, waiting for Reg to get home from nightshift to save her from nothing.

I could never work out why Mum was so scared all the time. In time I worked out that the prowlers, who seemed to be lurking in the shadows wherever we lived, never existed, except maybe in my mum's mind. But I couldn't work out why she thought 'they' were coming for her, not to mention who 'they' were. Was there something in my mum's dark past that we didn't know about that kept her on her toes, desperately trying to stay one step ahead of them at all time? Had she done something that made her feel so bad about herself that she had to run away all her life, even from us, the ones who loved her and needed her more than anyone in the world? Or was it that she just didn't fit in anywhere?

Maybe she couldn't stop roaming until she found her place; a place where she could just stop and breathe. I think it might be as simple as that. I know it has taken me most of my life to just be; to stop for the first time and breathe.

CHAPTER SIXTEEN

the time our worlds collided

The school holidays were great once we lived with Reg. He was happy to show me where he'd played as a child and worked as an adult. It wasn't long until I knew my way around that area like the back of my hand. I liked the place, and still do. It was a very working-class area and quite tough but unlike Elizabeth, the people seemed reasonably happy. You could even walk around the place and not get stabbed or kicked to bits. People passing you on the street would stop and help you if you needed directions. This is what life in Australia was supposed to be like. I was still very young but I felt safe walking around the Port by myself. Maybe I wasn't, but compared to where I'd been this was Disneyland.

It was just around the corner from where I used to escape to when I lived in Elizabeth. I could walk to the beach if I wanted to and the Port River ran right through the place.

Where I came from in Glasgow, the River Clyde was dark and cold and the wind howled through the trees on its banks. It didn't breathe life into you, it sucked you under and held you down. I've read stories about nice rivers that sing to you and whisper secrets that you can hear if you listen carefully. But not the Clyde. That river cried like a mother who had lost a child and all its secrets were buried on the bottom or washed out to sea with the rest of the rubbish.

The Port River railway bridge was not for the public. We had to jump a fence to reach the small service paths that ran along each side of the railway tracks – wooden slats, with guard rails that led across the bridge. Half of these slats were missing so it could be quite tricky to get from one side to the other. This was where we would sit and do whatever we wanted. The trains that crossed the bridge moved so fast that we couldn't see into them so we presumed they couldn't see us. They shook and rattled the bridge so much we sometimes thought we were about to fall off.

The bridge was right towards the end of the Port River. Just past the bridge was the Causeway, a stretch of road that by-passed the Port and led to the beaches. This was built after the Port had lost its shine. It used to be the driving hub of the whole area; now it was just an old main street with too many pubs and not enough people to fill them. Even the cargo ships never came down this far anymore. They docked at Outer Harbour with its high-tech facilities and new roads in and out. Beyond the Causeway, the river turned into swamp, spreading out into a wet land that should have been home to all sorts of birds and native animals. But because of years of industrial pollution, there was only a swamp, made up of very tough plants that hardly broke the surface of the red-stained ground, burned from the chemicals and rust. All across the swamp there were pools of evil-smelling liquids oozing out of the ground. Nothing lived in there except feral cats and snakes.

The Port in some respects was a lot like the Clyde. Both were murky and dangerous but the Port rolled along a little slower. There was something about it that helped me forget about Elizabeth. And as I sat on the railway bridge, life beyond where I was moved faster and faster. Much faster than the river flowed, and faster than the trains that whooshed past me on the bridge.

I was sure I saw the water police fishing the odd body out of the river just down from where I would fish. And I heard stories of murder in the area but I wasn't scared. I was too smart to get caught by any weirdos. And I was too fast to be caught by any drunks. Looking back, maybe I was just lucky. Kids did go missing in the area but I never wanted to hear about that from anybody. I was free. I was taught how to fish in the river by Reg's dad. It became my playground.

I used to go swimming in the river with a few friends. One of my friends' dads owned a little dinghy and used to let us borrow it. We would row around the river and jump off the dinghy whenever we felt like it. In the summer this was great fun. The sun would be blazing down and it would be stinking hot. We could dive off the boat and swim whenever there were no big ships passing by. There were cargo ships and fishing boats, big and small, but we just swam around them. Occasionally someone would yell out at us, 'Get out of the way, you stupid little bastards.' We just jumped back in the boat and rowed away laughing at them.

The water wasn't blue and inviting like a normal river, it was black and threatening, and what we saw floating on the top was only half of what was in there. I'm sure there were things that were weighted down to the bottom too. This river, like the Clyde, had stories it would not give up.

We did see suspicious-looking characters dumping things into it. And I heard about companies dumping chemicals too. The river was dark and dirty but we dived into the depths without even a thought of what lay beneath the surface. It's a wonder we never got sick from the cocktail of shit that was tossed into it. We were kids and we were tough so we never thought about that at all. I wouldn't swim in there now. Especially when I think of the things that floated past us.

There was a couple of guys who used to go dynamite fishing in broad daylight. This was in the middle of a busy waterway. They would pull up in their boat and throw a stick of dynamite over the side. A few seconds later – *boom!* – there would be an explosion. Next thing, fish would just float to the surface and they would scoop them up with a net and move on down the river to their next spot. We would follow behind, grabbing any fish they left, but these guys didn't want anyone watching them and would threaten us whenever we got too close. How they got away with this, we could never work out, but it did reassure us that there were plenty of fish in the river, waiting to be caught by us.

We would row up to places you couldn't get to by foot, so we felt like we were going somewhere we shouldn't have. Somewhere top secret. But there wasn't a lot going on behind our backs; we just imagined that there was. And we kept our eyes peeled for anything that might interest us.

There were a few nights we went out with Reg and Mum and sat on the railway bridge until sun-up, fishing. We didn't catch too much, just enough to keep us there. Staring at the end of our lines, saying nothing, waiting on a bite. It was great just to have the silence, occasionally broken by the sound of a train, clicking in time like a drummer, as it passed over the bridge.

We would have something simple to eat, Vegemite sandwiches and tea from a Thermos, to keep us going all night. It was like camping. We didn't have to talk much. We would sit and stare into the water or up at the night sky. Every now and then Reg would think of something to tell me about one of his brothers or one of his cousins.

Reg used a language I wasn't used to. People we knew spoke Scots or would be swearing and slurring. But he'd say things like, 'Tom was a real scallywag and Mum and Dad would scare the living Christ out of him and chase him with a switch.'

It was like he didn't speak English. In Scots that would have been, 'Wee Tommy was a bit of a lad and his ma and da wid frighten the shite oot o' him, and skelp his arse wi' a stick.'

That would have made sense to me. So at the start, I would have to listen really carefully, just so I could understand him. But I just nodded along with him as if it was normal to me.

Mum used three or four voices. I used to think that they were just because she was insecure but I've since worked out that it was so she could be understood. The Scottish accent is hard to understand sometimes but the broad Glaswegian accent is almost impossible to catch unless you're used to it. Even then it can be hard, especially if someone is yelling at you.

So later on in life when we had a phone, I would hear Mum on the phone sounding like she had a plum in her mouth, saying things like, 'Oh yes. I see what you mean. I will get onto that right away.'

We would all laugh and tell each other that Mum was pretending to be posh. But she was probably trying to get something done for the house, or paying a bill. She still uses that voice when she answers the phone to this day. I've heard it when I ring her.

Then there were times that she sounded like she was in the markets in Glasgow, swearing like a sailor, bagging Dad or someone else but laughing and sounding young. 'Ma man is fuckin' useless, he's no like me, good at everythin'. Ha ha ha.'

In those times I could hardly understand her, but I was glad she was happy. A Glaswegian woman can sound as rough as guts if she gets wound up. It's frightening.

Mum had another voice that came out when we'd done something wrong. This voice was shrill and piercing and could peel the paint off walls. It sounded like a starving pterodactyl swooping down on a small furry animal that was too slow to keep up with its mum. When we heard that voice, it was time to leave the house by the back door as fast as we could.

'Did you make this mess? I just cleaned this hoose. I'm goin' tae murder ye when I get ma hands on you, ya wee bastard.'

The last voice was soft and loving and made me think that everything would be all right. 'You know I love you, my son of gold. I'm here so you don't have to worry.'

But I never heard that voice unless something drastic had happened.

There were days when I used to go down to the mudflats with a shovel and dig up these long slimy things called blood worms to use as bait. Then I'd sit on the old railway bridge and fish all day by myself and never feel lonely. Life was good. This was the same bridge that Grandpa used to fish off when he was young. And the same bridge that he taught Reg to fish from. Not that Reg was a great fisherman. By the time our worlds collided, he only went fishing because he knew I liked it.

I would catch tommy roughs and take them to Grandpa's house. He'd show me how to clean them and then he'd cook them up and we'd sit in the backyard and have a feast. I felt like Huckleberry Finn, living by the river, catching my own meals and needing no one. Well, I needed Grandpa to clean and cook them.

Grandpa used to give me slices of fruit cake with a cup of tea. He called it racecourse cake. Now, I used to just wolf it down like any hungry young lad but after a few visits I had to ask him why he called it racecourse cake. He smiled at me and told me he'd do better than tell me, he'd show me.

He stubbed out his cigarette in the ashtray and said, 'All right, let's go and get some racecourse cake.'

I went on the bus with him and he didn't say where we were going or where we would find this fantastic cake. But I soon worked it out when we ended up at the racetrack. Now Grandpa wasn't a gambler; he wasn't one to waste money frivolously. Maybe he liked to look at the horses, who knows? But he took me to sit in the racecourse cafeteria and have a cup of tea. Guess what they served the tea with? That's right, fruit cake.

'This is the best place in the world to get this cake,' he said. So that's what I've called it ever since – racecourse cake.

Grandpa had false top teeth that he never wore and he laughed all the time. He was a great guy to hang around with. I loved listening to him tell stories about the Port and how much it had changed over the years. He told me stories about fishing and about boats and ghosts and any other things he thought I would like.

He told me a yarn – that's what he called stories – about years earlier, when he had been out fishing in his boat. But first he sat down and lit a cigarette, breathed in a huge cloud of smoke then he began to talk.

'Now I was out in my boat this day. It wasn't that big, maybe twenty feet long at the most and that was with the outboard motor.' Laughing and coughing out the smoke he had just sucked into his lungs. 'I was at the channel marker about three miles off of Largs. Don't tell anyone about this place. It's one of my secret spots for catching sand whiting.' He gave me a knowing wink and a grin. 'Well, I noticed a big bloody shark cruising around and under my boat. I'd seen plenty of big sharks out there before; there are always loads of them. They cruise up and down the coast. So I wasn't that worried.'

He flicked the ash carefully off his cigarette; it floated down into the ashtray. 'Now,' he continued, 'the sun was setting and a full moon was coming up. She was lighting up the sky like a bloody beacon. I was sitting there alone in the boat, contemplating life. As you do.' He laughed again. 'When I felt this bloody big bump. I nearly fell out of the boat. The bugger had come back and was after a taste of my boat.' He nervously sucked on his cigarette, as if it had all just happened.

'I was a bit tired but suddenly my eyes were wide open and I could see everything that was in the water, big or small. As clear as day, I could see this bloody thing swimming around my boat. That's when I really started to worry.' A cloud of blue smoke fled his mouth and floated off into the sky. 'Then there was a big splash and the bastard hit my boat even harder. Now I was panicking.'

He lowered his voice and looked at me as if he was trying to see if I was scared yet. 'Suddenly –'

I jumped, he was almost shouting now.

'This big bastard came up out of the water behind the boat. I tell you, against the night sky he looked massive. He lunged towards my boat with his mouth wide open and ripped the bloody outboard motor off.' He took another drag of his smoke. 'If he was big enough to eat the motor I figured he was big enough to take down the whole bloody boat. I tried to keep calm and I slowly picked up my oars from the bottom of the boat and began rowing back to shore.'

If this was just a story, he had me sucked right in. 'All the way back I was waiting for the bastard to come back for his second course, which I assumed would be me. But he left me alone. Probably didn't like the taste of the oily old motor. I made it to shore in one piece, albeit in need of a new pair of underpants. Ha ha ha.' He coughed. 'Next day my boat was up on the trailer at home and I found a couple of big teeth stuck into the hull. The bloody thing had tried to eat my boat.'

I was beginning to think he was an old sea dog telling old sea tales. Then he went inside and came out with a couple of big shark's teeth he kept in a drawer in the house. I never doubted him again.

I never really wore shoes that often. I was always in and out of the water. Anyway, one day I was out on my bike about two miles from the house, fishing off the rocks next to the railway bridge at a place called the Causeway, a good place to catch bream. I was standing on a big rock when I got a bite.

Now I had a feeling this was going to be the biggest fish I'd ever caught. In fact, in my mind this was going to be the biggest fish ever caught by anyone from this spot. So I worked my way down to the river's edge to pull it in. I took one wrong step and slipped and sliced my foot open on a barnacle on one of the rocks. These shells were like razors and it cut me right to the bone so I tried to get the fish in as fast as I could.

I could see a pool of blood spreading in the water all around me, getting bigger and bigger, and by this time I was up to my waist in water. I suddenly remembered the stories Grandpa had told me about the big sharks who followed the boats in from the harbour, up the river to feed.

Catching that fish went from being the most important moment in my life to being meaningless, when the thought of being eaten overwhelmed me. I jumped out of the water. Then, when I looked at the wound on my foot and realised how big the cut was, I dropped my fishing rod and got on my bike and rode home. I left a trail of blood the whole way back to our house. I was taken to hospital and stitched up – again. As a kid I always seemed to be being stitched up for something.

The next day I followed the trail of my own blood back to where the accident had happened and stood and stared out across the river wondering if that fish knew how lucky he was. I'd be back for him soon. The battle was not over yet.

CHAPTER SEVENTEEN

don't let the name down

By this time, I was nearly ready to start high school and Reg wanted me to go to the same school he and his brothers had gone to in Semaphore South. So he signed me up to start at Le Fevre Boys High, one of the best schools in that area.

I loved the school. Reg had told me about his name, along with the names of his brothers, on the honour roll on the office wall. He got me a second-hand uniform and new shoes and a schoolbag ready for my first day. I think he was more nervous than me.

'Now this is a special school, son. Your uncles and me were students here so don't let the name down. If you work hard here you'll be able to do anything you want in life.'

It all went well; I was smarter than he thought. All my old tools were still working well. Work hard and get the teachers to like you. This would be easy.

Reg talked to me about how important this phase of my life was and how much work it would take for me to get the most out of it. But I'd never had to work really hard for anything, mainly because we didn't have anything to work for before, so the idea of responsibility for myself was completely new to me.

'Son, I know you feel like playing with your mates all day but if you want to get ahead in this world it's going to take hard work. You get nothing for nothing.' I could see he was almost crying so I knew it meant the world to him.

'Your brother John had so much promise but he's ruined his life by leaving school and wasting his time with bands. Don't do the same, son.'

Reg went to his mum's place and came back with a desk to help me study. Not just any old desk, but the desk he'd had as a young man when he went to the same school as I was going to now. It was a great desk with a map of Australia stained into the top of it.

This desk was made by his father for him and I knew how much it meant to him. It meant the world to me too. I placed the lighthouse lamp he had given me on the desk, spread my papers and pencils and sat and thought about working. But I had the attention span of a small soap dish and very soon the idea of sitting at any desk, studying, wore off. And I was once again daydreaming about football or trouble or something else, anything but work.

With high school came new challenges. Going from the top of the primary school to the bottom of the pecking order at high school didn't feel safe. It was a new world and I would take a while to settle in. Everyone paid some sort of price to be there, bullying or some form of intimidation. But I had to ride that out. It would get worse when I went to Elizabeth again.

I started borrowing clothes from John's wardrobe and dressing cooler than all the other kids. He had cool clothes because he was in a band. John later said that the rule seemed to be 'first up, best dressed'. Seeing as I had no good clothes for him to pinch, I was always going to get the best end of that deal.

There were very strict uniform codes at Le Fevre, and I had long drawn-out fights with the staff. I would sneak in slight changes every day. Some days they wouldn't even notice. I would be in full uniform but my shirt was a little different. My tie would be missing one day; the next I would be wearing R.M. Williams boots. I would tell the school, 'Mum and Dad can't afford the right shoes to go with the uniform.' But my boots cost more than the official shoes I was supposed to wear. That negated that argument. Letters were sent home to my folks and I started to sneak clothes out of the house.

I loved the fact that this was Reg's school, and it was my first school where they really cared about how the students looked and felt about themselves. But for some reason I didn't want to look like they wanted me to look. And I didn't feel the way they wanted me to feel. I was at the stage in my life when I wanted to look like me, or so I thought. It's pretty funny when you think about it, because I was pinching my brother's clothes. So I was probably trying to look like him.

I was still the best student in my class so the teachers were at odds as to what to do with me. They didn't want to suspend me but I was creating unrest in the school. Some of the older boys thought it was cool and started wearing different shoes or shirts too.

Every week I would be in the headmaster's office declaring my innocence. 'I'm sorry, I'm only wearing these flares because I don't have the right pants. Dad is working two jobs to pay for our uniforms.'

Slowly they loosened the rules. By the end of my first year of high school I was dux of the year and there were no compulsory uniform rules to fight against.

I was becoming more and more rebellious and I liked the feeling. This would be the start of more troubled times for me. And once girls were added to the equation, all bets were off; I would be running wild whether they liked it or not.

There was a girl who lived not far from our street who was just a little bit older than me, but she caught my eye and for some reason I caught her eye too. We would meet on the way home from school and walk together. It was quite innocent at first, but slowly the games began to change.

We would walk down to where I used to fish and sit by ourselves and she let me kiss her. I'd kissed girls before and, as I told you, I'd even seen girls without their clothes on, but I knew that this was different. This was a new feeling, better than anything I'd ever felt. Before too long we would end up hiding near the railway bridge where she would take off her clothes and let me touch her and kiss her. One day she put her hands on my crotch and then pulled down my trousers and what she did to me with her hands under that bridge changed my life forever. This was the best I had ever felt.

'We can do this any time you want to. Just don't let anyone else know about it,' she whispered. It was our secret. But I felt that I was finally in control of my own happiness.

We went to the bridge often and there was not a lot of fishing done by either of us.

Well, it was time to move again and Mum wanted to be back in Elizabeth. A big question I keep asking myself is why was Mum drawn to Elizabeth, over and over again? When we first moved there, things didn't work out. That was nothing to do with the place as far as I know but it held nothing but bad memories for all of us. Especially her. But it seemed that Mum would escape from Elizabeth, vowing never to return, only to announce a few months later that we were moving back once again. The past was forgotten and we were all going to be happy in yet another part of Elizabeth. No sooner would we move in than she would curse and swear about how much she hated it and couldn't wait to leave again.

I guess it's like going on a roller-coaster. It looks like fun from a distance. So you jump on and as it pulls itself to the top of the hill you suddenly remember that you shouldn't be there. But it's too late. The whole world falls from beneath your feet and you get turned upside down. Mum was a thrill-seeker but every time she stepped into the void she dragged us with her. All we could do was shut our eyes and hope for the best.

I didn't want to quit my school, so every day I would be up at five to take a train and a bus to school. It would take me a few hours to get to school and a few to get home. This was almost the same trip that I used to take when I would run away from home as a kid. But I was always getting home after dark and I seemed to be constantly tired. My schoolwork was suffering and I decided that as much as I loved my school, I would have to change and go to a high school in Elizabeth.

This was a hard move for me; for the first time I had felt like I was beginning to settle into a routine. I could have gone to stay with Reg's parents, but they were old and it would have been too much for them. Not to mention that their house looked haunted. I remembered all the stuff Linda told me about seeing dead people walking around and talking to her there, so that was out of the question. I could fight other people but ghosts were a different story. I would have to try to survive in Elizabeth again.

I moved to Elizabeth West High School. This school was much rougher than Le Fevre. Every student went through some form of initiation. Some had their ties cut off, some were made to be slaves to the older boys. Some were beaten up and had their head shoved down the toilet and flushed. No one seemed to escape without some sort of scars. But nothing happened to me. I surely wasn't that intimidating that I scared off the big kids? After a short time, I worked it out. The tough kids were terrified of my brother John so I got away with murder. Even some of the younger teachers knew my brother and were afraid of him.

John had fought from the day we arrived in Elizabeth. It was as if he had something to prove. I don't know what that was. At primary school his kilt was like a red flag that he waved at everyone. Daring them to say a word. If they did he would swing at them. He spent a lot of time in the headmaster's office with blood on his face and knuckles. When he moved to high school he refused to be intimidated by older kids and often fought with them, winning a lot of the time. As I said before, he was asked to leave after knocking one of his teachers to the ground.

Once out of school, John got mixed up with the hardest people in Elizabeth, sometimes through choice but often by chance. He fought with the gangs that roamed around the streets and shops and anywhere else. By the time I came through the system, he had established himself as a force to be reckoned with. Everyone saw him as fierce and unafraid, but I knew a different John. He was always a gentle, caring big brother to me. But I soon learned from others that if he was cornered he could be frightening. His reputation as a street fighter saved me a lot of beatings as I grew up on the streets.

The first thing that I noticed was I didn't care as much about my schoolwork. Well, the first thing I noticed were the girls, this was a co-ed school. Girls were all I was interested in. I loved them all. I wasn't worried about fighting or playing up; the only thing on my mind by this time was girls.

There was one girl at the school who took my breath away. I was smitten with her. She was a beautiful, blonde, smart girl but she had no time for me when we first met. Girls didn't go out with guys their own age, it seemed. This was something that I would have to put up with for a few years. I couldn't work it out. What did the older guys have that we younger guys didn't have? Besides cars, money, self-confidence, a vocabulary and good skin?

I heard through the grapevine that she was seeing one of the teachers and this seemed very weird to me. Surely that was illegal or something? We were only fourteen years old and it had me baffled why she would be seeing someone so much older than her when she could be seeing me. I adored her, but to be fair I hadn't told her that; I don't think I had spoken to her at all. Every time I got the chance to talk to her, nothing came out. It was like an affliction of some sort, acute nerves.

I watched her all day in class. She was my first love. She had style and grace and I had none of either. But I was smart and tough and persistent and I began to build up the courage to speak to her. Then I did it whenever I got the chance.

Once I could actually get a few sentences out, I could tell she was warming to me; I made her laugh. She probably laughed at me, not with me, but she laughed all the same.

'Why are you going out with that teacher? Isn't that a bit wrong?'

'None of your business. He's very nice anyway.'

'He's a bit of a dork, don't you think?'

'He's gentle and sophisticated actually.'

'That's what I said, a dork.'

'Very funny.'

'Why don't you go out with me? I'm sophisticated.'

'You don't even know what that means.'

'Okay. But I'm gentle.'

'No you're not.'

'But I know you like me. I've caught you looking at me.'

'I wasn't. I was looking behind you, not at you.'

'Yeah, yeah, sure you were. You like me. Admit it.'

'Why am I talking to you anyway? I've got better things to do.'

'Like what? Come on. You know you like me.'

One day before school, we were talking and she said, 'Come over to my house after school. We can have some fun.'

I had no idea what I would say to her when I got to the house. What sort of fun was she talking about anyway – board games, that kind of fun? I had no idea but I couldn't wait to be alone with her.

'Sure, that would be great,' I spluttered out, hoping my voice wouldn't break.

That day at school felt like the longest day of my life. It dragged on forever. I couldn't concentrate at all. She was in every thought I had. Whatever she wanted of me, I was ready to give her. Or was I? What if she didn't really like me and she was bringing me over to let me down gently?

I got to her house five minutes after school got out. I ran the whole way. Pretty quickly I worked out that things would only go well if we did things her way, and to my surprise that included having sex.

By this point I'd had sex a few times but it was always rushed, in a paddock or a shed somewhere, with girls who were as confused by it as I was and were equally as scared. But with her it was different. It was at her home, in her bed, and it was the best thing I'd shared with anyone.

As usual, the voice in my head was saying, 'You're from the wrong side of the tracks for her and this will have to end badly.' And eventually I made that happen. We broke up. Either I was too uncomfortable around her or I turned up late one too many times or missed a date completely. Whatever it was, I pushed us to the end quite quickly.

I don't think her parents knew how serious I was about her

and they certainly didn't know we were having sex but they were always nice to me and made me feel at home. She still makes me smile when I think about her.

This was a significant time for me in other ways too. I became very interested in music, not through the school but through my brother. At school, music classes were boring, ending up with the teacher wanting me to play the triangle or something equally as stupid. This was kids' stuff and it bored me senseless. The only classical music I had ever heard was in cartoons, so hearing it without the cartoons made no sense to me at all. This piece was where Mickey Mouse was in a car chase, another piece was where he became a wizard. So why were we hearing it at school? This wasn't music.

The music I liked moved me, made me think or feel something. It stirred something inside me that hadn't been stirred before. It was sexual or rebellious or both if that's possible.

I wanted to be in a band like my big brother. In fact, myself and a few mates started a little band with the intention of playing at the school dance. The band needed a bass player and as the guitar player had a bass going spare, that was it. I wasn't really interested in singing at this stage. I loved the band Free and thought Andy Fraser, the bass player, was the man. I thought the bass was the driving force behind the band. And chicks liked bass players. It was settled: I would be a bass player. There were only four strings too so there was less that could go wrong.

We worked and worked at learning songs in every spare minute we had and we started to sound pretty good. We did songs like 'All Right Now' by Free and 'American Woman' by The Guess Who. We were a rock band and thought we were really cool.

We all plugged into one amp because that's all we had — one amp. Even the microphone plugged into that guitar amp.

It couldn't have sounded very good at all. Our singer Stuart was also the goalkeeper for our local football team. He was a tall, good-looking guy who all the girls liked. He sang pretty well too. He was cool and he dressed just like us. Ripped blue jeans and T-shirts. But it all went horribly wrong when the day of the show arrived.

'Hi, guys, I'm so excited about this show. I couldn't sleep last night.'

We looked over at him. There he was, dressed up for the gig in a full David Bowie outfit. Now I liked David Bowie as much as the next guy but I didn't want to dress like him. Stuart was wearing fishnet stockings, high silver boots and full Ziggy Stardust make-up. We didn't know where to look. We weren't a glam rock band at all.

So we had no choice.

'You're not getting on the stage with us dressed like that,' we all said in unison. 'You're sacked.'

We couldn't go on stage with him dressed that way. It was a matter of personal safety. We were in Elizabeth remember, and anything even slightly showbiz could get you killed or at least badly beaten.

'Come on, guys, you can't be serious. Are you? I could lose the boots if you want.'

'No, it wouldn't help, just get out of here now before someone thinks one of us is dating you,' I said, winking at the guitar player.

Stuart wasn't happy but he did go on to have a career as a singer in a band that played on Countdown and had a successful single. His band was called Scandal and they were a bit of a glam band even then. Many years later, while I was working in London, I was looking for a sound guy to mix my band. And a guy was recommended to me by the record company. 'You must use this guy. He's the best sound guy in England. He mixes a lot of really big bands. And guess what, he used to live in Australia too.'

'Great, what's his name?'

'Stuart Kerrison. You might know him. He used to sing with a band called Scandal.'

Stuart turned up for rehearsals dressed in ripped blue jeans and a T-shirt.

'Sorry we sacked you, man.'

'Na, it doesn't matter Jim. I was a shit singer anyway. I make a lot more money mixing bands than I would have singing.'

I'm glad he had a sense of humour or my band could have sounded really bad.

But anyway, back at the school dance, we didn't have a singer. Well, I'd been singing all my life but never rock songs and never in a band.

'Who wants to be the singer?' I asked enthusiastically.

It appeared the rest of the guys couldn't or didn't want to sing at all. So I was the obvious choice, in fact I was the only choice.

I had never been so nervous in my life. I couldn't play bass and sing at the same time, so this meant that anywhere there was singing, there was no bass playing, and anywhere there was bass playing, there was no singing. This was interesting but not good. It was a concept that would not catch on with bands, not even ours.

The audience were as young as us and it appeared their ears were as musically trained as ours were. They clapped but not all at the same time.

'If you're going to clap your hands like that, shut your mouth or someone will throw a fish into it.' I had all the good stage patter.

The band broke up. I can't even remember our name, but it couldn't have been good. I hope it wasn't Spiders from Mars.

* * *

I was spending a bit of time at the gym, getting fit and learning to box at the place where my dad taught my brother to fight. I wanted to be like John and I thought boxing was a good place to start. Followed closely by drinking.

I thought I was getting pretty handy with my fists. But in fact I wasn't. Well, not handy enough, I was soon to find out. Apparently it was a lot easier to hit a punching bag than it was to fight a human. Two things are important here. Firstly, the bag doesn't move a lot. And secondly, and this is the most important thing, the punching bag doesn't hit you back or try to kill you. But I was about to find all this out, and, unfortunately for me, I found it out just a little too late.

I got a message from one of the trainers asking me to be involved in an exhibition boxing match at the local school. I hadn't done this before, but how hard could it be? You walk around the ring and wink at a few chicks and throw a few punches. I'd watched lots of fights and I thought I could do it. They told me that the guy I was to fight had just started training and I would have to take it easy on him. Cool, I'd dance around the ring and float like a butterfly and all that good stuff that I'd heard boxers say. And do my best not to embarrass the poor young guy too much. Simple.

'Look, I'm very busy but I'll do it just this once,' I said as if I had a busy schedule.

They were right, he had just started boxing, but within a month he was state champion. He was an absolute natural, one of the most natural fighters my trainer had ever seen. I made it through three, three-minute rounds with him. It was the longest nine minutes of my life. If it had gone any longer you could have sold advertising space on the soles of my shoes.

'Why didn't you tell me this before I went in there?' I spluttered through my newly fattened lips. 'You sent me into the ring with a killer and let him beat the shit out of me.'

I gave up boxing that day and started fighting dirty.

* * *

Mum and Reg moved away from Elizabeth again, and rather than change schools I moved in with friends of the family – Aunty Mary and Uncle Eddie, who I'd stayed with before, when times were really rough with Dad. We all wanted my school marks, which had gone rapidly downhill since joining a co-ed school, to improve and Mum and Reg thought moving would not help that cause. Besides, I was slipping back into life in Elizabeth again.

Aunty Mary was the mother of one of Mum's mates. She tried to save me whenever she could. She took me to stay at her house in Broadmeadows, just across the paddock from where we lived in the old days. Aunty Mary's house was exactly the same as most of the houses that made up Elizabeth. A small, grey, three-bedroom duplex. From the outside they all basically looked the same. Some had nice gardens and some looked like bomb sites. Aunty Mary's was somewhere in the middle. She was too old to work in the garden as much as she would have liked but you could tell that she cared. She kept the garden tidy and had a few roses growing in the yard.

Inside, the house was like a lot of other Scottish homes. Clean, but nothing fancy. Aunty Mary would scrub the floors until they were so clean you could eat off them. She had crocheted toilet roll holders and doilies to place her ornaments on. There were tartan dolls and black-and-white dogs, the kind you saw on whisky bottles, sitting on the mantelpiece. She was sweet, as was Eddie. They were both quite old, and had a grown-up son named John.

There were no fights in Aunty Mary's house. She was a tough and loving old lady. She reminded me a bit of what my mum would have been like without all the problems that alcohol brought into her life. Uncle Eddie drank but Mary ran the house with an iron fist. Neither Eddie nor John ever said a bad word to her and when she said to stop drinking, they would. It was quiet and peaceful.

At night the four of us would sit and watch television and have tea and toast with Anchovette or pepper steak spread before bed. Uncle Eddie worked and we would all be up early getting ready for work and school. I would leave just after he did and walk across the paddock to high school. This worked well for me as it took less than half an hour to get there. So I would be at school on time, fed and ready to work. Well, that was in theory. The reality was I was in a co-ed school and rapidly losing focus. So sometimes I didn't get there on time or ready to work. Sometimes I met people on the way to school and got side-tracked. But most days I made it eventually.

Aunty Mary seemed a lonely old soul as Eddie and John spent a lot of time at the pub after work, so she loved having me around. I'd get home from school and she'd be sitting at the kitchen table with her only other friend, Billy the budgie, sitting on her shoulder, talking to it like it was a child. 'Oh you're a beautiful wee boy, aren't you, Bill? Come on, gie us a wee kiss. What a boy! Mwaa, mwaa.'

As soon as I walked through the door she would put Billy carefully back into his cage and find something to feed me and then sit and tell me about her day. 'No too much happened the day, Jim. I just sat wi' ma wee bird and drank tea,' she'd say. 'I've cooked mince for Eddie and you for dinner. I know you love it.'

Then we would talk about everything and nothing. She would ask about my mum and dad, as if she knew stuff that I didn't. It was a little strange sometimes and I was not always sure I knew where the conversations were heading. But she never said a bad word about them; there was just something in her tone that made me feel that she didn't really like them both.

'Your mum's had a lot of problems you know, son. But we've all got problems, Jim, it's just how you cope wi' them that matters.'

She was always worried about her son John too. Life wasn't easy for him. He was a lovely chap but he spoke with a terrible stutter. He had very few friends and was struggling with life. His parents loved him and cared for him but they were from Glasgow and probably had their own problems to deal with.

One dark, rainy night when John was walking home from the pub someone ran him down with a car, which didn't stop. He was left lying in the middle of the road bleeding and alone and was hit by a second car. They didn't stop either. I can't imagine what was going through his head as he lay there on the road. Maybe he was happy it was over, I don't know. I like to think he was out cold and didn't know what happened.

When the news came, Uncle Eddie was already in bed but Aunty Mary and I were sitting up, waiting for him to come home. She would not sleep until she knew John was home safe. He was her angel. The police turned up late that night and gave her the news and she just fell apart. Her golden boy was gone. Uncle Eddie died not long after his son. Aunty Mary was never the same after that.

I stayed with Aunty Mary for about three months. Enough time for me to complete the second term of high school before I moved back in with Mum and Reg and changed schools. I didn't see Aunty Mary for years, but I know that staying with her was one of the good times in my life.

CHAPTER EIGHTEEN

everybody thought I was fearless

Mum and Reg moved again, back to another part of Elizabeth. They were working their way around every part of the place. This time they moved to Elizabeth South. It was hard to get to my school in the west from there. I was beginning to get in trouble at that school anyway. So it was time to change again and rather than go too far I moved to Elizabeth High School, the roughest school in the area – and that was saying something.

Our home in Elizabeth South was another housing trust house that looked the same as every other housing trust house. It was in an older part of the town, so there were a few more trees, but it was not a lot different from anywhere else. Still, it was only a short walk from the town centre, which meant I could get into more trouble if I wanted, and I often did.

It was the start of term three in Year 9 by the time I went to my new school and it wasn't long before I found new friends. These friends weren't like the guys I knew at Le Fevre, or even at Elizabeth West High. They didn't do any work at all. All they did was create havoc and cause the teachers grief. The school looked like something from a bad movie. It seemed every kid there was from a broken, dysfunctional home, and all the problems they had at home made study impossible. These kids were hooligans. By the time I moved there, so was I. My studious days were over. It didn't help that this new school was co-ed like the last one, so I was completely distracted by girls again. We spent most of our day trying to impress the chicks – if we weren't terrorising teachers or other students.

We must have looked like extras from *Blackboard Jungle*. We all wore leather jackets and did whatever we wanted. Some of the teachers were quite young, on their first posting. They weren't ready for what they had to face when they came across us. They would be enthusiastically teaching us English and our gang would be sitting with our chairs tilted against the back wall of the class, showing no interest whatsoever. When they thought they were doing really well we would get up and walk to the fire escape near the front of the class and kick it open, walk out onto the oval and lie down and smoke cigarettes or pierce each other's ears with needles.

There were big fights in the schoolyard too. I soon found out that at Elizabeth High things were different. Everyone was much more vicious than I remembered and I had to sharpen my fighting skills very quickly to survive. The guys in this area didn't think twice about stabbing people or kicking them half to death. In fact, they thought it was funny and did it as entertainment. I wasn't like this, but I had to find a way to make them think that I was, before I was found out and became one of their victims.

I learned something in that school that served me well: a barking dog doesn't bite. In other words, the guy who seems the scariest, with the biggest mouth, isn't always the best fighter. If he talked about fighting too much, he probably wasn't that good at it. So I would always wait until the biggest, ugliest bloke pushed me around a little or mouthed off trying to impress the other guys and then I'd turn on him and give him a hiding. It was simple.

'Hey, you, I'm going to bash your fucking head in, mate!'

Bang! Before he had even finished the sentence I would be tearing into him, hitting him with everything I had. Everybody thought I was fearless but in fact it was the opposite – I was terrified. Pretty soon I was accepted into the gangs with the toughest kids in the area. I had them all bluffed. They thought I was an animal just like them so they would never push me. I could fight if I was cornered, but my heart wasn't in it.

Some of the teachers were very nice, like the English teacher we drove to the brink of a nervous breakdown. She was just a young woman trying to make a difference to some kids' lives. 'Today we will be reading poetry from …'

Smash! Down went the fire escape again and four or five of us would walk out of the class onto the lawn and lie back in the sun. After a month with us I think she quit teaching. She probably never went back to it. Looking back on those days I feel ashamed of my behaviour, although I was one of the nicer students at the school. Some students beat up the teachers and the strangest thing was no one ever seemed to get expelled or even reprimanded. The school was just a place where we could gather and do whatever we liked. A meeting place for the gang.

I think it was only there to get us out of our parents' hair. In the few months I spent there I started caring less about what anyone thought of me and just did whatever I thought would be fun. My schoolwork went further down the drain. Don't get me wrong – I was still a very quick learner. But the things I was learning now could have had me locked up, and the key thrown away.

* * *

The hard guy in our year was a guy called George. He was big, he was wild and he had no fear of anything or anybody. I worked out on the first day that if I was going to survive at this school, I would have to have him onside. He was a smartarse who wasn't that likeable, but I was a smartarse too and I was smarter than him, or so I thought.

He had the worst taste in music and he insisted on singing everywhere he went around the school. To make it even more unbearable he had a really bad singing voice. But he loved music, I could tell, and so did I. It wasn't long before he and I were friends and I was playing some decent music to him. He, in the meantime, was scaring the other hoodlums away from me.

After hanging around with George for a while I realised that he wasn't dumb at all; he just didn't care. Whatever had gone on in my life, had also gone on – maybe even worse – in his life. That's why he didn't give a fuck about anything. Under his brutal exterior there seemed to be a brutal interior. But I could talk to him and see the tears welling up in his eyes. I could play a song and he would have to pretend he wasn't crying. I knew that underneath he was really a softie. We became good mates. We got each other into a lot of trouble but we watched each other's back and where we lived nobody else did that.

I was too cool to listen to pop music but George used to sing 'Sylvia's Mother' all the time. Was he doing this to provoke people?

'La la la … Sylvia such and such,' he would sing in a voice that sounded like fingernails on a blackboard. 'I love you whoever you are … la la la.'

He would make up his own words, singing at the top of his voice while walking down the street, especially if we walked past girls. Then George would sing even louder and stare into their eyes, whether he knew them or not.

His shirt was untucked and he walked with the kind of

swagger that only a dangerous teenager can muster. Guys from the older gangs around the shops would sometimes get sick of him and have a go at him. They hated that song. But George would take them down. He was hard. At the start I hated that song too but now I really like it because it reminds me of George and his stupid antics. We would fight and drink and run amok all over Elizabeth and always managed not to get caught by the cops; we were too fast. No one else anywhere near our age could push us around or tell us what to do. We ran the place.

I lost contact with George not long after I left that school and I was really sad to hear that soon after he died in a car wreck. He acted like a thug but underneath it all he was a good guy and deserved a better life. But he didn't stand a chance from the start. He was never going to escape Elizabeth and I wondered if I would either.

I can still hear him. 'Sylvia ... la la la.'

In the meantime, my brother John had decided to join the army. I think that he was so out of control that it scared even him and he thought the army would straighten his life out. He wanted stability and routine and to feel safe. He later told me he wanted to buy a house of his own so he didn't have to rely on anyone. Somewhere he could be safe from the world. The only way he could see himself doing that was to join the army and get a service loan. So, at a time when everyone else in the world was marching to stop the war, he marched straight in and saluted. I can imagine him saying, 'Put me in, I'm ready to kill.'

He went to basic training and things didn't go as well as he expected. 'Who the fuck are these people who think they can tell me what to do?' No one told John what to do. 'I'm out of here.' He ran away from base. But it wasn't long until they caught up with him. He was back and in trouble. But he pulled his head in and knuckled down to work even though he knew the army just didn't suit him. How he thought that the army would work out for him when even high school discipline was too much for him was beyond me, but he tried. He was learning to be a cook for a short while. By this point he had already volunteered for Vietnam but his volatile nature at that time lead to his discharge before any active service. This suited John just fine. He went back to singing in the trenches of the Australian music scene and fighting hand to hand on the street. At least there you knew where you stood.

John told us of many people he met during his time in the service of his country, including officers who were real psychopaths. People who didn't feel anything for anyone, and who felt no remorse for anything or compassion for anybody. One of these people was a guy who I'll call Shane. John had become close to him until the day that Shane went up to another soldier in the mess hall and stuck his thumb into the corner of his eye, popping it out onto his cheek and then smashing it on his face simply because he wanted his seat at the table. Now, John didn't mind exaggerating a bit if it helped to make a good story even better. But when John told me about this I could tell that even he thought it was too much. So I don't think he was embellishing at all.

This guy was an absolute nutcase, but for some reason John had given him our address. And soon after John got out of the army he turned up at our door. John had told me that story and a few others about this psycho so I was afraid of him. He should have been locked away but instead he was at our door. Not only that, but it didn't take that long until Mum asked him to move in with us.

We seemed to have strange and dangerous people staying with us all the time. Mum said it was because she felt sorry for people and wanted to help them out but I'm not sure it was that simple. She liked to help people and had trouble saying no to anybody, a trait that her kids all seemed to inherit. But I think there were other reasons too. Maybe she needed other people around to help her put up with us or life in general. Maybe she didn't want to be in the same house as Reg.

Shane was a classic Australian conman and he had my mum conned. He was not a good-looking bloke but was brim full of confidence and smooth talked any vulnerable women that came within earshot. Reg didn't want him anywhere around us. He could always pick the people we should avoid. He had no control over Mum though, so she just let whoever she wanted get in close.

Mum and Linda in particular were taken in by this cheap conman; the rest of us had not a lot to do with him. John, in the meantime, hardly spent any time at all with him. I think John knew how dangerous Shane was and didn't want to be responsible for him or anything he did.

It wasn't long until Shane was the chosen one in Mum's eyes. She fell for his lies, hook, line and sinker. Pretty soon he had the run of the house, much to Reg's dismay. He had something going on with Linda while they were both living in our house, even though Linda was only about seventeen. No one seemed to care but Reg.

Soon he was getting drunk in the house and playing up with my sisters' friends. This was not a good thing. But he could talk his way into anything.

One day he asked if he could take me out to help him with some work. I had no idea what he had in mind. I'm sure Mum didn't know either, but she agreed that I could go, and the next day, very early, there was Shane at the end of my bed. 'Get up, Jim, we've got work to do.'

We left the house before the sun came up and headed down to the docks near Port Adelaide. He had a bag with him, full of photos and videos.

'I want you to just walk around with me while I talk to a few of these blokes at the bar,' he said.

They were all merchant seamen and shift workers. Who else would be drinking at the early opener at seven in the morning?

'Just pretend that you're my little brother. But don't fucking speak, all right? Don't say a fucking word. Just agree with me and that's it. Got it?'

Shane kept reaching into his bag and getting what looked like picture books or magazines from it. It didn't take me long to work it out. I wasn't allowed to handle the merchandise but I wasn't stupid so I knew what was going on – he was selling porn, and he was pretending to be looking after me. 'I need money to look after the young lad here. His mother left us and I'm all he's got.'

A couple of guys didn't want to be hustled. They'd been working all night and just wanted to drink. 'Fuck off and leave us alone, you scumbag. Can't you see we're talking?'

Shane beat them senseless and then we left in a hurry and moved on to the next pub. After a couple of hours, he turned to me and said, 'Well done. That was a bit of fun, eh. Time to go home now, but I've got to make a stop on the way.'

We were at this house and I could hear banging, screaming and moaning coming from the next room. He and the woman who lived there had left me to look after her young children while they went to talk about a few things. I tried to talk over the screams and thumps coming through the walls. I didn't want the kids to be afraid but it sounded like he was beating her up in the next room. I just kept playing with the little ones, knowing they were as scared as me.

He came out and looked at me, grinning. 'That's a lot fucking better.' He picked up her purse, took some money from it, and we left.

Shane stayed with us for a few months. Towards the end I think that even Mum had had enough of him. He was an animal.

* * *

Linda always had wild people around as well. Sometimes they were dangerous and other times they were just crazy.

She had a friend who was a little older than her. This girl was cute with a bob haircut and big teeth. She was maybe twenty years old. She would stay at our house and when everyone had gone to bed she would come into my room and go down on me, right there in the house. Or she'd wake me up in the middle of the night.

'Hey, Jim, psst Jim! Wake up and come with me. I've got a little present for you,' she'd laugh.

Then she'd take me out to the backyard and fuck me. This became more and more frequent, even getting to the point where it was affecting my schoolwork. I didn't mind but I was getting very little sleep and couldn't think about anything else at all.

She spent more time with us every week and she seemed to find more time where we could get away. At the time I thought that this was great, being a young lad. But it was wearing me down. The more she stayed with us, the more I wanted to fuck her. I was becoming just like her.

She hung around for a long time and she started to get angry with me when my interest in her dwindled. I wanted to chase after the girls at the centre with my mates. Things turned nasty towards the end and I had to keep away from the house as much as I could.

Around that time, Mum opened the door to the Mormons, who door-knocked in short-sleeved white shirts, riding pushbikes. No sooner were they in the door than Mum wanted us all to get baptised and join the faithful. She was an easy touch for anybody with a story and the Mormons were very good talkers. At least these guys never meant us too much harm. In fact, sometimes I think Mum was trying to make up for all the shit we had been through by saving our souls. Lord knows they needed saving by this time.

It seemed that every day the house was full of these Mormon guys and the coffee table was overflowing with pamphlets that none of us wanted to read. We had no need for the coffee table anymore anyway, as Mormons didn't drink coffee or tea, much to the dismay of Reg. Tea was his only vice and Mum had seen to it that that particular avenue of pleasure was cut off.

'Reg, if we're going tae be proper Mormons then aw the coffee and tea must be oot the hoose. I don't need it and neither do you.'

'All right, love, whatever you say.' Once again, Reg went along with anything Mum wanted. But he was becoming more and more miserable. He already felt close to his God without a bunch of American lost souls trying to ram their faith down his throat. I think he secretly wanted to kill those Mormons. How dare they take away his tea?

The family were invited to barbecues at the homes of other Mormons. And we were expected to hang around and play with the little Mormons. But by this point we didn't want to play with anyone or anybody. We were delinquents. But Dot and Linda, like my mum, were easy touches and so Mum, Reg, Dot, Linda, Alan and Lisa all agreed to get baptised into the Mormon faith. Well, Mum did and the others didn't have a choice. John and I just told them to leave us alone. I don't think those were the exact words we used but they certainly got the message quickly.

The ceremony involved all of them being laid back into a swimming pool until they were submerged completely. Apparently this was the way to let the Holy Spirit in. He would only come in if you were saturated. Lisa told me later that her long, thick hair wouldn't go under the water and they had to keep trying to get her completely submerged, dunking her head under the water quite a few times. She was worried she was going to drown, but apparently God won't talk to you if your hair doesn't go under the water. He's very fussy. He hates dry hair.

They were all successfully baptised but after about a week of Mormon life my mum got bored and made all the family quit the faith. We were heathens again and happy about it. Of course the rest of us, including Reg, had seen this coming right from the start. The Mormons stopped trying to save our souls and Mum started swearing at us again. Things got back to normal very quickly, and Mum never mentioned the Mormons again unless it was, 'Those fuckin' Mormons.'

Reg got to have his tea in peace. 'Put the kettle on, love.'

We did whatever we were doing before Mum saw God.

Linda found new and more interesting people to hang around and it wasn't long until she invited me into the fold.

One guy Linda took a shine to looked like another conman to me. I was fifteen by then and I'd seen enough conmen to pick one when I saw one. There was definitely something wrong with this guy but Linda liked him and they ran away to Melbourne.

After fighting with Mum one too many times, I decided to go and join her. So I hitchhiked to Melbourne. Linda was living in an apartment in St Kilda by this point. I turned up on her doorstep late one night and said, 'I'm here, where's my room?'

No one looked up. They were all drunk. So I made myself at home. I could see piles of things stacked around the room. There were televisions and stereos with the leads all wound up neatly lying on the floor. Between what I was seeing and what was being said in the flat I soon worked out what the guy was up to. He was a thief. He had been making all his money breaking into homes and robbing people.

Now I never wanted anything from anybody but I was wild and wanted to do anything that was illegal by this point. I could climb anything and had no fear at all. So he recruited me as a cat burglar. I didn't steal anything, all I would do was shimmy up poles two or three storeys high and break into apartments. Then I would open the door and walk away. He didn't mind that I wasn't interested in taking things, he just wanted me to help him get into places.

I could see in my heart that this was wrong. But I did it. I still feel guilty about that time in my life. Just what I needed – one more thing to regret. But back then I tried not to think. I could have died, climbing up five storeys on the outside of an apartment building in the rain. But I didn't care about dying either.

I didn't die, and every day I would wake up, and there I'd be, ashamed, afraid and guilt-ridden, waiting for the world to catch on to me. I'd tell myself, 'I'm not doing this ever again.'

But the next day, off I would go. The world was a fucked up place and it was never going to get any better.

I only lasted in Melbourne for about two or three weeks before I wanted to go back to Adelaide. The guy had a Dodge Phoenix, a big American gas guzzler. That's the car, not him. He said he had an offer for me. I got the feeling he wanted to get rid of me.

'I'll drive you to Adelaide, but you've got to help me steal the petrol first.'

I agreed and off we went, the guy and me. We pulled into a car park, stopped the Yank tank next to a nice-looking car and jumped out.

'You start siphoning the petrol and I'll keep watch.'

'Why do I have to do the work?'

'It's my car, mate.'

I seemed to be getting the bad end of the deal here.

When I finished filling the can, and spitting the petrol out of my mouth, he came and took the can off me and left the hose in the other car's tank. Then he started filling his car with a funnel.

Suddenly we heard a noise. The guy he was stealing the petrol from was walking back to his car with his girl. We hid quietly, a little way away.

'Shit,' Linda's friend whispered. We had left the hose hanging out of the other guy's car and the funnel in ours.

'What the fuck is going on here?' The guy scowled and turned to his girl.

It didn't take long before he worked it out. He looked around but couldn't see us. So he started siphoning the petrol out of our car to put back into his. As he was in the middle of it, the police drove into the car park.

Like a bullet, Linda's mate shot up and called out, 'Help, these bastards are stealing my petrol.' He was screaming hysterically, at the top of his voice.

Now, if you had just got there, that's exactly what it looked like. The police grabbed the poor guy who had done nothing and let us go. Linda's friend was a very good talker. He gave a false address and we left. The car must have been stolen too so they could never trace it back to us.

With a nearly full tank of gas we headed back to the flat to get Linda before driving to Adelaide. I had the feeling she didn't want to be there anymore either.

By the time we got to Adelaide the shine had well and truly worn off this guy. Linda didn't like him anymore. He was dull; the only thing he had going was that he was a smooth talker and we had heard everything he had to say. So Linda gave him the flick, much to his disappointment.

He pleaded with her to let him stay. 'Come on, Linda, come back to Melbourne with me. This town's a hole.'

Linda was a needy girl but she'd had enough. She didn't need him anymore. The last thing we saw of him, he was driving at high speed down a little laneway in Elizabeth, screaming 'Fuck you,' at the top of his voice.

Linda had something similar to say to him, but I don't think he heard it. She moved back in with Mum and so did I. All was forgiven. Mum was just happy to have us all home again and not locked up in jail.

I went back to school and tried to study but all I really wanted to do was chase girls. The biggest problem was, I kept catching them. Girls liked me. I was different from the other guys we hung round with. I was softer and not as violent. I liked to hang with them and not the guys. I was running around and had different girls for every day of the week.

I started taking time off school and going to different girls' houses during the day while their parents were working. We would drink and have sex all day and I loved it. One day the parents of one of the girls came home early and I had to hide under their bed until I could escape. They were in the room, telling off the girl for skipping school. She must have looked very dishevelled but they never worked out I was in their room, under their bed. Her dad would have killed me. He went out about twenty minutes later and I lived another day.

CHAPTER NINETEEN

a murderer but a good bloke

One day I came home and there living in our house was a guy named Davey. He had a huge scar across his face where someone had sliced him with an open razor. It made him look very scary.

Later I heard he had killed someone in Glasgow and he had to get on a ship before the cops could arrest him. The boat brought him to Australia and Davey jumped ship because his brother had moved here a few years earlier. He was in Australia without a passport or any papers. He could not go back to Scotland without going to jail for life. Apparently he couldn't live with his brother because his brother's wife didn't want him near the kids – and so he ended up living in a room with me.

To this day I don't know why he ended up at our house. It troubled Reg as he didn't really want strangers living with us but he had no choice. He was always too nice to stand up for his rights; my mum walked all over him. It made me sad to see him treated with so little respect. But he did warm to Davey. He might have been a murderer but he was a good bloke. He came from a place where the straight blade ruled and he had to use one to survive. It was the same place that I had come from, so God knows if I had stayed there I might have been like him. He still carried an open razor with him everywhere he went, except of course when my mum would search him. I used to see her frisk him before he went out on a Saturday night.

'Right Davey, before you go anywhere, let me gie you a wee pat doon. I might search you too. Ha ha ha.'

He would always have a razor or a diving knife strapped to his leg.

'Come on son, give that to me. There's naebody trying to kill ye here,' she'd say as she was checking him head to toe.

'Are ye sure o' that, Dot? I think that I heard a couple of lassies saying they wanted ma body.'

'Come on,' she'd say again.

'Aye aw right, I'll gie ye the knife 'cause you're so good lookin'. But naebody else is gettin' it from me.'

He was always respectful of Mum. She took the knife from him but I got the feeling he carried another one somewhere. Just for security. He never liked to be unarmed. He was terrified all the time, like me. This made me think about how frightening parts of Glasgow must have been.

He loved the family though; he was like a big brother. Davey eventually got a job and met a girl and wanted to move in with her. Life was starting to look good for the first time for old Davey.

'Well, Mr and Mrs B, I know you all loved having me here and you're gonnae be heartbroken when I leave. But I've got tae go and spread the love. Ye cannae keep a good man like me all tae yersels.'

He had even reconciled with his brother and his wife. They were all out at the shopping centre one day, buying some tools to hang pictures for his new house, when out of the blue a policeman came up to him in the coffee shop. The policeman didn't want him. He was only going to ask a simple question but

Davey panicked, thinking that his past had caught up with him. He wasn't going to be arrested and sent back home. He started swinging. Things quickly escalated and before he could stop himself he had hit the policeman over the head with the hammer he had just bought. It was over in seconds.

'My fuckin' god. What've I done?'

He ended up in jail for life and maybe was sent back to Scotland to serve out his sentence. This was the one thing he had been running from for years. But life always catches up with you eventually. I think I would rather have been in jail in Australia than Glasgow but by then I'm sure it didn't matter. He was alone and his life was over. Poor bastard never stood a chance.

By this time all the years of fear and abuse had pushed me beyond the point of no return. I was bad and everything I was doing now was a result of my own choices. Choices that were all wrong and only getting worse. I came close to getting locked up quite a few times while I was at Elizabeth High School.

I had started drinking every weekend with my new friends. We were getting ourselves into a lot of trouble. Lots of fighting and generally getting on the wrong side of the law. We were stealing things from the shopping centre and we had no respect for anyone or anything.

Every kid at the school stole from the shopping centre – stupid stuff they didn't need. I learned to steal things that I needed: clothes and food and music. I learned how to steal records from the department store and this allowed me to hear records that I couldn't afford. But I didn't like the idea of doing this. I had been involved with people who stole before, in Melbourne, and I felt bad about it then. Shoplifting was not as bad as what was happening then but there was something about taking something that didn't belong to me or I hadn't earned that didn't sit right with me. It still doesn't and I regret any involvement I ever had in that sort of thing. So my career as a shoplifter didn't last very long. I felt bad whenever I did it – not because I was taking someone's royalties, I wouldn't find out about that until much later – but because I knew that it was wrong. I knew right from wrong and this was something I had to deal with while I was going out of control. I tried to be like all the other guys and it made me feel even worse about myself. I already felt worthless so this just made things more unbearable. I was a loser, and I was behaving like one, more and more. I couldn't live with myself so I would just numb myself as much as I could, whenever I could.

One night while I was sitting in the coffee shop at the shopping centre waiting for the rest of the gang, I saw a group of guys beating up this young guy I knew. I ran to help him. I immediately hit the ringleader of the group as hard as I could, knocking him to the ground. His friends scattered like rats. I then proceeded to give him a beating and left him whimpering in a pool of blood.

As luck would have it, the guy I hit was the son of a local magistrate and I ended up in court charged with assault. My life was unravelling.

Mum screamed and yelled at me. It all went in one ear and out the other. Reg was once again disappointed in me and as much as I shrugged this off, it did make me feel ashamed. But I would get over it.

Luckily other people had seen what had happened and the guy had a very bad reputation, even worse than mine. Although I was found guilty, I was let off with a caution. I was still a minor and no charges were put on my record, but I would have more run-ins with the law as I got older.

* * *

I was in trouble quite a lot and my folks were starting to crack down on me. Well, they were trying to crack down on me. I didn't respond well to being kept in line.

'You're grounded, boy,' Reg would say and I would walk straight out of the door. 'Your mother is going to give you a good belting when you get home.' This was desperation on Reg's behalf. He didn't like violence and I knew he wouldn't even tell her.

'Yeah, Dad, I love you too,' I would say as the door slammed behind me. At times like this I felt funny calling Reg 'Dad'. He had been a real father to me for quite a while now and I loved him, but treating him with so little respect made me think about how little my family really cared for one another. We always said we loved each other and that we would never do the wrong thing by one another. Then we just did whatever we liked. This wasn't the way you spoke to someone you loved. I would never have spoken to my real dad that way – not because of respect or love but because of fear, being afraid he would knock me out. Mum tried to threaten us like that but it never worked. Reg would never really threaten me. Families are very confusing.

Anyway, I was fighting with them all the time, but they were used to it, as all the kids fought with them. They were fighting a losing battle as far as we could see. We were wearing them down.

At that time, in 1971, Myponga Festival was staged on the Australia Day long weekend. Black Sabbath were the big headliners and I was desperate to see them. I was a huge fan, along with most of the teenage guys in Australia at the time. My brother was going and my sisters told me they were going, so I presumed I would go along with them and their mates. Not a problem, they said, so all I had to do was run it past my mum.

'Mum, there's a little rock show on this weekend. I'm going to go with John and Dot and Linda, okay?'

Mum was dead against it. 'You're goin' nowhere. You're grounded. You're stayin' here wi' me.'

I had been a little wild at the time and probably needed to stay home but I wasn't going to make it easy. 'This is the only chance I'll have to see this show. I'm going.'

The house was quiet except for the sound of Mum's fuse burning down. 'You're goin' nowhere.'

Mum sat in the corner. Her lips had disappeared and she was waiting to strike out at me. I continued to push my luck.

The fuse had burned to the end and Mum exploded. She screamed and tried to grab me so she could give me the slapping I deserved.

I was out of the door before she could get to me. 'I'm going and you can't stop me.'

I was gone down the street. I had already planned to meet Linda and her mates later that night. I would climb out the window.

I came home after a while, having left enough time for Mum to cool off. She was sitting in the lounge room saying nothing so I went to my bedroom. I put on John's best clothes and I had one leg out of the window when suddenly Mum was standing there, waiting for me. She must have been getting wise to me running away by that time.

'Get intae that hoose, right now!' she shrieked.

I could see Linda's friend's car speed away into the night. I knew I'd be going nowhere. I was shattered. This was one of the bands I really liked and I wanted to see them live. But there was no way I could talk her into letting me go without a physical fight. I decided for once that it was better to be cool and do what she said rather than just fuck off and cause trouble for everyone, including Reg.

My sisters came home after the festival absolutely raving about this band. I didn't want to hear about it. 'Yeah, I know. Black Sabbath are great.'

But it wasn't Black Sabbath they were talking about. It was an Australian band called Daddy Cool. They were raving about this singer. 'He danced around with a fox tail attached to his arse and a guitar player who had a propeller on his head. It was the best.'

Sounded weird but I guessed you had to be there. They said Daddy Cool was the best band they had ever seen. I was so pissed off that I had missed this chance to check out a new band. I'll never forgive my mum for making me miss that festival.

I soon found out I had some advantages over the other guys, one in particular, which had helped me earlier in school – my brother John. Like I've said, John was wild, but by this point in his life he was absolutely out of control. We all were, but he was wilder than anyone I knew.

All the older guys hung around at the Elizabeth shopping centre, fighting blokes and shagging chicks. Anybody our age who went there would be roughed up and sent packing, but John was one of the craziest and most violent members of the gang and this, I soon worked out, meant that I could do almost anything I wanted. No one wanted to touch me or hit me because they knew that John would kill them.

John was one of those guys you could never win against, even if you beat the shit out of him. He would wait. It didn't matter if he had to wait months. He would wait until you least expected it. Maybe one night, six months later, you'd be getting home late at night and there would be John behind a bush holding a lump of wood with your name on it. You had to kill him to beat him. My dad taught us that. Never give in.

I found out later that John was even more frightened than I was. This is what made him such a very dangerous person. If he was cornered, he would take on anyone. To top this off he was also drinking a lot by then and taking copious amounts of drugs, and that made him very unpredictable. No one messed with him.

Even the most vicious guys in Elizabeth thought twice before they would go up against John.

Around that time, I fell in love with an Irish girl from Elizabeth High. She was beautiful. She had black, black hair and green eyes and wore the shortest miniskirts and the highest shoes I'd ever seen. Her legs seemed to go on forever; she was breathtaking. I used to look at her shoes and work my way up. I could only dream about her. She was the same age as me but used to go out with the much older guys in the area.

But I was lucky. I was always hanging around with John's friends. I was a part of the older guys' gang. Every night around the pool hall I would hang out with them. Slowly but surely some of my younger friends joined me, so it became more normal for us to be included in the things they got up to. We would tag along to their parties and even get involved in their fights.

She was always there and I was always watching her. She would smile at me and talk to me whenever we had the chance. I knew she liked me but I was too young. I didn't have a car and I wasn't allowed into the pubs yet. So that love affair didn't last long but I felt a lot for her and I thought of her all the time. I would see her in the back of some idiot's car with his hands all over her and it would break my heart, but I never let anyone see it. She saw me looking at her a few times and I could see she was hurting too but we could never talk about it. It was over for us before it started.

As we got older and my mates got cars, we began to hang around the centre more often with the other guys, but if the word came that John had left the pub, my mates would scatter, terrified that he would see them and slap them around just to keep them in line.

He was frightening but he never hit me at all. Never in my life did John even raise his hands to me. He was always there to protect me. He made me feel safe when he was around even when he was totally out of control. For many years I wanted to be just like him.

I remember one night at the shopping centre, John was walking through the car park on his way to a mate's wedding. This car park had been the scene of many a savage beating. He was dressed up in a suit and looked very sharp, but no one dressed like that around the shops, not even John, without getting some sort of attention.

A couple of bikies had just got off their bikes as he walked by. They made the fatal mistake of commenting on his clothes. 'Hey poof. Where do you think you're going?'

John stopped and turned towards them. He didn't react, he just started a conversation with them. Pretty soon they were laughing and chatting along with him. I told you he was charming. After a little while John started commenting on their bikes.

'Wow, they look good. Did you paint them yourselves?' he asked, sounding really interested. 'Really good job, guys.'

Soon these poor bikies were completely sucked in. They were so proud of their bikes. Then John said, 'I noticed that your helmets are painted really well. Could I have a look at them?'

They, by this point, thought he was a funny guy who posed no threat to two big blokes like them and without hesitation handed over their helmets.

As soon as John got the helmets in his hands he proceeded to beat the shit out of these guys with their own helmets. He didn't stop until they were on the ground bleeding and pleading for mercy.

John then kicked over both bikes and spat on them. As quickly as he had turned, he regained his composure and straightened his tie. 'Get some fucking manners, boys. And sharpen up your dress sense a bit while you're at it.'

Then he just walked away and on to the wedding. Myself and a few mates were sitting maybe twenty yards away on the steps of the pool hall, watching the whole thing and we couldn't believe it. It was like a scene from a movie. John was my hero again.

Mum and Reg got to the point where they never left anything to drink around the house because one of the kids would take it, which was fine for them because they hardly drank at all. But Mum always had something hidden somewhere in the house, saving up for Hogmanay, and John knew it. So John used to work out inventive ways to make them get out the alcohol. Some of these cons were very funny.

One night he came home at about two in the morning with a few mates and what appeared to be a very nice girl, called Sally. He woke up Mum and Reg and most of the household. 'Mum. This is Sally and we're gettin' married. I know I've just met her but I love her.'

Mum was ecstatic and immediately went to her cupboard. 'Oh my God, that's great. This calls for a wee celebration. Get the other kids up.' She then produced a few bottles of nice whisky she was saving for Hogmanay and we had a party.

'Alan, you move into the girls' room and Jim you'll have tae sleep on the couch tae gie the lovebirds some privacy,' Mum shouted after a few drinks.

The next day Mum got up and asked John, 'Where's Sally, son?'

John looked at her with bloodshot, glassy eyes and said, 'Who are you talking about?'

He had forgotten her name. It was only then that Mum realised she had been conned.

John had met this girl at closing time and told her, 'Hi, darling, do you fancy a wee drink when the pub shuts? I've got nice things to drink at home if you want to come with me.' It was only when she got to our place that she worked out what role she would be playing in this elaborate hoax.

Luckily for John she was a good actress and loved to drink. The two of them had a great night all round. We never saw her again. Mum cleaned up the mess and never said another word about it.

The pool hall was a meeting place. Most nights started out there. The girls would be there with the older guys, and all of our younger gang would be hanging out there too, hoping the girls noticed us.

The smoke hung heavy over the tables. The whole place smelled like an ashtray. One guy ran the place at night. He was a hard-looking bloke who wore a sort of butcher's apron. In the front pocket of the apron he kept his money that he collected from the tables, the keys to the office and to the pinball machines. He regularly had to open up the machines to free the balls that had become jammed from one of us banging and shoving the machines around.

'Hey you. If you bang that machine again I'm going to toss you out of here on your arse. Okay?'

'Yeah, yeah. It was an accident, mate. I fell on it.'

'Well, don't fall on it again or my fist will fall on your face. Understand?'

'Yeah mate, I understand. Can I get some change? This machine is a rip-off.'

The front of the hall was where the younger guys hung out. Playing pinball and watching to see who was coming in and out of the place. Towards the back, where the light was dim, the real pool players hung out.

On the weekends, as it got late, groups of people would drift off to the pubs or to parties. Some of us had nowhere to go and we would wait in the pool hall. Waiting to find out where there was a place to go. Us younger ones would get one of our mates who looked old enough to go to the bottle shop and buy us booze so we could get drunk and act like the older guys. Someone would turn up with an address of a party that none of us were invited to and the place would empty. These parties always ended up as bloodbaths.

Fights often broke out in the pool hall too. Money was usually the reason for fighting but sometimes it was over one of the girls who would be standing around in short tight skirts. Most of the blokes played better when the girls were there. Letting them take a shot or two as everyone watched as the girl leaned over the tables, struggling to keep their dresses below their waists. The girls weren't there for the pool. They would smoke cigarettes and laugh as they waited for the real party to get started later on in the pub or in the back of someone's car.

The police would visit the hall some nights and the place would suddenly go dead quiet. Everyone would stop playing at once. The bells on the machines would go silent and all eyes would be on the cops as they walked through the place trying to get their eyes to adjust to the light, squinting to see the faces in the darkness. Blokes would be running to the back door or lying down under the tables in the dark, waiting for them to leave. Sometimes someone would be dragged out swearing and kicking to the cheers of their friends. The cops knew that if they needed to find any troublemakers, this was the first place to look.

I began hanging out at the pool hall more and more and became a pretty good pool player myself. I tried to make a bit of money, beating the odd sucker who came into the place after work.

Kelly pool was the game of choice. Each player pulled a marble out of a bag. This marble had a number on it. Each number corresponded to a number on one of the pool balls. The idea was to place your small ball on the side of the table, not letting anyone else see what number was yours, along with a sum of money, whatever you'd all decided to play for. You had to pocket as many balls as you could until you got the chance to pot your own. But if someone else potted your number you rolled the small ball over and you were out of the game and had lost your money. The first person to pot his own ball took all the money.

Before too long I owned my own pool cue, which was kept behind the counter with the real pool players' things. Some nights I could hustle enough money to buy drinks. One of us always found some money for drinks.

One day I did lose but not to another pool player, to my mum. I took my pool cue home for some reason and had it sitting in my bedroom. That day I had a fight with my mum over something unrelated and I was giving her a bit of lip. Mum came into my room to have a swing at me and I made some smartarse comment. Now Mum wasn't afraid to grab herself a weapon when she was ready to fight and she looked around the room for something to belt me with. She spotted my prize possession, my pool cue, and she grabbed it and swung it towards me.

'You gie me any more o' yer lip and I'll murder you.'

Bang! She broke the cue over my head, smashing it into pieces.

I just laughed. 'Do you think that hurt me? It didn't. You can't hurt me.'

She was crying her eyes out because she couldn't hurt me. I was a bit unhappy because she had broken my pool cue. And as she ran from the room crying, I kept laughing. I had worked out a few years earlier that if Mum was really trying to hit you hard, all you had to do was laugh at her and she would fall apart. It was a bit cruel but so was life and she didn't have to smash my cue. I never bought another one and my career as a pool hustler was over.

CHAPTER TWENTY

cheap speed and beer

It sounds clichéd but the booze led us straight to harder things and we were soon chasing any drugs we could get our hands on, just like the big guys we looked up to. The older guys became noticeably more dangerous as harder drugs came into the picture. And so did we.

All my mates started out as potheads, happy to smoke weed and sit around and laugh at each other, but that didn't work for me. I was watching the older guys taking cheap speed and acid and I noticed some of them doing smack.

I wasn't a fan of weed as it made me too laidback and a bit more introverted, which was the last thing I needed in Elizabeth, so I started swallowing handfuls of cheap speed tablets, washing them down with beer or spirits.

I found that I could drink all day and night if I took these pills and as drinking was our main pastime this suited me down to the ground. Instead of getting drunk and sloppy, I would get drunk and aggressive, which was a dangerous thing for anybody who messed with me. We all started doing this, which led to us getting into fights with any strangers who walked near the shopping centre.

* * *

The gang would grab girls and some booze and head up to Uley Road Cemetery, an old place up in the hills above Elizabeth Downs. Now, Uley Road had a few benefits. It was out of the way of anything or anyone, and it was a bit scary so it was a good place to take girls because they wouldn't leave your side. We would sit up there and take drugs and drink and tell stories and make out with chicks.

A lot of the guys used to tell the girls to put out or walk home but I thought this was all wrong. I didn't want the blokes to think I was soft so I would pretend to do the same but let the girl know what was going on. We seemed to get away with it. I never really liked going up there for that reason and I thought that it was fucked up to have parties on people's graves, but I quite often ended up there. It was one of the few places we could go without being hassled or having to fight anyone. Sometimes we ended up fighting each other but not often and only when we were very drunk.

I don't think that any of us were that comfortable there, but in a group we were all much braver. Occasionally one of us would walk through the cemetery with one of the girls. It's funny how brave we were when girls were involved.

Uley Road had one road in, and one road out. I liked a place that was well lit and easy to get away from. I wouldn't go anywhere without an escape plan. Even at clubs or parties you would always find me with my back to the wall and in clear view of an exit. No one was going to sneak up on me.

I progressed from speed to acid, LSD. A lot of my friends were spending thirty dollars on a bag of weed. I thought that was a waste of time and money, so I would buy six tabs of acid and take them over the course of the next four or five days. Half a tablet on the Thursday, a whole one on the Friday, a couple on the Saturday and anything I had left on the Sunday. Then more of my mates started doing the same and things changed. Most people I had heard of who took hard drugs like this sat and listened to music and contemplated the universe, but not us, we wanted a challenge – and doing anything on acid was a challenge.

There were guys who hung around the gang who could do incredible things while they were wasted. One friend of ours played first division football for Elizabeth City and he used to take acid and play the games. So we would all take acid too and go and watch him play. We would all be amazed at how he did it, but he not only did it, he played really well. Meanwhile we were having trouble sitting in the car drinking beer, just watching him.

He was amazing. He was the team captain and the main striker, so it was not like he could avoid the play. He was right in the middle of it. He told me later it was like the whole game was in slow motion, and he had so much time to make his decisions and get himself into the right position. I don't know if I could have done it but, in saying that, many years later I used to take acid and go on stage with Cold Chisel and not tell them. They never noticed but I know it was incredibly hard to concentrate.

We would still get into fights, even on acid. We did other stupid things too. Here's the sort of smart thing we would do: we used to wait until the drugs kicked in, and we were hallucinating, then walk over to the local police station and ask directions to places that didn't exist. Just to see if they noticed that we were tripping.

'What can I do for you ... Hey, you ... Over here. What can I do for you? Over here, mate.'

'Sorry, er. Yeah, I'm looking for a place to watch er ... movies.'

'You mean a theatre. Is that what you want? Look at me when you're talking to me, son.'

'Er, yeah a theatre. I want to see a movie.'

'There isn't a movie theatre here, son. This is a police station in case you didn't notice. How old are you? I think I've seen you before, haven't I? Just stay there while I come around from behind the counter and see if I can help you. Have you been drinking or something?'

'Er … No. Er … Bye, sorry mate, I'd better go.'

'Take it easy, son. I want to talk to you a minute so just hold on there.'

'Bye, got to go, thanks mate.'

Out the door I went, running as fast as I could out of the car park and back to the safety of the shops.

The boys would be waiting, glassy-eyed and laughing. 'That's so cool. What did you say?'

'What? Er … I don't know but it was funny. Your turn.'

That progressed to some of the guys actually trying to get arrested to see how they coped being locked up while they were tripping. That still wasn't enough though; we kept pushing it further. A couple of our friends who were particularly crazy decided that they would not only get arrested but see how long it would take for them to escape.

The local police had a lot to deal with, as you can imagine, and they were known for their heavy-handed tactics. Looking back I can see why they had to be that way. A lot of the boys would fight with the cops at any chance they were given and this led to our next game. The idea was to take the acid and wait until you were peaking, hallucinating so much you hardly knew where you were, then you had to get yourself arrested. Now as I said, the police were a tad violent, so they were easily provoked. What you had to do, once they locked you in the cell, was scream and yell at them until they decided to shut you up.

They had a system whereby if someone was a difficult detainee they would take them out the back of the cells and beat them. At this point our guys would turn on them and smash them to bits. You've got to remember that these mates of ours were very hard guys and they were on very heavy drugs, so they had incredible strength and no fear. After they belted the cops they would jump the back wall of the station and run back to the shops where we were waiting. Of course, we were timing them and it became a competition to see who could do this the quickest.

The police would turn up minutes later looking for them but they would be gone, off with some girl or hidden in the boot of the car, anywhere the cops couldn't find them. This kept us amused on the odd night but more often we would go out to start trouble somewhere else, where the cops didn't know us.

I started hanging out with a guy called Mick. As we both knew loads of girls, we spent most nights getting drunk or fucked up and chatting up chicks.

Both Mick and myself were different from the other guys around the area. We were smarter. We didn't want to fight and get chased by the cops all night; we preferred to cruise around getting wasted and listening to music, singing along to the radio and pretending we were singers in bands. We both fancied the idea of getting into a band but it was Mick who was most likely to do it. He had better clothes than me and he knew more songs than me and he was more outgoing than me. He had the front to chat up the girls and win them over, but he was pushy, where I was just easygoing. He made it clear to girls what he wanted where I was just out for some fun. So a lot of the time I ended up with the girls, which suited me fine and drove Mick mad.

* * *

Night after night Mick and I would drive around looking for chicks. Talking shit and getting smashed.

'Come on, sing along. This is great.'

'I don't want to sing along with that.'

'But it's huge, Jim. This band has sold a shitload of records. It's one of the biggest selling records in history I reckon.'

'Yeah I know, but it's hippie shit. I don't mind listening to it when I'm out of it but I don't want to sing along with it.'

'Why not? It's cool.'

'If I wanted to be in a band like that I'd smoke pot.'

'You do smoke pot.'

'Just drive the car and shut up.'

'You love pot.'

'You smoke pot. I just have to drive around in the fucking car with you while you do it.'

'I hear Led Zeppelin smoke pot.'

'Just fucking look at the state of them. Hey, watch the road, would you.'

'What? I'm watching the road. Now that sounds cool.'

'No it doesn't. I like music to fucking smash you in the face. I don't want to go see a band and sit around and watch the light show. Fuck that. I want music you can fight to. Like The Who or Jerry Lee Lewis. Not Pink Floyd.'

'You like Pink Floyd.'

'I know I do, but that's not the point.'

'Hang on, man, try to look cool. And act like you're enjoying yourself for a minute.'

'Yeah, yeah.'

'Hey girls, what's happening? Are you looking for a party to go to? We got one going in the car here. Why don't you jump in?'

'Nice car. Maybe we will. Hey, cool music.'

'Shit.'

* * *

It seemed that everyone our age in and around the north of Adelaide had nothing better to do than fight. Not only in the north – there were stabbings and even shootings at the clubs and pubs around Adelaide – but it always seemed to be traced back to Elizabeth. Whether it was gangs like us from the north heading to town to start trouble or motorbike gangs based in the north fighting in the clubs, the police ended up looking for culprits in Elizabeth and most of the time they were right.

The gang would change from night to night. Some nights there were thirty or more, mostly young guys who had nothing better to do. They couldn't or didn't want to stay home. We all went out looking for something we couldn't find anywhere else, especially at home – ourselves. Sometimes it was easier to find yourself in the eyes of someone else. A young girl who saw you the way you really wanted to be. Soft, caring and even, God forbid, sensitive. Or sometimes you saw yourself in the eyes of one of your mates. Cold, angry and rebellious, ready to smash anyone that came within swinging distance. There were a few of us who were always there. We were the ones who never stayed home. We had nothing to stay home for.

Jeff was about six foot two and English and as hard as nails. But the same guy could tell if you felt alone or worried and would reach out and say things to you like, 'Jim, you don't look like the same old you tonight. Is something wrong?'

'Yeah, mate, I'm in trouble. Things aren't going well at home and I don't know what I'm doing with my life. It's all going down the drain.'

'No, mate, you're fine. You just need to shake it off.'

'But I can't, Jeff. I've got myself into huge trouble and I can't see any way out of it.'

'Well, I'm here if you want to talk about it.'

'Thanks, mate.'

'If you don't want to talk about it we could always go over to the shops and bash someone's head in. That'll cheer you up.'

Mick, on the other hand, was more like me in a lot of ways. He liked music and didn't want to fight all the time like the other guys. But he was so wounded he was even more alone. He needed no one. He could be warm one minute, then selfish and cold the next.

'Hey Jim, I thought we'd go out tonight and find a few chicks and have a good time.'

'That'd be great. Where did you want to go?'

'I don't care. How much money have you got for petrol?'

'I'm broke, but I'll get some tomorrow and slip you a bit for gas.'

'Na, fuck it, Billy's got money, I'm going to see him instead. Maybe I'll see you tomorrow.'

'Thanks, mate, that's nice of you.'

'Fuck it. I'm not running a taxi service here.'

'Yeah, fuck you too.'

It seemed the more of us that got together the more trouble we got ourselves into. The size of the gathering fed the need to be violent – with each other and anyone else. One or two of us could have a laugh or see a movie but any more than one or two and we would only want to drink and fight. Young blokes, driven by fear and testosterone with no morals and no sense of decency. It was frightening how quickly things could change. From laughing to leering; from friends to fighting. It all turned on its arse in a matter of seconds.

I have been sitting in a car laughing while everyone smoked pot and drank beer one minute and the next someone they didn't know or didn't like walked by and it became a near-death experience for one of them.

Most of the guys didn't seem to care if they really hurt someone or not. We all wore R.M. Williams riding boots with Cuban heels. I wore them because I thought they looked cool but my mates wore them because they did more damage when you jumped up and down on people's heads. Pounding them into the ground and smashing them into the gutter on the end of their boots. Leaving people bleeding and gasping for air while they laughed out loud and shouted for one another to come and join in. It was frightening.

These fights were not just about knocking people down, they were about hurting people as much as you could. Somehow that was meant to make you feel good about yourself, but it didn't make sense to me.

I don't know how people weren't killed in these fights. Maybe they were. I'm sure some of them must have been left with permanent damage but I tried not to think about this. I went along with it all, trying to get through without killing someone or being killed myself.

Eventually the gang ran out of people to fight around Elizabeth, so they would pile into cars and go into town and find people to fight there. There were always more people just like us, wanting to belt things to get rid of their frustrations, and it wouldn't take us long to find them.

Fighting wasn't the only thing we did but it did seem to take up most of our time – either fighting or bragging about our fights. In Elizabeth there were two types of people, fighters and victims, and I wasn't going to become a victim for anything or anybody.

The gang were like a pack of wolves, looking for weakness – if you looked weak, even for a second, one of them would turn on you. But most nights I was ready and struck out at one of them first. Whoever I would hit, I had to hit really hard. This normally made them all back off in fear they might be next.

There is one night I remember very clearly, when things didn't go as easily as I thought they would. I was in the coffee shop and there was a new guy hanging around the pack. He was very big and I think my mates, if I could really call them that, wanted to find out how dangerous he was. These guys were your friends while they were scared of you or needed you. If they didn't need you, you were a target. Anyway, one of them told me the guy had been talking shit about me. We'd all been drinking so it didn't take a lot for the rest of them to get themselves whipped into a frenzy.

'This fucking guy has been telling people you're scared of him. He lives near your house and he says you avoid walking near him,' one of them said, baiting me to see if I would react.

'Yeah, get him. Go on, hit him.'

Their voices were getting higher pitched, louder and more desperate. They wanted someone to get hurt. I don't know why. Maybe it was because they got hurt all their lives at home or maybe they were just animals.

'I've hardly seen this guy. I wouldn't know him if I fell over him.'

'You'd know him. You can't miss him. He's fucking big. I reckon he'd knock you out,' one of them sniggered.

'What am I supposed to be, scared because he's big? Is that it?' I was a bit but I didn't let on to them.

'Yeah. I reckon you are, and I think you're letting him talk about you because he could do you in.'

I could see their eyes turning to knives and suddenly they all looked like they were after my blood, not his. I had to protect myself. I had to fight or risk becoming a target whenever they got bored.

I walked over to him as he was standing outside the coffee shop. 'What the fuck have you been saying about me? If you want to get yourself killed, I'm happy to do it.'

He looked me straight in the eye with the look of a man who wasn't bullshitting and said, 'I haven't said anything about you. I don't talk about people I don't know.'

This seemed like the right response to me. What more could he say? So I walked away and back towards the guys. Suddenly I knew they could taste my blood.

'Why didn't you hit him? You are a fucking coward just like he says.'

I had always hated these stupid thug games. I'd seen them since I started school in Elizabeth and I knew if I wasn't careful, I was next on the menu. I had to do something. It was either fight him or fight six of these animals – my so-called mates.

I turned and walked after him. By this time, he had moved away from the shops and was heading home. The rest of the boys were walking behind me, snapping at my heels like a pack of starving jackals.

I had just about caught up to him as he started walking over the bridge that led over the railway line to Elizabeth West.

I could feel the train racing under the bridge, rattling it as I approached him. The wind was blowing and it suddenly felt colder. My heart was jumping out of my chest.

I reached up with my hand and grabbed his shoulder, spun him around and swung. I caught him hard right on the chin. He swayed, clearly stunned, but he didn't fall so I hit him again. This time even harder.

He shook his head and then turned on me. He smashed me to the ground and began to beat me senseless. This was the worst beating I had had for a long time. I couldn't help but think to myself as I lay on the ground being kicked to death that I deserved everything I got. Probably worse.

Meanwhile the jackals scattered like scared dogs, disappearing from sight, their high-pitched whining voices fading into the distance. Leaving me lying alone on the ground as he sunk another boot into my ribs. He left me bleeding, dazed and stunned.

After a minute I felt a hand pulling me up. It was him. I expected to be hit again but instead he helped me to my feet and stood and looked at me.

'I told you I didn't want to fight you but you pushed me.'

I felt even dumber than I looked. I was an idiot and I knew it.

'I live just down the road from you. I'm going home now. So do you want to walk with me?'

I'd never been belted then helped out by the person who beat the shit out of me before so this felt a bit weird.

'Yeah, why not.'

We walked along saying very little to each other.

'Sorry for starting you,' I muttered quietly.

'Didn't hurt a bit.' He laughed as he looked at me.

'That makes me feel a lot better.'

I had learned a big lesson. I would make my own decisions and do what I thought was right from then on, no matter what the consequences were. I'd rather get beaten for doing the right thing than the wrong. It was as simple as that. I never picked another fight in my life.

There were so many nights I sat alone, no longer afraid of where I came from but of what I was becoming. I was becoming just like the people in my darkest memories from Scotland. The same dreams that haunted me as a child were becoming a reality as a young man, twisting me around so much I wanted to die.

There was nothing for me at home. There never really had been. Home was a place that no one wanted to be. Mum stayed because she had to. Our home had been shattered and put back together and was in the process of being shattered again. Mum was a human wrecking ball when she had lost interest in something or someone. She had held it together long enough for us to basically get through school and now she was ready to move on again. Life was crumbling around us again but this time she would not be picking up the pieces. We would have to do it ourselves.

She and Reg fought and there were other people around all the time. There was nothing for me to stay there for, so I wanted to leave. I hadn't worked out where I was going or what I would do. All I knew was I felt better around a gang of young guys who drank too much and ran out of control than I did near my parents and home.

There were nights when I walked through the shopping centre and there were no crowds of guys or girls hanging around, just rain falling on the footpaths where I'd seen so much blood spilled, and the wind howling around the shopfront windows. I wondered how long this life would go on before I would be made to pay for everything I had done wrong. I felt I was constantly running, only just keeping one step in front of everything that had haunted me in my nightmares.

Most of the guys had families or jobs and spent most of the week away from the shops but I didn't. They would stay at home with their mums or girlfriends and then on the weekend come out and turn into some sort of animal, but I felt like an animal all the time. I didn't want to be at home and I had nowhere else to go. I would sit alone on the steps of the pool hall waiting for someone to turn up, anyone who could distract me from my own thoughts.

Some nights other guys, even worse than me, would walk through the shopping centre. Drunk and dazed, looking for someone to hurt, they would walk from the pool hall to the coffee shop until they found someone to let their pain out on. I would be sitting in the shadows, watching as the police dragged them into paddy wagons, beating them with truncheons. I couldn't help but see that this was what they wanted, to pay for their fucked up lives in their own blood and misery.

I would pull back even further into the shadows, ashamed, not wanting them to see me and know that I saw their pain. Then I would walk over the bridge and down the street to our house and sneak in so no one noticed me or spoke to me. I had nothing to say to anyone.

Some mornings, walking home just before sun-up, I would see the milkman delivering milk to the houses on his route. As the sun came over the horizon and shone a little light on the dark road, I would wait until he had gone out of sight and nip in and grab myself a bottle and drink it on the way home. I knew it wasn't the best thing to do but if you were broke and really thirsty, surely it couldn't be such a sin to steal one bottle? I kept telling myself that I would go back to the same house on another night and give them a bottle back but I never seemed to get around to it.

It was early 1972 when I had to run away from home to go to the Sunbury Rock Festival. My folks were trying to be tough with me by stopping me going again but I was way beyond that. They had no control over me by then. I snuck out my bedroom window and headed to Melbourne with Linda and her mates. They had a full car but they squeezed me into the back of their station wagon along with all the camping gear. I lay across their stuff for eight hours or so, smoking joints and drinking beer with them, and by the time we arrived at Sunbury they were all shit-faced, as was I. We staggered out of the car park and towards the gate of the festival.

Now, the reason I wanted to go was to see Billy Thorpe. He was my hero. He played louder and faster than anyone else in the country. So I was really excited at the prospect of seeing him in such a great setting. I planned to watch a few bands that I liked over the weekend and generally have a good time until Thorpie came on stage on the Sunday. The best laid plans and all that ...

We walked into the festival and found a place to set up camp and also a place to watch all the bands from. We were all organised. It was my first rock festival and I was ready to watch every band that was playing. Then one of Linda's mates pulled out a handful of pills that I found out later were Mandrax, a very strong sleeping pill that was taken in those days for fun. When you mixed it with beer very strange things happened. But they were all taking a handful or so of these tablets and they gave me the same.

Then we decided to check out what was going on at the festival, so we went for a walk. The Sunbury Festival site had a lovely river running through it where people swam naked, as you do at rock festivals. So we were down by the river admiring the view when the pills started to take effect. I sort of remember the whole world slipping into slow motion and it felt like my tongue had swollen up and I couldn't talk. 'So far so good,' I thought. Then things took another sharp turn sideways and the last thing I remember was slipping down the bank and into the river. A veil of blackness covered me and then nothing.

I woke up in a tent. I didn't know where I was but as I looked around the tent I saw people strapped into beds next to me. It took a while but my head cleared and I realised I was in some sort of hospital tent. I looked around and saw a sign saying 'Buoyancy Tent'. Now I had seen this tent when I arrived and knew it was a place where people who had taken too many drugs or were having a bum trip went to be looked after. I wasn't having a bum trip; in fact, I'd had a great sleep and felt refreshed and ready to rock.

I got up out of bed while no one was watching and left the tent, dancing out so it looked like I had just danced into the wrong tent by accident. No one noticed, so off I went to find the gang. I walked back to where Linda and her friends were watching the show; they were all in various stages of falling apart, staring blankly at the stage. I don't think that any of them could even see the stage. No one knew I was missing. No one cared anyway. I could have drowned and I doubt that Linda and her mates would have even remembered that they had brought me with them. But the good news was, just as I got there Thorpie walked on stage to start his set. It was a perfect night. I had a great sleep, got hammered and got to see my hero Billy Thorpe. It was a perfect weekend really. Then we drove home.

who had hit who

On one of those cold and wet nights when none of the gang were hanging around the shops, I was sitting in the coffee shop waiting to see if anyone would show up. The Elizabeth Centre coffee shop served bad coffee and bad food to a clientele that changed from families and shoppers through the day to packs of young hooligans who came out looking for trouble at night. We used to drink the coffee and listen to the jukebox when it was too cold to hang around the corners and the car park. The pool hall and this place were all that was open after five-thirty.

None of my mates made it. Pink Floyd was on the jukebox. The sound of the cash register being tallied up for the night blended with the music, drowning out the snoring and mumbling of the only other person in the shop. This was one of my brother's friends, a bloke I'll call Steve. He had had a big afternoon and was sitting in a corner with a bottle of beer in front of him. Steve was the size of a house and looked like he was made to fight, so even though booze was not allowed in the shop, nobody was going to stop him bringing it in. By the time I got there Steve was nodding off over his beer. He had a bad reputation around

Elizabeth for his explosive temper and everyone who knew him gave him a wide berth when he was in this state.

I wasn't scared of him because he was a mate of John's and treated me like his little brother. Anyway, tonight I thought he was way beyond fighting so I wasn't worried. But he was starting to stir. Slowly, like a giant waking from a deep sleep. Mumbling under his breath. He was not happy.

'You fuckin' … I don't care who you think you … I told no … Shut up and –' It didn't make any sense. Occasionally he would shout out at someone who he thought was sitting opposite him. There was no one there. He was best left alone and although I wasn't scared of him, I didn't really want to be there if he exploded. I got up to leave.

'Bye, Jim,' he said without looking up.

I decided to walk over to the pub and see who was there. As I walked I put on my jacket. The rain was starting to come down quite heavily and I zipped it up to my chin. My leather jacket had saved my life on many a night. It had saved me from broken glass when I'd been knocked to the floor fighting and it had kept out the cold when I had nowhere to sleep. A good leather jacket was a must for a young guy growing up in Elizabeth.

I walked past the pool hall and went to cross the car park. Through the rain I saw three or four guys get out of a beaten-up old Holden and head towards me. Now these guys didn't look like they were out for a late-night cup of tea and cake. They were looking for someone to terrorise and I was the only one around so I guess they settled for me. I turned around as quick as I could and made a beeline for the coffee shop where there was at least one person who might help me. I knew if big Steve was awake I would be all right.

Steve was still in the corner when I ran in. He knew there was something going on straight away. He looked up and kicked away his chair. He was drunk and out of his mind but instinctively he knew that there was trouble to be had, and he wanted to be involved in it. I don't think he cared who it was with, he just wanted to fight someone.

The guys from the car were no boy scouts, they were big ugly motherfuckers, but when they saw Steve start towards them they bolted for the safety of their car. But the car wouldn't start. I could see the terror in their eyes as Steve and I turned up outside the door of the choking car. They locked the doors as quickly as they could and for a second there was a look of relief on their faces.

This was enough for me and I laughed a little at how quickly the tide had turned, but scaring these guys was not enough for Steve. They kept trying to get the engine to turn over but it wouldn't; they'd flooded it. Steve was at the door and in one movement he turned the beer bottle in his hand around and smashed it straight through the side window, into the face of the bloke sitting in the passenger seat.

'You're fucking mine, mate,' he screamed at the top of his voice. Blood started spurting out of the guy's neck. The bottle had broken going through the window and was now lodged in his throat.

I tried to pull him off but Steve kept stabbing repeatedly until I thought the guy was dead, and then he turned to go around the car to get the driver.

'Right,' he bellowed, 'your fucking turn, mate.'

The driver was panic-stricken and kept turning the key, hoping the car would start and get him out of there.

Steve staggered around the car to the driver's door just as the car roared into life. The driver managed to jam it into gear and skidded out of the car park, jumping the kerb and side-swiping a telegraph pole as they fled.

As quickly as it all had happened it was over and once again I could hear the rain falling on the ground around me. It was like waking up from a nightmare. I was covered in sweat and hyperventilating and my heart was pounding like a jack hammer.

Steve turned to me, wiped the blood from his face and quietly said, 'Let's go, I'll buy you a beer.'

He walked off into the night laughing to himself. I don't know how much damage Steve did in that attack; I never heard another thing about it. But I kept as far away from him as I could from then on.

A couple of years later, Steve was jailed for murder over an unrelated fight where he went too far and someone died. I wasn't surprised and I'm almost certain that wasn't the first person he killed. He was an absolute psychopath, but he was just one of many psychopaths we hung around with.

The local bike club, like a lot of other gangs, was filled with thugs and criminals. But around Elizabeth that didn't mean that you ruled the streets. There were as many thugs and criminals walking around the streets dressed in suits and the poor bikie gang regularly got a hiding from the Elizabeth guys, fuelled up on the same booze and speed that the bikies were on, only the non-bikies were much nastier and had less to live for. My brother and his mates used to get hammered and head to Salisbury where the bikies had their clubhouse and attack them with knives and baseball bats and anything else that came to hand.

One night I remember there was a huge fight after a couple of the bikies were beaten senseless in the city by some Elizabeth boys. They got as many of their mates together as they could and rode into the Elizabeth shopping centre en masse, ready to kill anybody that was there. Unfortunately for them, we were expecting them and lay in ambush waiting for them to arrive.

They rode in full of bravado and booze, only to be met by a big mob of young guys, ranging from the ages of fifteen to thirty, all drunk and ready to make names for themselves. The way out was cut off by cars and the bikies had no escape. As they rode in, the boys opened the boots of their cars and produced bats, clubs, knives and bottles and ran at the bikies, going berserk. They bashed them, burned their bikes and stomped their heads into the concrete. Then drove off before the police could arrive.

It was the bloodiest battle I have ever been involved in or seen for that matter. We ran away from the shops to the sounds of sirens and bikes screaming in the night. A constant stream of police cars and ambulances passed by as we hid in the bushes, no more than two or three hundred yards away.

That night went down in local folklore. But unless you were actually there, you couldn't have imagined how brutal it really was. I was very afraid and felt lucky to be alive but I couldn't tell my friends. Instead we all bragged about who had hit who and how much damage we had done. 'Did you see the size of that guy I king hit? He was the size of a fridge. Ha ha. He went down like a sack of shit.'

There were guys who hung with us who didn't fight all the time but they were all up to no good of some sort. A favourite thing to do was stop at the house of someone we didn't know in the middle of the night and lift their car up. This was something we would do when we were very drunk and very bored. We obviously picked a house with a small car. Then we'd put it in a place that it was impossible to get out of. The car would end up turned sideways in the driveway. Impossible to drive out. Small things amuse small minds.

Another thing that kept us amused was the drive-in movie shows. On many a night we would all go to the Shandon Drive-in to see movies and have a bit of fun. Quite often we didn't watch a lot of the movie. Instead we would drink and fool around with girls.

We would wait until a few cars were going in and then the guy working didn't have time to think too much.

'Right you guys, get in the boot and shut up.'

'But it's my car, I don't want to get in the boot.'

'But you've got no money to get in. I have, so you're in the boot.'

'Fuck off. This is my car. You give me the money and you get in the boot.'

'I bought the beer as well. So I've got to buy the beer and give you the money to get in?'

'I've got the car. Do you think cars run on nothing? I had to put petrol in.'

'All right, I'll get in the boot but I'm not sitting in the back. You never get to see anything with your big fuckin' head in front of you.'

'Just shut up and pull your feet in so I can shut the boot or we'll miss the start of the movie.'

A couple of us would jump the fence and meet up with the car inside; others would be crammed into the boot while one guy sat in the front and drove in. It must have looked strange. I don't think normal people went to the drive-in by themselves. A stream of cars would be lined up to pay to get in.

'One, please.'

'You want just one ticket to get in?'

Beep, beep! The car behind us was in a hurry. 'Hurry up, we're going to miss the start.'

'That's what I said, didn't I? One ticket.'

'What's that noise I heard in the back?'

'Nothing mate. Just my shockers. They're buggered. One ticket please. And hurry up or I'll miss the start.'

Beep, beep! 'Come on, get a move on would you?'

'Yeah, all right then. In you go, but I'm not stupid you know.'

'Thanks mate. If you weren't, you wouldn't be working here would you?'

The car would speed through the gate and find a place to park up near the kiosk so we could buy ice-cream and chips. Then the rest of the gang would come walking across in front of the cars already parked and pile in. Sometimes it was too packed in the car so we would sit on the ground around the car or reverse the car in and lie on the boot and drink beer. No one ever said a word to us.

While I was still at school, I worked part-time in the local garage pumping gas. I thought it was pretty cool to actually make some money but I didn't see a future in it unless I owned the oil company, which was never going to happen. But I did make enough money working there to buy my first car.

Reg had already taught me to drive in his almost brand new Toyota Corolla. He was really proud of that car so he would give me driving lessons, hoping that I was growing up and driving might make me more responsible. It didn't help. I didn't get my driver's licence straight away either. I got it after three tries. The same guy took me for the test all three times and I didn't get any better after three attempts. I think he felt if he didn't give it to me I would never get a driver's licence, or worse, he would have to get in a car with me again. So I was ready to rock and all I needed was to get my own set of wheels, and it would be good if they had a car attached to them.

As luck would have it, a teacher who came into the garage asked me if I knew anyone who wanted to buy a cheap car.

'It's really good,' he said. 'I'm only selling it because I have to move away for work.'

'I'll take it.'

I made the deal right there and then and bought my first car. It was an old Morris Oxford. I paid twenty-five dollars for it and it had a full tank of gas and six months' registration. It was a good deal, as far as I could see. What could go wrong?

He brought it over to me at the garage that afternoon and as soon as I finished work I was cruising around the shops. I thought I was so cool. All the guys around there had cars like EHs or FBs – things that sounded really cool. Morris Oxford didn't have the same ring. They drove hot rods with straight line gear shifts and loud exhausts and even racing strips across the bonnet. My car went about thirty-five miles an hour, with the pedal flat to the floor, downhill, with the wind behind it. It didn't look very cool and I don't think any amount of GT striping would have made it look any better or faster, but it was mine and I loved it.

Owning my own car meant that I didn't have to rely on anyone to get around anymore. I was free. I felt like Easy Rider with the wind blowing through my hair, but that was only because I couldn't wind the windows up. I could see this was going to be a problem in the rain but I would burn that bridge when I came to it. In the meantime I had to pray it wouldn't get cold or wet. I'm not sure the wipers worked either.

That night, myself and a few friends decided to go to the drive-in in my new car. There was a movie we all wanted to see called *A Clockwork Orange* and it was on about twenty miles away at the Gepps Cross drive-in. So we scored some acid, took one each and headed off to the drive-in.

It was all going well, we were nearly at the drive-in when we started to hit a little traffic.

'Take it easy, Jim, there might be cops around here,' one of my mates said.

By this time, things were starting to look a little different because of the blotting paper acid we had consumed. So I decided I'd better slow down to about thirty miles an hour. The guys were all singing and yelling out and generally having a good time. I put my foot onto the brake pedal and applied some pressure – nothing.

'Hey guys, I don't want you to panic but I think the brakes are fucked.'

Everybody in the car went silent.

I applied a little more pressure, still nothing.

'Stop fucking around, Jim,' one of them said but I was concentrating too much on driving to answer.

I slammed my foot to the floor – nothing at all.

'You're going to have to help, lads,' I yelled, trying to slow the car down by shifting back through the gears. Soon we were going slow enough to pull off the road.

'Jump out and stop us, boys.'

They all jumped out of the car and we managed to stop it.

We sat there scratching our heads for a while. None of us knew anything about cars so we just sat, saying nothing for a minute or two. I had bought this car that very day; you would think that the vendor would mention something as important as the brakes being shot.

'Maybe he didn't know the brakes were gone when he sold it to me,' I said, shaking my head in disbelief.

'Yeah sure, Jim. He saw you coming, pal. I hope you know where to find him.'

'Right, guys, we need to work this out,' I said. 'I guess we leave the car here and hitch home.' But the drugs had kicked in. 'Or we could keep going without brakes and you guys stop the car.'

We took a quick vote and decided to keep going.

'We'll be fine, boys. Brakes aren't that important. I'll drive slowly and when we need to stop you guys jump out and get in front of it and stop it.'

We made it just in time to see the movie. We had decided that none of us were going to jump the fence because we needed everyone to stop the car. We did get some very strange looks when we pulled up at the ticket gate, with all the guys falling out of the car, laughing and throwing themselves in front of the moving car. Surprisingly, they said nothing and let us go straight in. My friends, the brakes, got back in the car and we cruised into a spot and settled in to watch the movie.

We loved the movie, though it reminded us of ourselves a bit too much.

'We're not that bad are we?' I asked as we left but no one answered me.

We spoke like they did in the movie for months after that night. It must have driven our parents mad.

'Well, well, my old Babooshka. What have thee for brekky my lovely?'

'Hey you, I'm yer mother. I don't like it when you speak tae me like that.'

'Oh apoly logy my old mumsy. Serve it up now and don't make me tolchock you.'

'I don't know what you're sayin' but I don't like the sound of it. So speak English or don't talk at aw.'

'Just hand over the pretty polly and I'll be gone.'

'Get oot, now!'

'Enough of this chumble, I'm offskie my lovely.'

Anyway, it was time to leave and we set out on the big adventure of getting home. I dropped off two of the guys, then the other two got out together and I was left alone in the car. I had, of course, not taken into consideration that I would have no brakes at all when I got home. The acid had affected my judgement a little.

So I drove very slowly and turned into my street and then into the driveway of Mum's house. It was then I realised I couldn't stop. In front of me was Reg's Corolla, and I didn't want to hit it. So I turned the wheel and slammed the car into a tree that was in the middle of my mum's front yard. It looked like there was a cloud of steam coming from under the bonnet, but it might just have been the drugs. The car had stopped and I was still breathing. I shook my head, turned off the engine and went inside.

It had been a big night and I never even thought about it again until morning, when Reg came in and woke me up to see if I was okay.

'What the hell happened, son?'

I got up and had a quick look outside and then at myself in the mirror. 'I'm fine but that car turned out to be a bit of a dud, Dad.'

Then I got back into bed and went back to sleep. That was the end of my first car. It lasted one evening. But it was worth every cent I paid for it. We had a great night and nobody died.

* * *

My sister Linda started going out with a guy who rode a motorbike. I'm not sure if he was a bikie but he rode a Kawasaki 900 and he was a scumbag. He wasn't real smart but what he lacked in intellect he made up for in stupidity. Also, to top things off, he had absolutely no social skills that any of the family could see. He was a dropkick. Linda fell for him, hook, line and sinker. This was the guy she had been waiting for all her life, apparently.

Mum hated him, and even Reg, who gave everybody a chance, pleaded with her to break up with him. The rest of us just put up with him. So after going through a very quick courtship they moved in together. This went well; they only came to blows a few times. So they decided to stay together a little longer. This went smoothly enough for Linda to make an announcement to us after a few months.

'I'm getting married,' she said with a tear in her slightly black eye.

'Are you fucking serious?' was the general reaction from her siblings.

But she was certain. 'Come on, guys. This is it. He's the one for me. I love him.'

Mum had been waiting all her life for one happy marriage in the family. To all of us, it seemed she would have to keep waiting. This was not going to be it.

So the wedding was arranged. Mum and Reg hired a hall in Port Adelaide and the wedding went ahead as planned. By now Linda and this fellow were getting to know each other better – but regardless of this, they decided to go ahead with the ceremony.

We all got dressed up in our Sunday best and got ready to party like there was no tomorrow. The party was big, and in true Scottish tradition there was drinking and dancing and fighting. Not necessarily in that order. Mum cried, Reg hoped for the best, as he always did, and the rest of us took advantage of the free booze and tried to have as great a party as we could. We all wanted the best for Linda and if this really made her happy, so be it.

Linda looked beautiful in white, with white flowers setting off her long dark hair that hung down to her waist. Around her neck was the beautiful cross laden with rubies, given to her by her dead step-great-grandmother, still walking the earth for some reason. This was the cross that would protect Linda for the rest of her life. This was the perfect day. She threw her bouquet to her friends at the end of the night and drove off with her husband to spend the first night of eternity with the man she loved. I guess the cross didn't see this guy coming.

Unfortunately, the man she loved had drunk way too much. A few miles down the road he stopped the car and dragged her out by her beautiful flowing hair with the flowers in it. He wrapped it around a barbed-wire fence and proceeded to beat her within an inch of her life. He then ripped the cross off her neck. No one is sure whether he took it with him or threw it into a field but it was never seen again. Linda was left alone and bleeding, draped across the barbed wire like an angel at Gallipoli, unconscious. She was found a few hours later and taken to hospital. She's never been the same wild girl since that night.

CHAPTER TWENTY-TWO

white trash

I spent most of my time thinking about girls. Well, girls and music. I never thought I could play music for a living. I just wanted to get into a band and escape from the day to day boredom of my life. Every day was the same as the last in Elizabeth. We waited all week for the weekend when we could go wild. But if I was in a real band, every night would be the weekend and there would be girls whenever I wanted them.

These were just dreams. I was going to be trapped in the life I had until I worked it out, died or was locked up.

I was heavily influenced by the music my brother John had played me, so I was way ahead of the other kids my own age. When they were listening to The Archies, I was listening to Jimi Hendrix.

An old school friend of mine called Malcolm lived around the corner from the Elizabeth Fields shops at that time. We were trying our best to learn about life. We were also trying our best to get drunk and to get laid as often as we could without getting killed. We were both listening to as much music as we could take in.

Malcolm wasn't part of the gang that fought and made targets of themselves at the centre; he was too nice for that. His house seemed to be a lot better than mine, and his family seemed more stable. But, like me, he spent way too much time getting very drunk and throwing up so he must have had his own problems.

On many a night we would end up back at his house after drinking too much, playing records until we passed out. He had the stereo of doom, a great reel-to-reel tape machine that he used to copy all my records onto. It was obviously his dad's but he didn't mind us using it. Malcolm and his brother were listening to nice music until they met me. I changed their musical tastes drastically.

I used to turn up at Malcolm's house with an armful of records, take off whatever was on the turntable and say, 'Listen to this' and put on 'Death Walks Behind You', 'War Pigs' or 'Easy Livin''.

I was like the local DJ. My collection was made up of stuff I'd found or stolen from my brother. Free, Deep Purple, Grand Funk Railroad (a particular favourite of mine at the time), Humble Pie, Black Sabbath. Depending on how many I could sneak away from John's collection and how many I wanted to carry. Some nights, I might have Atomic Rooster, Uriah Heep and Led Zeppelin, depending on what caught my eye at the time I was leaving. My records could easily wake up the neighbourhood and quite often did.

I wanted to play bass like Andy Fraser and scream like Mark Farner. And I wanted my band to be heavy, so heavy it made my parents sick. In fact, made all parents sick. That was my plan. And to try to make that a reality, I would sing at the top of my voice along with Paul Rodgers, Stevie Marriott, Mark Farner and Ozzie while I was playing records in Malcolm's living room. Most nights we would have a bunch of guys with us, a pile of beer and a few girls. If we had no money, which was quite often, we would drink any beer that Malcolm's folks left in the fridge. Then we would crank up his stereo until it nearly exploded.

'How come your dad never makes us turn it down?' I would ask while rummaging through the fridge looking for more to drink.

'He's not here a lot and even if he was he wouldn't mind.'

'What about drinking his beer?'

'That's okay with him too.'

I guess his parents were happy we were doing this at their house instead of in a paddock somewhere. Malcolm was my best mate for a long time. I used to escape the shit that was my real life and have fun with him and his brother. They were normal blokes and we shared a lot of laughs. Many a night he found me asleep on his front doormat. I had passed out while I was knocking on the door, trying to get him up to let me in.

Mick and I were driving around one night, looking for something to do or to destroy, when we ended up at a dance at the Elizabeth Community Centre. This was a place we only went as a last resort. The community centre had nothing going for it. It consisted of an entrance hallway (so brightly lit by fluorescent lights that no one looked good), where you could buy soft drinks, which led into the bigger room where the dance was held. This room had no stage, no dance floor and no real lighting. The other essential ingredient that was needed for a dance was atmosphere. The community centre had very little. The more lights that were turned off, the better it looked. It probably looked best when it was shut.

Anyway, the local community group held dances here every Saturday night. Sometimes they had a band but most nights someone played DJ, playing bad music that no one wanted to hear. The only people who went were dorks, unless they were like us and desperate or looking for trouble. A few girls would hang around at the dance though, which is why we were there.

But this night there was a band playing. And the singer, as fate would have it, was the same singer who had been in my school band, the guy with the Ziggy Stardust obsession. Anyway, he was sick or drunk and couldn't sing that night. He missed a lot of gigs this guy.

We tried to talk Mick into singing. He was the extrovert of the gang and we all thought he was the guy who was cut out to be a rock star.

'Go on, man, sing with the band. This is your chance.'

'Fuck that, I'd rather get drunk somewhere. I'm out of here.' The reality was he was too lazy to get up with the band. He took off in his car with a girl, leaving me stranded.

Now I'd had a few drinks and somehow got talked into singing. I was probably nearly as lazy as Mick but I'd drunk more than him. Enough to get me up there with the band. I stood with my back turned to the audience and started to sing along. The guys knew lots of songs by my favourite bands, so I knew some of the words. What I didn't know I just mumbled. No one was paying that much attention so it didn't really matter.

After a while we had a few people watching us. Even cheering us on. But they were mostly our mates.

I sang on and off for a set or two, singing every song in my repertoire. There weren't many songs in my repertoire, by the way. Come to think of it, I didn't know what a repertoire was. But I sang every song I knew; in fact, I think I sang most of them twice. The gig was a huge success. All five people watching liked us.

I had taken a very small step up the social ladder in Elizabeth that night and I knew it and it felt good. A couple of girls who wouldn't speak to me before suddenly thought I was cool and wanted to hang out with me.

'Are you coming here again next week?'

'Yeah, maybe. The band want me to sit in with them again if I'm not singing somewhere else.'

As if I had somewhere else to sing. This band thing was pretty good. I might have to do it more often.

Mick turned up later and had the shits because he wasn't the centre of attention and left soon after. But I'd made some new friends and I decided that I wanted to be in their band. Luckily for me they wanted me to join too.

This was really my first band. With the addition of Michael Smith on bass we became Tarkus, the band I played with until I joined Cold Chisel. We weren't that good but it was our training ground. Michael and I would go on to have careers in the music industry; the others really never made it past the garage band stage.

We started doing the odd show at local community halls. I'm sure we were shit but we thought we were destined for greatness – as long as you could be great doing bad covers of other people's songs.

For years my brother John smuggled me into gigs. 'Hey Jim, come and carry my drums for me and you can get up and sing at the end of the night. You might learn something if you're lucky.'

So that's what I did. I would help him carry his drums and I would get up and sing with them at the end of the night. In the meantime, I would drink all the free drinks I could get from the staff and anyone else at the shows.

By the end of the night I would be pissed and singing on the stage. Girls seemed to like me when I sang and I had more confidence when I drank. This would become a wild roller-coaster ride that I would be riding for a long, long time but I liked it and I wasn't jumping off.

'Hey Jim, get off your lazy arse and carry my drums back out to the truck. That was the deal remember.'

'Yeah, right away John.'

I would stagger to the stage and do some work for a minute or else he wouldn't let me go with him the next time. I knew a good thing when I saw one.

John and his band would take me back to their band house and we would drink and take drugs until the sun came up, every night of the week. The house was in the suburb of Paradise, which was quite fitting when I think about what went on there. The band were all good musicians who loved soul music and real rock-and-roll. Unfortunately for them this was not how they made their money. They had to play the hits of the time and the odd Chuck Berry song to audiences who never cared that much until they were pissed and trying to impress each other. By this time, they danced to the band but the only thing they had in mind was who they would be sleeping with that night. Fortunately, by that time, the band had the same thing on their minds. So quite often they would end up at Paradise with a car full of girls and pockets full of drugs. And I would be there with them.

They played great music to me, each of them taking the time to add songs to my listening repertoire. It was as if each of these guys played a part in my music education.

Life was good and I wanted to get into my own band, a real band, not like the one I was in, but a band where you got paid to play and girls followed you around and wanted to be with you. Just like one of John's bands. I didn't think I would make a lot of money, but I didn't care. I just wanted to be out of control, like him.

I was getting better at singing too. John turned me on to an album by Edgar Winter's White Trash called *Roadwork*. I listened to it every night for a year. I was like a sponge. Every note they sang I copied. I learned how to scream from the singers on this record. Johnny and Edgar Winter, Jerry La Croix, these were the singers I wanted to be like, wild Texan and Louisiana boys who did whatever they wanted and screamed like banshees. They played loud and fast and soulful and I made up my mind that when I found a band, this was how we would play. Well, loud and fast would do. It might take a bit longer to find some soul. Especially when you didn't know where to look or what you were looking for.

CHAPTER TWENTY-THREE

what are we going to do now?

Like most young men, Mick and I were obsessed with sex, but unlike most young men our age, where we lived there was no shortage of sex to be had.

The girls we knew came from the same sort of homes we did and all they wanted to do was escape them and get some control in their lives and they thought that sex gave them that control. Unfortunately, we thought the same thing.

We were constantly looking for girls who would make us feel good about ourselves, even if it was just for a second. Most of the guys were too screwed up to be able to talk to girls and this led to more fighting than fucking but I found it easier to talk to girls than I did to guys. Girls didn't want to beat people senseless. They just wanted to feel someone cared about them, even if it was only for a short time, and I was the same.

So whenever we were at parties or the pub or even the centre, and all the guys would be beating their chests and getting too drunk to speak, I always found myself talking to the girls. This seemed a much better thing to do than smashing beer bottles into other guys' faces. I had found my calling.

* * *

'Where you going?'

'None of your business, Mum,' Mick said as he got to the door. I was already sitting in his car, waiting for him.

'You better be home early tonight. You've got work tomorrow and you better go or your dad will kill you.'

'That drunken old bastard wouldn't even know if I was alive.'

'Don't talk that way about your dad.'

'Why?'

'Your dad loves you, Mick. He just has a few problems.'

'Yeah, sure. Fuck him.'

'Have a good night, son, and be good. You two look after each other, okay boys?'

'Yeah, yeah, yeah.'

Mick ran across the lawn and into the waiting car.

'What are we going to do tonight?' Mick asked.

'I've got no money again and I don't get paid until Thursday.' This was becoming the usual answer from me. Just like my dad really: I got paid and the next day it was gone. And I had to make do until the next payday came around.

'I just stole fifty bucks from my mum's purse. Let's get some acid,' Mick said as he wound down the car window and turned up the music on the radio.

'Get It On' by T-Rex screamed across the night as he spun the wheels of his car and we left his mum waving at us in a cloud of dust.

His mum always looked a little sad to me. She was sweet but didn't have a clue what her son got up to once he left the front door. I don't think many of our parents really knew what went on. I don't think many of them really cared either.

It was like getting a weight lifted off your shoulders when you walked out of the door. No more nagging and lectures, no more yelling. You were free to do what you wanted and answer to no one. Free to tear apart the town or anything else that got in your way.

'Gino's going to be at the pool hall and he has some really good acid. He'll sell us some.'

Gino was a mad Italian lad. He was the only Italian, in fact the only non-British guy, hanging around with us. We used to drive into the city to fight with the Greeks and Italians on the weekends. But Gino had to work really hard to get accepted. He was crazy. He would dress like the manikins in John Martin's, the local department store. Then he'd sneak in and stand in the windows with the other manikins. We would all be standing around outside laughing. When he got bored he would grab something he wanted from the window display and walk straight out. He was so brazen he never got caught. He could steal anything that wasn't nailed down.

One night he came driving through the car park at the shops, standing on the roof of his car. His car, by the way, was an S series Valiant, a very woggy-looking car but it looked good on him. This night he had rigged up ropes to steer the car. He was funny wild and all the chicks liked him. And he knew where to get good drugs. He could fight too and wasn't scared of anybody.

Tonight would be a typical night in Elizabeth. Get a few drinks into us, take any drugs we could find. Fight with anybody we didn't know that dared to walk through the shops and try and find some chicks.

We never stayed home. Most of us had to escape something at home. Who wants to see their mum and dad fighting every night?

So it was out to the shops, get as mindless as we could and find someone to kill.

* * *

It was after one of the shows at the community centre that Kim, a girl who had been a friend of ours for a while, turned up. Now we didn't go out or anything but we were part of the same gang. I don't think we'd ever thought about each other all that much before that night. We just got on well and had a good laugh together and liked to get drunk with all our friends.

Somehow at the end of the night it ended up just me and her.

'Shall I walk up the street with you?' I asked ever so casually.

'Yeah, that'll be good.' She smiled at me as if she knew what I was thinking.

I don't know if she was so impressed by the show that she could no longer keep her hands off me. I knew I hadn't been struck by a bolt of lightning when I looked into her eyes. I suspect that it was that we both had just drunk a little too much. And in the heat of the moment, heat being the operative word here, we ended up getting way too close.

We made out behind the shops at Elizabeth Field. Somewhere between the milk crates and the security doors. It wasn't romantic and the earth didn't move for either of us. We did it because that's what we thought we were supposed to do. We straightened up our clothes and then started to walk home.

We were both a bit awkward and didn't really know what to say to each other, especially after what had just happened. So there wasn't a lot of talking going on.

We passed a place that sold motorbikes and I turned and said, 'I'm going to get enough money to buy one of those one day and then I'm out of here for good. This place is a hole and I feel like I'm dying here.'

'I want to get out of here too. We could go together.'

We both knew that I would never be able to afford to buy a bike. The only way we were leaving was on foot and it wouldn't be together.

Kim was a good girl and I got the feeling that we weren't that much different from each other. Just like me she drank hoping it would make her feel better about herself. But in the end it didn't. Like me she drank until she felt nothing at all. We both stayed out as late as we could because we didn't have anything to go home for. And like me she thought that if someone liked you for a little while it was better than nothing at all.

'Goodnight Kim. That was fun. Maybe I'll see you later.'

'Yeah it was fun. Goodnight.'

Next time I saw Kim she told me she had missed her period. I was shocked.

'What's a period?' I asked. Only joking. Even back then I made jokes when I was panicking. It was more like, 'Oh my god. What are we going to do now?'

It wasn't like I shouldn't have expected this to happen at some point. I had been sleeping with different girls every night, sometimes two or three girls in the same night, and using no protection. But I was shocked anyway.

I had heard stories about girls trying to trap boys by getting pregnant. A few of my mates who hung around the centre shops had married girls because they thought it was the right thing to do. It never worked out.

Kim wasn't like that. This was no trap. She was as shocked as me. We didn't want to get married, we didn't even want to go steady. I'm not that sure we even wanted to fool around that much to start with. It just happened. We were both totally unprepared to deal with something as important as a baby. We were only about sixteen.

My first thought was to run away. If I ran away, maybe I wouldn't have to deal with it. But I couldn't run away. I had nowhere to go. I had tried to run away from home and it didn't help that much. But running is something that I became good at. I have been running all my life. The thing I've learned about running is that as soon as you stumble or stop, whatever is behind you will catch up to you or at least get close enough to grab onto you. Then the trouble starts.

We didn't speak for a while. I think we were both hoping it would go away. But nothing goes away until you deal with it.

I would see Kim out with the gang and she would look pale and her stomach was starting to show. We didn't talk to each other while there was anyone else around.

'What are we going to do?' she would whisper to me when no one was listening.

But I had no answers. I started to avoid her. I couldn't look at her.

We were still running around the shops, hanging out with the gang. I was still drinking. Still fighting. Still playing music. And behind all of this was the looming worry of the responsibility for another human being. We weren't ready. I didn't grow up at all when I got the news. I just got more scared.

I was scared of facing up to life, as I guess any young man would be. But more than this, I was scared of being responsible for bringing a baby into this world. The same world that had been a painful place for me. No one deserved to go through the kind of life that Kim and I had but here we were bringing an innocent child into a world we didn't really understand.

What were we thinking? We weren't thinking at all it seemed.

We knew we would have to tell our parents but we put it off as long as we could. I thought this was going to be the hardest day of my life but it wasn't really. My parents and Kim's had both come from poor backgrounds. Wild kids regularly got themselves into trouble where we came from. They weren't as shocked as we were. But I could see that same look on Reg's face that I'd seen a lot of times before. I had let him down again.

Instead we listened to what everybody was telling us:

'You're too young to have a baby. You'll never be able to look after a child.'

'You're still kids yourselves. The baby will suffer.'

My mum immediately wanted to adopt the baby. 'Let me look after the wean. I'll give it a good home and you can still see it whenever you like,' she said in her warmest Glaswegian mum voice. I hadn't heard this voice since I was two.

But Kim's mum thought that would be wrong. I agree with her now but probably not for the same reasons as she had. Mum had had enough trouble trying to bring us up. It wouldn't have been fair to do that to any poor unsuspecting baby.

Kim's mum was the next to come up with a plan. 'The way I see fings, this baby, God bless its little heart, should be adopted out. Give the little fing a chance in life. What have you got to offer it? Nuffin'. And it would be too hard on you two young ones if the baby is around.'

Something about the English accent makes me suspicious. It's genetic I think. But it all sounded reasonable at the time.

Without telling any of my family, Kim's mum adopted the baby. This was completely the opposite to what she had said was the best thing to do. She decided the child was never to know who his real parents were. Just for his own good.

I should have been ready to change and become a man and start to deal with the consequences of my actions but instead I returned to life as if it had never happened. Learning nothing and not growing at all.

This was one more thing that I would try to shove to the back of my head, knowing full well that I knew better. The guilt brought another layer of darkness into my life. I had done the wrong thing again.

I don't know if Kim's mum did the right thing at the time or not, but one thing I do know. The world seems to have a way of making things work out. As frightening as it was at the time, it was one of the most important moments in my life.

My son David came into the world on 6 August 1973. It was a time of confusion and fear for me, but from the moment he arrived, he was a beautiful human being and he brought nothing but joy to everyone around him.

I watched his progress from a distance. He wasn't allowed to know who I was. And I tried to pretend not to care. I didn't have a lot to offer him at that time when I look back on things. Apart from Reg – who maybe came along a bit late – my parental role models hadn't really been the best so I have no idea what I would have done had things ended up differently. David spent his childhood without a father. I can never change that or make it up to him. I was allowed to pop in occasionally to see him playing. But I could never get too close. The situation, Kim's mum, and my own fear stopped me getting close to my son. I know now how great that loss was. He needed a dad. If I could go back in time I would spend every minute I could with him.

But you can't go back. You can't live life regretting what was or wasn't. All I can do is go forward and make things right now.

It was only once I became famous that suddenly it appeared to others and myself that I had something to offer him.

I would go over to Kim's mum's house and be introduced: 'David, this is Jim. He's a good friend of the family. Why don't you go and spend the day with him and get to know him a bit.'

It must have been very strange for the young lad. One minute he's playing around the house, next he's going off for the day with his bleary-eyed, leather jacket-wearing uncle. He probably couldn't work out what side of the family I was connected to. Must be the distant Scottish relatives that no one ever spoke about.

As he got older we even started to spend weekends together. This was hard for us. We didn't really know what to say to each other. I tried to make things as easy for him as I could. David was always a gentle boy. He was soft and caring. He made it easy for both of us.

I don't need to say too much more about this time. Not to you guys anyway.

CHAPTER TWENTY-FOUR

you'll hear more if you shut up

By this time, I wanted to leave school and was looking for
work. When I say looking for work, I've got to say I didn't
look very hard. I only needed a little bit of money, enough to get
trashed with my mates. I realised no one was going to give me a
job with a future. Because I had no future. I had no plans.

At school there were supposed to be people who came
around and gave career guidance but they never came near me or
gave me any advice. The only thing I remember anyone telling
me was to leave school as quickly as possible and get a job in a
factory. No talk of university or extra study or anything. Just
get a job. Didn't matter what it was, just get a job. I think the
teachers by this point just wanted me out of their hair and away
from the school, as far away as possible. They'd done all they
could. I was a lost cause.

Reg didn't want me to leave school without getting an
apprenticeship. 'Son, you're going nowhere without a trade. I
don't want you to leave school without one. You need a job to fall
back on when you are ready to settle down.'

He really didn't want me to leave school at all.

'I'm really worried about the way you're turning out, Jim.' I know he'd all but given up on me, but he was still worried.

'I don't want you to be a good-for-nothing like your friends.' I was probably already worse than any of them by that time.

He insisted on making me apply for a few different apprenticeships. I never expected to actually get a reply from anyone but I sent them out anyway to keep him happy. He was a good guy and I owed it to him to at least try to improve myself after all he had given me.

Now, every good boy I knew ... let me just clarify that, I didn't know too many good boys. But the ones I did know wanted to be mechanics or carpenters or the like but I didn't really care. I had no real interest in any job at all. I thought that there was a good chance that I would be working in a factory for the rest of my life. And I didn't know or care how long that life would be. I thought that whatever happened would be out of my control.

But lo and behold, in early 1973 I got one reply to all of my many applications. The letter was from the South Australian Railways. They wanted me to become an apprentice moulder. Now I wasn't really sure what a moulder was, but I was ready to take any offer that made Reg happy.

'Hey Dad, I got an answer to my applications for an apprenticeship,' I announced one night at dinner. 'It's with the South Australian Railways. I'm going to be a moulder.'

'That's so good, son. I'm proud of you. You'll thank me for pushing you into this one day. You mark my words, Jim.'

They seemed to like me at the railways and I got the job. They must have been really desperate. One minute I had no future, the next I had a chance to make my name in the coveted world of metallurgy. I was already staying out all night most nights. And I soon found that I had to pull my head in a little if I was to get through life in this line of work. It involved, among other things, pouring molten metal at about two thousand degrees centigrade and could be very dangerous with shaky hands.

I found, like I did with most things, that with very little effort I was pretty good at it. I might even have a future that would work for me if I made an effort, and I did for a while. Not for long though. Soon I was distracted again by girls, booze, drugs and music. These seemed to be the only things that interested me and the only things that I would make an effort for.

The guys in the foundry liked me and one particularly gnarly old guy took me under his wing and looked after me. His name was Tony Matthews. Tony had been at the foundry longer than anyone else in the place. He was the boss as far as I was concerned. He would take me aside and say things like, 'Come on, young fella. Don't be a stupid bastard all your life. Knuckle down and do your job and life in this place won't be too bad to you. Just pull your bloody head in, would ya? You got to work hard to get ahead in this life. I've bloody worked hard for forty-five years and life is okay for me.'

Was that what I wanted? A lifetime of slaving at a job I didn't like just to be okay? I wasn't sure.

The foundry was huge, broken up into sections. Each section had a different job. Each job played an integral part of the big picture. Casting and shaping brakes and wheels for the trains they were building at the railways. There was constant noise. Sirens to tell you to get out of the way. Sirens to tell you to take a break. Sirens to let you know there was danger and sirens to relax. The whole foundry screamed at me all day. I was constantly looking over my shoulder, waiting for something to fall on me. Sparks exploded from the moulds as metal so hot it flowed like lava from giant buckets was carried across the floor by cranes the size of dinosaurs. Then there would be a deafening bang as the bucket was slammed on the floor to get rid of the waste. A siren would sound, telling everyone to move out of the way as the crane lumbered back to the other end of the floor to be refilled with molten steel and the whole process started again.

Tony pointed out what I needed to know about the foundry to get by. He took me to the front door and showed me where I had to clock in every day. 'It all starts here. Get here on time and the whole bloody day will go a lot smoother for everybody.'

'I know that.'

'Yeah. Well, just remember it. Too many of you young bastards think you can waltz in here whenever it suits you. You bloody well can't, okay?'

'Yeah, yeah.'

'Don't bloody "yeah, yeah" me, just listen and learn.'

'Over here is where we clean up the castings. You won't have to do that much but get a good look at it. You should be able to do every step of this bloody work.'

'Right, Tony.'

'This is Len's office. He's a good bloke. Nice and polite. Not like me but don't think you can pull anything over on him. He sits in that bloody office all bloody day and he sees everything that goes on in this joint.'

'What's he do in there?'

'He runs the bloody place. Aren't you listening to me? You got cloth ears from all that rock-and-bloody-roll you play. That's not real music anyway. So don't get me started on that.'

'I never said anything.'

'Good. Keep it that bloody way. You'll hear more if you shut up a bit.'

'Right.'

This went on through every part of the foundry floor. By the time we got to the other end, I'd forgotten what happened at the start. But Tony would tell me over and over.

He taught me everything he knew about moulding but sometimes I didn't listen close enough. 'Get the bloody hell out of the way you idiot. You might want to kill yourself but I don't want you killing me along with you. I'm going to show you this one more time and if you don't get it right you can fuck off out of this job.'

Of course he was right. One wrong step in the process could cause a mould to blow molten metal back up at you. It was very dangerous.

He would reason with me at times too. 'You know what, Jim? You could be the best apprentice I've ever trained if you buckled down a bit. I like you a lot. I look at you like my own son, so come on. Don't let us both down.'

I could see him tearing up sometimes when he spoke to me. He tried to be really tough but he wasn't. He'd been at this job for most of his life and before he retired he wanted to pass on his wisdom to me.

When it came time to initiate the apprentices I was ready to kill anyone who came near me and so was he. They grabbed all the new guys and painted their balls with some weird paint that burned like hell, but I made it clear that if they came near me with that shit they would end up getting it rammed down their throats.

'You bastards touch my boy and you'll have to deal with me,' Tony roared across the floor. They all laughed at him behind his back but no one was game to take him on head to head. He was a tough old codger and I found out later that they left me alone because my old mate had frightened them off, not me.

We worked together the whole time I was at the railways. He always looked after me, helping me learn new things. If I came in too wasted to work, he helped me out then too. There were sand bins in every section of the building.

'Get yourself in behind that bloody bin and sleep it off you stupid young bastard,' he would say and look at me with that same look of disappointment that I had seen so many times on Reg's face. I was getting used to it by now and really didn't care anymore.

After a couple of hours, he would walk up to the back of the bin and kick my feet shouting, 'Get up boy, here's a cup of coffee for you. You can't sleep all bloody day. We've got work to do here.'

I spent a lot of time behind those bins. By this time, I was going out to the pubs around Adelaide to see bands and chase girls. A lot of those gigs didn't finish until three or four in the morning so it was safer if I did sleep it off. This was as much for his safety as mine. But it worked out well for both of us. I would walk in at seven in the morning, red-eyed and shaky, and he would get me a cup of tea and send me to sleep. I'd wake up just in time for a break and then he would work me like a dog for the rest of the day. I was his prize apprentice and I was a wild boy. I got the feeling he'd been a wild boy like me in his youth and he wanted to help me get through this rough patch in my life. The difference between him and me was this wasn't a rough patch. My life had always been this out of control and it was spinning more and more out of control every day. So he was never going to be able to save me. I was the only one who could save me and I couldn't see that happening.

Some of the older guys in Elizabeth had been dabbling in heroin for quite a while and a few had become real casualties, losing their jobs and cars and even their families. That was bad, but what was worse was that just like in every other aspect of life, whatever the older guys did, the younger guys wanted to do the same. So some of my friends started using heroin.

This particular drug was not seen as cool by the real heavy guys in Elizabeth. You could get drunk out of your mind and beat your girl. Or take acid or speed. Being strung out on speed was all right because you could still fight on it; in fact, it made you want to fight even more. So that was cool. But heroin was wrong. If you did it, you were a fucking junkie. And nobody wanted to be that.

This meant that the guys who were doing heroin kept it on the down low. Because of that a few of my mates were well and truly addicts before I had any idea they were using at all. I was offered it a few times and said no. I don't know if it was good sense or brainwashing from my folks but whatever the reason, it worked, and I always managed to say no to heroin. I used to joke and say, 'I won't take anything I can't fight or fuck on.' But you could probably do both on heroin.

Some of the guys I knew started stealing from friends' cars and homes and it wasn't long before a couple ended up in jail. Over the years I lost a lot of friends to heroin overdoses, and to jails come to think about it. All drugs fucked us up, but this one seemed to do even more damage, and it seemed irreparable so I was scared to try it. This was a good thing but there must have been a better way to learn a lesson than by the death of your friends.

There was another apprentice who worked in our section. He was a quiet young guy and one day he invited me out to his house for a birthday party. So after work I hitchhiked home and got changed and grabbed a few of my mates from Elizabeth. We all took LSD and then headed out for a few drinks while we waited for the drugs to kick in. Then we would head to the party.

By ten o'clock we were mindless and ready to tear the town down. So we decided that we were ready to hit the party and find some girls to keep us company.

We drove up to my workmate's house, thinking he wouldn't be ready for what was coming, but in fact we were the ones who weren't ready for what was coming. We arrived at his house just after ten o'clock and knocked at the door.

'Hi Jim. Great to see you. Come on in. I thought you might not come.'

The mild-mannered young man I worked with was a drag queen in his spare time. And was taking hard drugs and listening to twisted music just like I was listening to. In fact, he played some music I'd never heard before.

As I walked in something was playing that sounded new to me. Not really like anything I had heard before. This was the first time I heard Lou Reed's *Transformer* and in the state I was in this was a life-changing event. Talk about different worlds colliding, his mates and mine were as opposite as you could get. My mates were dressed in denims, ripped and faded. With Adidas sneakers and T-shirts. This was the uniform we all wore so we didn't draw attention to ourselves, every single one of us as unrecognisable to the police as the next.

His mates were as far from us as you could get. Dressed to the nines in sparkling frocks that sent light dancing across the room, drawing your eyes to them. With shoes that were so high they looked fierce, like something we would use as a weapon back in the shops around Elizabeth. They had hair that was teased so much that they looked seven feet tall. And make-up that chiselled their features so they resembled statues. Everything about these guys screamed out, 'Look at me. Look at me. Look at me.'

But we all got on like a house on fire. In fact, we were all so out of it, the house could have been on fire and no one would have noticed. We had a lot more in common than either of us could have imagined. We were all trying to find out who we were in this world. I never looked at that guy the same again.

CHAPTER TWENTY-FIVE

wouldn't be dead for quids

The year 1973 was becoming a good one for me. I was learning about music and life. Every night had potential; it was all up to me to make it happen.

Mick and me would talk twenty or so guys into going to the Apollo Stadium, near the city, to see bands. None of us ever had any money.

'Hey, guys. I reckon if we kick the back door in the bastards could only catch one or two of us at the most.'

Mick and I had worked it out.

'The rest of us just keep running into the hall and mingle with the crowd. It'll be easy.'

'And if we don't like the bands we can leave. It'll cost us nothing.'

'What'll we do if the fucking bouncers catch us?'

'Just act innocent. They've got too much to do. They'll let you go for sure,' Mick told the boys. 'Otherwise belt them and run. What are you, pussies?'

We did this night after night and much to our surprise it never got any harder. We couldn't work it out.

'Maybe they just don't give a fuck. Or maybe they'll be waiting one night and bash our heads in.'

'Na. They don't give a shit,' Mick assured us all. 'Trust me.' We had trusted Mick many a night and it nearly got us killed.

I've got to say some of the best shows I ever saw were for free, after charging over a couple of useless security guys at the Apollo.

I remember one of the many nights that we took acid and ended up outside the stadium. We didn't even know who was playing. We didn't care. If it was bad, we would just walk out and go and start trouble somewhere else.

Bang! We kicked the door in and Mick shouted, 'Let's go.'

I slipped through the grips of an overweight body builder who was moonlighting as a bouncer and I was in. I made it into the middle of the crowd just as the show started. About the same time, coincidentally, as the drugs kicked in.

The room went dark and trumpets rang out. 'Fanfare for the Common Man' washed across the crowd. I felt that I was waiting for the entrance of the Queen, not a rock band. Low bottom end from the PA droned out across the hall, so deep that you couldn't really hear it but felt it in your stomach. Dry ice-created fog came rolling over the amps and cascaded from the edge of the stage like a waterfall onto the audience.

'Wow,' I whispered to myself, trying not to look too gobsmacked. 'This is great, isn't it?' I said, nudging the stranger with the headband who was standing next to me.

'They haven't started yet, man.'

I quickly got a hold of myself. 'Better try and look a bit tough or these hippies will punch holes in my aura.' As if.

I'd never heard anything like it before – or since really. It was Yes in their prime. I wasn't a Yes fan as such. Progressive rock took too much thinking for my liking. But as I stood surrounded by patchouli oil-smelling, sandal-wearing, kaftan-flowing hippies, I came to the conclusion that they were a fantastic band.

'Maybe it's the drugs,' I said to myself. 'Na, could be.' I've got to say, I still like them but they have never sounded quite as good as they did that night. Yeah, it was the drugs.

Everyone else got bored and left to look for more excitement but I stayed with my eyes glued to the stage, taking in everything that was going on between the band.

My eyes were darting between the lights and the PA system. I was watching roadies running across the stage making guitar changes. Subtle set changes between songs seemed seamless. This was the smoke and mirrors that you hear about in showbiz. Because my reality had been enhanced by the drugs or perhaps because the penny dropped for the first time, I saw the communication that was happening on the stage. I was mesmerised.

I think I had to hitchhike home but I didn't care; it was worth it. It seemed there was more to being in a band than just singing.

That year I saw Frank Zappa, T-Rex, Jethro Tull, Black Sabbath and Ike and Tina Turner at the Apollo. Every single show we saw for free.

Frank Zappa played songs that turned my ear to more adventurous music. Watching him play was like watching someone conduct an orchestra. Every move of his hands led every musician into another movement of the song. It was amazing.

Jethro Tull was a band that most of the young guys in Elizabeth liked, mainly because of their gross lyrics about snotters and girls. But we went anyway.

I stood watching what appeared to be cleaners in white overalls sweeping the stage. Only to find that one by one the overalls came off revealing that they were the band. Good trick.

Marc Bolan, who had made amazing music in the early seventies, was completely disillusioned by the time he came to Adelaide. British media had worn him down. It was clear you couldn't be openly gay and be allowed to make music without being driven into the ground. He had an empty, lost look in his eyes when he sang. The best thing he did all night was to bullwhip his guitar. He needed to lash out at something I guess. He died a few years later. I learned that the public and the press don't need to know everything about you or they might turn on you.

Ike and Tina were unbelievable. I fought my way down to the front to get a look at Tina and the girls.

'Excuse me. Coming through. Excuse me. Hey, I said get to fuck out of my way.'

I made it to the front row. I remember being mesmerised by Tina and the Ike-ettes, as any young guy would have been. But while I was in the front row watching the girls I saw this guy in the back of the band driving them all like I'd never seen before. That was Ike Turner. As I watched him I realised how important it was to push a band, and push them really hard. He was a brutal taskmaster and I could see the band jumping at his every gesture. He made the band great. But this same tyrannical behaviour made him a violent partner for Tina. She survived Ike's violence to go on to much bigger things – when he was washed up and good for nothing, Tina was just getting started. I think he should have kept the iron fist for the running of the band.

I learned something from every band I saw. I was like a sponge, soaking in everything I could. This was to become my apprenticeship – not the railways but rock shows all over Adelaide.

We would go and see Fraternity, the Coloured Balls, Billy Thorpe and the Aztecs and anybody else who came through town. But

Billy was the guy I liked the best. He was a rocker. No bullshit. Straight out rock-and-roll. I used to go and watch him at pubs I shouldn't have even been allowed into. Places like the Largs Pier Hotel, one of the wildest and roughest pubs in Australia. I started sneaking in there when I was only sixteen. I'm sure the bouncers knew I was underage but I didn't start trouble and they had their hands too full throwing people out to stop some young guy getting in.

There were no police threatening to take away their licences in those days; it was just jam as many people as you could into a small space and see what happened.

I saw Billy Thorpe in there one night with a whole wall of guitar amps. He was loud as hell but I thought he should have been even louder considering how many guitar amps he had up there. So I tried to speak to one of the roadies.

He was standing, trying to look important in front of a girl he was aiming to impress.

'Hey mate, you busy?'

'What do you think? Do I look busy? Someone's got to run this show,' he said, winking at the chick.

'There's a lot of amps up there. Is that normal?'

He looked a bit annoyed by now. I was obviously cramping his style.

'Fuck, yeah. It is for Billy. He's the man. The loudest guy in the country,' he said to the girl. Almost as if I wasn't there.

'I didn't think they were all turned on.'

Suddenly I had his attention. 'Listen, you little bastard, I've got fucking work to do. What do you want?'

The girl walked away.

'Sorry, I'm in a band too and Billy's a bit of a hero to me. I want to play as loud as him, that's all.'

By this time he knew his chances with the girl were gone but for some reason he started to soften. 'I'll let you into a little secret, son. Everything is not always as it seems. It's show business. Do you understand?'

'So I was right, wasn't I?'

'Look, I can't stand and talk to you all day. This is a show, that's all I'll tell you. Now fuck off and let me work.'

'Thanks, mate. Maybe you can work for me one day.'

I got a smile out of him.

I had worked it out. Billy had a bunch of amps he loved but the others were spares or even just dummies to make the show look bigger. This is something I've seen a million times since that night but Billy was the first. And I thought he was so smart to do that. He did it just to keep the punters guessing.

The Pier was happening. On a lot of nights, I was more entertained by the fights that broke out than the bands that were playing. There was one bouncer I remember very well. They called him the Beast, for obvious reasons; he looked like a refrigerator on legs. I would sit, off my head on whatever I could find, and watch as the Beast threw people through the plate glass windows, the glass smashing and spraying through the air like fireworks, while the music screamed in my ears and the hallucinogenics surged through my brain. It was like being an extra for *A Clockwork Orange*.

Every Friday and Saturday night I seemed to end up at the Pier watching the hardest and best bands that Australia had to offer at the time, playing so loud that my eardrums nearly burst. This was what I called fun, not hanging around the shops fighting and hoping to get laid.

This pub was full of tough blokes who looked like they worked on the wharves during the day. Some of their girls looked just as tough. There were bearded blokes with tattoos, arm in arm with tattooed girls drinking beer. There were handsome young fellows holding beautiful girls with wide eyes and beaming smiles, jiving around the dance floor to the music. I got the feeling that if you looked at the wrong girl for too long you would end up floating next to one of the wharves their boyfriends worked at. You were safe as long as you showed respect for the locals.

They were a strange mix of people but everyone seemed to watch out for each other and I liked that. One of the people that I met in the front bar of the Pier was a guy called Dennis O'Toole, who I had met many years earlier at the party where we first met Reg's family. Tooley, as we call him, has been a friend ever since we reacquainted ourselves at the Pier. He was a gentle soul but could fight with the best of them if he had to and he ended up working as a roadie for Cold Chisel and Fraternity when I joined them.

That pub became my home ground and soon I became friends with many of the regulars. By the time I was sixteen and a half I even ended up on a first name basis with the Beast.

'Hey, Beast. What's it like in there tonight?'

'It's really packed. In you go, have a good night.'

'Thanks, mate.'

'Hey. Hey.'

I thought for a minute I was getting stopped. 'Yeah, what is it?'

'It's Bob.'

'Pardon me?'

'It's Bob. Bob McKinnon. That's me name. Call me Bob.'

'Er, right. Thanks mate, er Beast, er Bob. Thanks.'

I felt even safer in the bar now. On many a night I ended up drinking until sun-up, on the jetty across the road from the pub with a bunch of mates and, if we were lucky, a few beautiful girls who were too pissed to go home or they'd get a hiding from their dads. We'd sit and look out to sea, thinking how lucky we were to be alive.

'Wouldn't be dead for quids,' Tooley would say. 'I wonder what the poor people are doing while we get to sit out here. Working probably, the poor suckers.'

He be laughing out loud. He thought he was really funny. 'We are the luckiest people alive. Look where we are. We got the water underneath us. A bunch of good mates and the pier to look at in the distance. Oh yeah and of course you girls are with us too.' Tooley seemed to care more about his mates than the girls but he was always a gentleman.

We'd sit there until the sun came up and then pile into a car and head for home. I'd be ready to sleep or keep partying with the girls but the others would head to the docks to work.

The Pier was my home away from home for many years after that. And even now, when I go back there I think about those days, when we were young and life was only about having something to drink and a pretty girl on your arm and a few mates ready to help you take on the world. And we did take it on, again and again. It became the place I learned about friendship and music. About love and loss. The Pier was our home. But the whole of Adelaide was our playground and we played hard.

One night we stood outside Memorial Drive in Adelaide. This venue was built for tennis but it became one of the great places to see a big band in Australia. I played there many times with Cold Chisel and as a solo performer and I always loved it. But this night we listened as Led Zeppelin played 'Rock and Roll' so loud that even outside the venue it was rocking. The crowd broke down the fence and thousands of punters who had no money got in for free. I remember being overjoyed at the chance to see them. Of the five thousand punters who crashed the fence I was the only one who got caught. I remember being dragged away to a paddy wagon as the sound of 'Dazed and Confused' drifted through the warm night air. They sounded good that night. And even from the back of a moving police car, I was happy to hear them.

Another night I stood outside and listened as the Rolling Stones played the same venue. I was wishing I could get in and see Mick and Keith do their thing. But it didn't really matter. I was happy to stand outside with the crowds or break in if I got the chance. As it happened, the Stones didn't sound so great that night. So I didn't feel too bad.

Our lives were like a Rolling Stones concert in a lot of ways. Some nights were great, some were bad. It depended on the night, the drugs and the company we kept. But it was all ours for the taking.

---

do you want to join our band?

It was about this time that I was visited by a roadie named Michael. 'Are you John Swan's young brother?'

'Why, who the fuck's asking?'

'My name's Michael. I work as a roadie for a new band that's starting up.'

'What, you mean this band has someone to carry their gear?' I was impressed but I didn't let on to him.

'Yeah, anyway we're looking for a singer.'

'You're in the band, are you?'

'Er, no. I mean they're looking for a singer.'

'Why didn't they come and ask me themselves?'

'Er. I live in Elizabeth and they don't. So we thought it would be easier if –'

'Yeah, yeah, I get it. I'm just giving you a hard time.'

'Look, I want you to know this up front. They really wanted your brother John to sing but he didn't even get back to them. I told them I heard he had a brother who sang pretty good.'

'That's great, so I'm second choice, am I?'

'Er, yeah. Are you interested in coming down for a jam? I could take you.'

'I'll get there myself if I'm going. Are they any good?'

'Yeah, listen man, they are great. It's a blues band and the guitar player is really fucking good. This young guy from Alice Springs is awesome. They're rehearsing on Saturday in the city if you want to go.'

When he called me man, I thought twice about it. 'What is he, some kind of fucking hippie?' I said to myself. But the idea of actually joining a band who were even remotely good appealed to me.

'Okay, man. I'll see you there.' I gave him a peace sign and walked away.

John was making quite a bit of money around the Adelaide scene at the time, so he didn't even consider this band. They were a bunch of guys with no experience. In fact, the only guy John knew was the piano player, a guy named Don Walker. He and Don had played together in an Adelaide blues band named Queen.

Don told me later that he had auditioned for a band in Adelaide and they were all very cool and hardly spoke to him. That is, except John. He said he was warm and tried to make it as easy as possible for him. Don also told me that he thought John was an amazing singer, and he figured if I was half as good as him I might be okay.

I'd never been around a band with a roadie before. Every band I'd been a part of carried their own gear and did everything themselves. Only big bands or overseas bands had roadies, so this was very impressive. Even if he was a hippie. I found out later that Michael was just a mate of the band, but he went on to become Cold Chisel's first roadie. He worked with us for a long time until we drove him crazy and he left. We seemed to do that to a lot of people; they'd come work with us for a while and then get burned out and need to leave.

Anyway, he was the guy who told Don that John had a young brother who also sang. As he had never heard me sing, he couldn't vouch for how good I'd be but he could find me and see if I wanted to audition.

I'd never tried out for a band before. My other bands I just walked into. Friends of friends or something like that, so it was always easy. This seemed more difficult and I wondered if I could be bothered. I didn't want to waste my time trying out for a bunch of dorks and I didn't want to go and be out of my depth. I didn't take rejection very well and would probably swing at them if they pissed me off. So I was a bit hesitant to go. I think I really wanted to try but needed some prodding.

I ran it past my mates at the shops. 'What do you think, guys? Should I have a look?'

'Just give it a go, mate. If they stink you can just tell them to get lost. Who needs 'em?' Mick said, not taking it that seriously.

This was true. I could just walk away.

'If things get bad you can always belt one of them. That'd be fun,' Mick laughed. 'I'll come with you and we could belt them all.'

The idea of taking a trip to the city alone appealed to me. Might be a chance to get away from Elizabeth. If things worked out, maybe for good. I'd go and see what it was like.

So I got the address of the place and the next Saturday I went to town. I turned up at the address and found myself at the Women's Liberation Centre. This was where they were rehearsing. It was in the middle of Adelaide and although I thought their choice of venue sounded more than a little strange,

I'd give it a try. Maybe one of their friends was a woman? I didn't know what women's lib meant at all. I only knew my mum had liberated herself from my dad but that was it. I had no idea what a feminist was. We didn't have them back in Cowcaddens, I don't think.

I was terrified by the time I walked in. They didn't look like feminists. The first guy I saw had thick curly hair that stuck out like an afro, bushy eyebrows and a big mouth. Ian Moss was a young guitarist from Alice Springs who didn't wear shoes and didn't talk at all. He seemed nice enough. Maybe they didn't speak English in Alice. He didn't really look at me. He kept his eyes down or on his guitar. Which was fine with me. What would he be looking at me for unless he wanted trouble?

Les Kaczmarek stood nearby, a young Polish bass player who had the best, shiniest equipment I had ever seen. He had long light brown hair and a pretty face. He was more self-assured than Ian and I thought he might run the show. If he didn't run it, he did a good job pretending that he did. He tried to make me comfortable right away. Les, I soon found out, also liked a drink and I think he needed a drinking partner in the band. The others were very straight.

There was another guy standing around who turned out to be the drummer. I really didn't get to know him as he was on his way out of the band as I was coming in. I'm sorry to say I don't even remember his name.

Then there was Don Walker – a bearded university student who looked way too intelligent to want to play rock. He was quiet and reserved. This made me suspicious of him immediately. I didn't trust quiet people and I didn't like university students. Quiet people were normally up to something where I came from.

When I say I didn't like university students, I didn't really know any. If they were that smart, they weren't hanging around the Elizabeth shops fighting. I thought that anyone who actually went to university was a spoilt rich kid with more dollars than sense. This was some sort of reverse snobbery, probably brought on by the fact that we had nothing for our whole lives and Mum resented anybody who got a break or had more than us. Everyone had more than us so she hated everyone. I think I got this wonderful trait from her. She didn't trust anyone. She didn't even trust us. And she taught us well – so well that we didn't trust her either.

I used to go and play football at the private schools when I was younger and I thought they were all pussies. We always beat them on and off the field and when it came to university students, the only ones I'd met were at university dances that we crashed while we were drunk and looking for trouble or chicks. In reality I was afraid of anyone who might be smarter or better than me.

Anyway, I was more than a little guarded with Don at the start but I soon worked out that he, in fact, ran the band. He was the one I was going to have to impress and I wasn't sure how to go about it. As it happened, I didn't have to. Don was a good guy from day one and all he wanted in the band was a good singer. How they ended up with me I'll never know.

'Shall we do a few songs,' Don said, rubbing his hands together.

'Sure. What do you want to do?' I was really worried.

'What about a Free song?' Ian piped up.

'Wow, I like this guy,' I said to myself.

'Do you know "The Stealer"?'

'Yeah. I think I know that one.' It was my favourite song at the time and I knew all the words like the back of my hand.

We did the song and there was an awkward silence.

'Yeah that was great. Give us some time to have a chat, would you?' Don said softly.

'Yeah well, just let me know. I'm fine if you don't want me. I got lots of things to do.' I started walking out the door.

'You want to just stay there a minute and we'll just have a quick talk over in the corner?'

I was getting defensive. 'You sure? I'll get to fuck out of your way if you want.'

'No, just wait.'

They went to a corner to discuss how I sounded. In the meantime, I stayed on the other side of the room, scowling at them. Pretending I didn't want the gig anyway.

Les was the first to speak. 'So yeah. We like what you do. Do you want to join our band?'

Now to tell you the truth I'd never sung with a band who could actually play that well. This band owned their own gear. They knew what they were doing. Ian was a great guitarist even in those early days. When they told me that Don was a songwriter, that was it. They had me. I'd never been in a band with someone who wrote songs before.

I acted as cool as I could and said, 'I'll give it a go and we'll see, eh?'

But inside I was really excited. They weren't the hardest band I'd ever heard but I was sure we could change that with a bit of pushing and shoving. Eventually I would jump all over these poor guys, fuelled by booze and cheap speed, making them play louder, harder and faster every night but that would come later. They didn't know what they were in for.

I joined the band and, like I said, the drummer was on his way out. So we were immediately talking about who to get to replace him. My brother John, besides being a great singer, was a great drummer too. I told you before John could do anything he put his mind to. In fact, at that time John was a drummer more than a singer. So I went to see him.

'John, the band I've joined needs a drummer. Got any ideas?'

'I didn't want to sing with them so I'm certainly not drumming for them,' he joked.

'Yeah, yeah, yeah. Do you know any drummers that might be good enough to try out?'

John didn't have to think for long. 'I met this English guy called Steve at a party. He plays really well. He might do it.'

Steve Prestwich had been in a band called Ice with Michael Smith, the guy who played bass in Tarkus, who went on to have a career as a music journalist. And Michael had also told me how good Steve was. I knew a couple of Steve's brothers and they were wild. As wild as me if not wilder. So I wasn't sure how we'd get on but we got in touch and Steve came down and tried out.

He was a great drummer. He was a bit cool and acted like he didn't really want to be in this kind of band. Ice had played covers of Yes songs and we were just a simple blues band. But he sounded great playing with the band so we asked him to join.

Steve ended up being one of my favourite people of all time. We toured the world together making music, laughing and drinking and fighting with each other, until he died a few years ago. What a loss.

Anyway, basically we had the band together and worked in that hall every weekend for months, trying to come up with a set of songs that we could play live, if we ever got out of the rehearsal hall. We all got on well and working with the guys was something I looked forward to. I would get out of Elizabeth and get to make music with a bunch of guys who played really well. Eventually we got ourselves a gig. It was in the local Polish Club. I'm sure we only got it because Les's dad put some pressure on them.

Now we had to find a name for ourselves, something that would be cool and let people know what we were about. We came up with the name Orange, a name that was not cool and didn't give any insight to where the band was coming from. It was a shit name. Maybe we weren't that good a band either, so the name probably fitted us. We got the name from a Jeff Beck album we liked – it wasn't called Orange but had a picture of one on the cover. This is still one of my favourite albums to this day. We were playing a couple of songs off the album in our very first set so it seemed like a good idea at the time.

The gig was not the best gig I'd ever been to. In fact, there were times when we were playing I could see members of the audience yawning and looking for something else to do. I'm sure I heard them whispering to each other in Polish, 'Let's get the fuck out of here.'

But my Polish wasn't that good so I could've been wrong. We played and got paid our very small fee and left thinking we were the best band ever.

It was great to get out of the rehearsal hall and into a place where people were watching us. Mind you, I think the only people who watched us were just so drunk they couldn't move.

I don't know if it was because of the Polish gig. I doubt it. But pretty soon we were offered another show, this time at Gawler Trotting Track just north of Elizabeth. We knew we would need a better name than Orange, so we went through our song list to see if anything stood out. By this time, we had two original songs. One was called 'Sorbonne Fender Chrome'. That was too long to be a name and even we didn't know what it meant. The other was a song called 'Cold Chisel'. This song had nothing to do with cold chisels and I didn't know what it was about either, but it was shorter than the last, and sounded remotely like a rock band's name. All the bands we liked were called Led Zeppelin or Deep Purple or something like that so Cold Chisel had a rock ring to it.

Anyway we would change it later when we thought of something better. That never happened. By the time we thought about it again the name had stuck and we couldn't change it. We were Cold Chisel for better or for worse.

The gig in Gawler was forgettable too. The Super Rock Open Air Festival went off with a whimper. It would have been busier if they let the horses come to the show. The stage was on the back of a truck and we would have been more successful if we drove it around until we found an audience. Not many people turned up and at a guess I'd say that the promoter did his dough. Not that we were being paid very much. Bullett were the headliners and no one really cared that much about them. Well, not enough to come to Gawler anyway. So we were hardly noticed. I've heard people say since that they saw potential in us back then but I think they were making it up. We were the only ones who saw any potential in us for many years after that. There are photos floating around from that gig; we look like kids, probably because we were.

The best thing that came from the show was that one of the members of Bullett decided we were gullible enough to buy a PA he had piled up in his garage collecting dust. He was right. We dived at the chance to own our own sound system. It sounded like a steal to us. We quickly paid him and left before he could change his mind. It wasn't great but it gave us the freedom to play shows all over the country. Not big shows but our own shows. We later found out that half of the speaker boxes didn't have speakers in them, but by then the guy who sold it to us had left town. He had ripped us off but we didn't care, it was ours and we could take it anywhere we wanted. Once we owned our own speakers we were ready to hit the road.

CHAPTER TWENTY-SEVEN

I was never coming back

I was still hanging around the Elizabeth shops with the gang. Drinking way too much and taking drugs four or five nights a week, while working days at the railways. When I say working days, I was sleeping at least half of the morning and recovering the other half. I was pouring molten metal during the day and tearing Adelaide apart by night. And singing in the band whenever we could get together.

Life at the railways was going downhill. Not the work really. I could cope with that once I'd straightened up. But actually wanting to be there was getting more difficult. I had known from the start that moulding wasn't my calling, but by this point it was starting to become an anchor around my neck.

If I wanted to stay out all night watching bands, I couldn't turn up for work. If I didn't turn up for work, I was in trouble and I had no money. Sooner or later I would have to make a choice between work and music.

There were more girls than I can remember. And more nights I couldn't remember. The band was getting better with every rehearsal and I was getting more and more out of control with every day that passed. I was living the rock-and-roll lifestyle and we had only done two gigs. I wanted to live fast and die young and leave a good-looking corpse, but surely I needed to make a record before that. Besides, dying seemed to be a much harder thing to do than I thought. It was going to take a long time and I would probably leave a trail of destruction in my wake. Even back then I would sit and look at myself in the mirror some nights and wonder what it would take to kill me. How much could I take before I reached breaking point? Maybe I had already passed that point years before.

I was finding it harder and harder to get up for work every day and it was getting more and more dangerous while I was there. It was an accident waiting to happen. Something had to give.

One day Don said to us all, 'I need to tell you blokes something important.'

We all sat around listening.

'I'm taking a year off to finish my master's degree at Armidale University.'

'What the fuck are we going to do?' I thought to myself.

Then one of the band had a brainwave. 'Why don't we go to Armidale and while Don's at university we can still get together and write some songs.'

'I'm going to be working a hell of a lot, but yeah, we could get together I guess,' Don said hesitantly.

But we had already decided. We were going to Armidale.

'We're coming with you, Don.' The rest of us by this time saw Don as the leader. He must have thought we were like puppies, following him around.

'Are you sure, guys? I'll be back in a year. You guys could just keep –'

'No, we're coming with you.' I cut him off mid-sentence. It was a done deal. The idea of leaving Adelaide appealed to me. In fact, I would have left right that moment if I could have. 'I'm ready. When do we leave?'

Don was the first to leave. He flew to Armidale to get ready for university. We were going to follow in the truck a little later.

But first I had to quit my job at the railways. I went in and talked to old Tony. 'Tony, I'm not good at this. I can't do it anymore. Music is what I want to do.'

'Don't be a bloody larrikin all your life, Jim. You've got a bloody good job here. If you just knuckle down a bit and do some bloody work, you could end up as the boss of the floor like me.'

I looked at Tony. He was a broken, tired, old man. Every day I worked with him I heard him complain about how bad his back was and how damaged his lungs were from smoke and gas. He had a coughing fit every time he laughed but he'd just light up another fag and keep working. This was not what I wanted.

'I'd love to do that, Tony, but I'm not as good as you,' I lied.

'Don't be a bloody idiot. You're potentially as good as I am or even better.' He was lying too. 'All you've got to do is keep your bloody head down and don't cause so much trouble. Your problem is that bloody boogie-woogie music you listen to. It's all just a load of rubbish, lad. This here is a real bloody job. Not prancing around the bloody stage in your bloody tight jeans. That's not a job for a man.'

'I've got to quit, Tony. We're moving interstate. You wait and see. We're going to be a big band.'

'Yeah, yeah, and I'm the fucking Prime Minister. You're a bloody idiot.' Tony's eyes were watering as he walked away. He hardly talked to me again. I hadn't lived up to his expectations.

Next I had to tell Reg. He wouldn't be happy either. I went to Mum and Reg's house in Smithfield, just on the outskirts of Elizabeth, to let him know.

'Dad, I'm quitting the railways and moving to Armidale with the band.'

'Oh Jim, son, have you thought about this at all? You can't run away from everything in life, mate. You have to settle down and finish your apprenticeship. Then you can do whatever you want. And you'll still have something to fall back on if it doesn't work out.'

But if I was going to fall, I didn't want a safety net. It was do or die for me.

'You're an eejit, Jim. You had a chance tae dae somethin' with yer life but no, you just want tae run away like yer dad. Off ye go then.' Mum never approved of anything.

Now I could drink and party all night and get paid for it. Or that was the theory. In fact, it appeared to me that the more I partied the more people liked me. And the harder rock-and-roll bands went, the bigger they would get. I'd read about them. That's what I was going to do. Go hard.

This was what I had dreamed about when I sat on the pier at Semaphore as a child, looking out to sea. This was what I had dreamed about listening to the rhythm of the train as I escaped my home to the sea. This was what I had dreamed about when I was hiding in the paddock across from our house. This was what I had wanted when we hid in the cupboards crying, trying to drown out the sounds of people fighting in our home. This was everything I had wanted for as long as I could remember. I was leaving and I was never coming back. I would miss my brothers and sisters but they had to save themselves, I couldn't help them. I'd made it this far and I'd be fucked if I was going to die in

Elizabeth. If Cold Chisel hadn't come along I would have hitched a ride in a truck or jumped on a freight train or walked if I had to, but I would have left somehow.

I'm going to take this denim jacket with me. I reckon it'll be cold up there. I know it's not mine but I like it. Anyway, fuck it. John won't miss it. He left. If it's still here he obviously doesn't want it. I doubt he even knows he had one. He left it with the rest of the rubbish. The shit he didn't want to see anymore. I was part of that rubbish, now that I think of it. So were the rest of the family. I don't blame him. I don't want to see him or any of this again either.

Even if I didn't listen I could hear Mum shouting at Reg while I packed. That voice that sounded like an open razor, slashing everything it came close to.

Mum's house held a lot of secrets. It always looked so clean. Everything she didn't want to see she swept under the carpet and pretended it didn't exist. Or she burned it. Everything that ever caused her pain. The past, our childhoods, Dad, the mistakes we all made. Pushed into a pile somewhere and burned. If she didn't see it, it never happened.

I sang to myself to block out the sounds of the house. I couldn't sing loud enough. This time I was leaving before I got thrown away again. The truck would be here soon. I was just about packed. I didn't have much. Fuck it, I didn't need much. I would go out to the front of the house and wait for the band to arrive. The sooner I was out of here the better.

Yeah. I'm taking this denim jacket with me.

I climbed into the back of the band's truck. It was an old Tip Top baker's truck that had done way too many miles delivering bread to be carrying a band's equipment all over the country. It didn't look very flash but I had a feeling it would get us to where we were going. There were no lights in the back. I could see the outline of the guys sitting around in the dark. I threw my bag on top of the gear and sat down on the floor.

Steve was as happy to get out of there as me. He was singing at the top of his voice in his broad Liverpudlian accent, prodding Ian, trying to get him to join in. Ian sat quietly, looking down. He was always quiet. I knew this wasn't the first place he'd left behind and I got the feeling he felt all right anywhere. Les, on the other hand, looked worried. Like he really wasn't ready to leave the safety of his mum and dad's home.

A strange sense of freedom came over me. It was just the band and Michael the roadie and me. No family, no friends. A new start. Michael shut the door; suddenly it was pitch black. I felt around for the bottle of cheap whisky I had in my bag and pulled it out. Opened it up and closed my eyes and breathed in. Tilted my head back and swallowed down as much as I could without throwing up. It tasted like fire. As we left Elizabeth I wanted to feel sad but I didn't. I wasn't scared anymore. In fact, I felt nothing at all.

EPILOGUE

———

Another thing just before I go.

Mum left Reg for Ray, who she has lived with ever since. Reg moved back into his mum and dad's house, alone, except for the ghosts of his childhood and memories of the Port in its heyday, when life was good and people didn't hurt one another.

Even though Mum left Reg, us kids couldn't leave him. He was our dad. But as we grew older Mum and he grew further apart until I don't think she could stand the sight of him. I know that they only got together to save us but we had prayed that they would be happy too. I guess that was too much to hope for.

Although we stayed in touch, we didn't see him enough. We lived in another state, so he was essentially alone and I think he might have been happier that way. I know he missed us but I don't think he missed that pterodactyl voice telling him what to do.

Many years later, about forty or so, as he got older he became sicker and sicker until he could no longer live alone and we had to move him out of his home and into a nursing home. He didn't want to go, but the house was falling down around him. He was a hoarder and had kept every scrap of paper and piece of junk that reminded him of the old days. He even kept scrapbooks about my career. I know he was proud of me and happy for me.

So the day came when we had to move him out of the home he was born in, the home he grew up in. As he drove to the nursing home I hope he got a final glimpse of the river where he had spent his childhood, the river he shared with me. He died peacefully in hospital, talking to ghosts he saw in his room. He told us they were all with him, waiting to take him over to the other side. Grandpa and Grandma and his Aunty Dorrie and probably that Red Indian that watched over him too. And I believe him. If anyone was going to be helped into the afterworld, it was Reg.

About six months after his death we got a notice from a lawyer in Adelaide. Reg had organised to sell his house and anything else he owned and had left his insurance money to us kids. Even in death he was there to save us. It wasn't a lot of money but this was treasure to me. Pure unadulterated love. What a guy. What a fine example he was to me in life and in death.

I didn't know what had happened to the piano. I thought after they split up maybe Mum had got rid of it, or burned it to spite him. But not long ago, I was visiting my youngest sister, Lisa, and there in the corner of her dining room was an old-looking piano. It was beaten up and looked the worse for wear but I recognised it immediately. It was Reg's old piano, the one he played at home. I felt a warmth come over me. It was like seeing an old, old friend.

I asked Lisa, 'Where did you find it?'

'It was in a corner of Grandma's house. I found it there after Dad died.'

I had a lump in my throat as soon as I saw it again. Lisa's dining room looked a little crowded. She'd had to squeeze it in.

'I couldn't leave it there alone. The house was falling down on top of it.'

'Do any of you play it?' I asked and opened up the lid and played a chord. It sounded completely out of tune, just like when Dad played it. I just stood for a second, unable to talk.

Lisa must have sensed that I was nearly in tears. Out of the blue she said to me, 'Would you like to have it, Jim? I'm sure Dad would be happy if it was getting played a bit.'

'I would love it,' I said quietly.

I'm having it moved to my house and then I'm going to finally take the piano lessons that he offered to give me so many years ago. And whenever I play it he will be there with me.

Mum and Ray live on the Central Coast of New South Wales. They are as happy as my mum can be. Ray's a good man. The life Mum was dealt is not what she wanted but at least after meeting Ray she has had less heartache. Mum still moved around a lot for a while there. She has a bit of a restless spirit, we all have. She has moved in to her own house now, with Ray. Lisa and her family live upstairs and try to keep an eye out to make sure she's okay. I haven't heard her talk about prowlers for a long time so I hope the bastards have left her alone so she can get some peace.

She doesn't talk about my dad at all and she doesn't talk about Reg either. If we accidentally mention either of them in front of her the conversation abruptly stops. 'Sorry, were you talking to me?'

It's like that life never happened.

Like I said at the beginning of this book, I don't blame her or Dad for anything. Life is what it is, and we all do the best with what we have. I have great memories of my dad and I try not to dwell on the bad stuff. I have fantastic memories of Mum too. I still remember that for the first years of my life, the only time I felt safe was in Mum's arms. I try to just think about that. The rest doesn't matter.

My mum was tough and survived a life that would have made most people throw in the towel. I like to think I got my ability to stick it through really tough times from her. She is soft and gentle too. She used to cry very easily and was always the first person who opened her door to help people, even when it meant she suffered for it. She would give away half of all she had to help anyone. I like to think that I got my generosity of spirit from her.

I look at pictures of Mum now. Everyone says I look like her. As a child I always thought she was the most beautiful person in the world. Children see people the way they really are, I think. So I was right, she is beautiful.

Dad died of emphysema in hospital in Geelong. After running all his life he had fear in his eyes as he gasped for his last breath. Life isn't fair. He came back to see us years earlier, a long time after he left us, and we had a chance to sort through some of what happened in our lives. Not all of it, but I hope enough for him to rest in peace. He was a good man. He taught me to make the best of what you have. He didn't want too much, just peace and quiet and to be able to sit and watch television with his dog. Dad also taught me not to brag about anything. He was a quiet assassin, the quiet one in a room who should not be taken lightly. He could fight and he had stamina. I got my stamina from him. I'll tell you more about my dad in the next book.

I got a lot of bad traits from both of them too, but hey, you have to take the bad with the good.

I learned about love from my family, especially my siblings. That's all we had, and it helped us through some horrible times. These days we don't talk enough and we don't see the love as much as we used to when it was the only thing there. But I know it is still there and I want to thank them all for helping me survive the life we shared.

We all have lives of our own and other people in those lives to share the time with. But those days growing up made me who I am, and I'm thankful that I went through them with my brothers and sisters, because I like who I am now. It took me a long time to get to this place but I made it. For all the sad things I've remembered in this book there are a thousand other moments that made me smile. When we thought we had nothing, we had each other.

I had a huge career with Cold Chisel, selling millions of records. During that time with the band I met Jane, the girl of my dreams. The one person in the world who could eventually make me feel safe. Jane is the most beautiful girl I have ever seen and the most important person in my life. I remember the minute I saw her. She took my breath away. I loved her then, I love her now, and I will love her forever. We have a beautiful family that is still growing, and these days, life is good.

The chip I had on my shoulder that had weighed me down for years became an attribute when I started writing songs. 'You've Got Nothing I Want' came from a young guy who had so many doors slammed in his face that he felt like the Avon lady. 'No Second Prize' came directly from my need to win at all costs. There was no other plan for me – it was sink or sing. And singing 'Working Class Man' was a match made in heaven for me. I wouldn't put anyone else through my life, but fuck it, I survived.

I went on to have a career as a solo performer that included selling as many, if not more, records than Cold Chisel, and having so many platinum albums I ran out of walls to hang them on. So I built more walls and eventually I worked out that walls and awards weren't going to make me happy. I was going to have to look longer and harder at myself, even if it hurt. My battle with my past and the scars that it left on me has been the cause of a life that was a roller-coaster of emotions, from great highs to unspeakable lows. Along the way I have laughed and loved, lived and lost. But I have always tried. I have tried to break the cycle that my family has been caught in. I've tried to hurt as few people as I could in this wild life I have lived. I've tried be a good man but the journey has not been easy for me or the ones I love the most. And I know that I have wounded many people along the way. I never meant to. I try every day now to pick up the broken pieces of my life and make a better person of myself.

I want people to read this because I know there are other people out there, just like me. People who think they are alone in life and that their cards have been dealt and that there is nothing they can do to change anything. That's how I felt too for a long, long time. I nearly killed myself because of it. But now I know there's always time for change and there's always a better path. You just have to look for it.

This book was my first real step in looking for hope.

Peace and love

Jimmy

ACKNOWLEDGMENTS

How I became Jimmy Barnes is a bit of a long story. In fact, it's such a long story that I've had to write two books to tell the whole thing. This book is the story of what shaped my life. The good, the bad and the very, very ugly. It's the book I had to write first if I was going to make any sense of what was to come. Everything I am is because of the things that I talk about in this first book. In the second book I will try to tell you about how all this early stuff shaped what came later – the rock'n'roll years.

It wasn't easy to write. There's a lot of my past that I wanted to push out of my memory and never see again. But I couldn't. I tried to drown my past in every possible way, but as long as it was festering inside me I could never really move on. My childhood affected every step I took over the rest of my life. It twisted the way I thought and the way I interacted with normal human beings. Eventually I realised that these wounds needed to be brought out in the open and aired if I ever wanted them to heal.

So I started trying to write things down. My first attempt was actually back in the early nineties. At the time I'd almost gone broke and it had me wondering what I was going to do with my life. I seemed to be on a downhill slide. So I started to write my story, not really knowing what I was trying to achieve. I thought that maybe I could skim across the surface of my past, dealing with as little as possible, and then it would stop haunting me.

I'd written about thirty thousand words by the time we moved to France in 1994. Moving away from Australia brought me a short period of relief. My past – like everything else – seemed a long way away and my writing slowed down. My computer sat on the bookshelf collecting dust until one day we were robbed and the computer was gone. I hadn't backed anything up or written anything down, so my first attempt at writing this book ended there.

I didn't try to write it again until about the year 2000. Everything I wrote that time was twisted by copious amounts of drinking and all the drugs I was taking. I still have that stuff somewhere and some of it's almost funny, but there's nothing in that version about the real issues. I actually can't bear to read it now. I skirted around everything and made light of the worst moments of my life. Once again I got to around thirty thousand words and came to a brick wall.

Eventually I realised that I was never going to be able to write this story until I faced up to a lot of things. It then took me many years of therapy, battling alcoholism, drug dependence and guilt, to see some light at the end of the tunnel. I'd seen that light before, by the way. In the past it always turned out to be a freight train coming to run me into the ground, but this time I think things have changed for good.

I remember the exact moment when things changed. It was about eighteen months ago. I was sitting in a hotel room somewhere in the middle of a tour. I'd watched every movie on the movie channels except one. It was a dark South Australian murder story called *Snowtown*.

I was suddenly dragged back to my childhood. Don't get me wrong, we weren't serial killers – well, not that I know of anyway. But everything in this movie looked like where I grew up. It looked like our street. In fact, it looked like our house. The floodgates opened and I couldn't hold back the past any longer. It just washed all over me. So I began to write. I really didn't lift my head again until I had well over a hundred thousand words. Suddenly a year was gone and I'd written down most of the stuff that I'd been running away from for most of my life. I felt at peace for the first time since my earliest memories of being a little boy back in Glasgow.

One day I was talking to a mate of mine, Neil Finn, and he asked me, 'So, what are you going to call your book?'

At that stage I had no idea, but if you've ever heard Neil's songs you'll know that he's very good at painting a picture in just a few words. Anyway, he said, 'You'd have to call it *Working Class Boy*, wouldn't you?'

I thought, 'Shit, I wish I'd come up with that!'

The name stuck from then on but apart from that one bit of help from Neil it's entirely my story. It's a story that I had to write on my own – the story of a working class lad from Glasgow who grew up in the northern suburbs of Adelaide where things definitely weren't pretty.

This book would not have been possible without the love and understanding of my family. My wife and children have watched me work my way through this stuff long before I even knew I had stuff to work through. They were there with me when I was at my highest, and believe me I was high. And when I hit my lowest they were there to reach out and help me up. They laughed with me and at me, and cried with me.

I sat and read parts of this to my two dogs, Snoop Dog and Oliver, when I was too ashamed to read it to anyone else. Thanks boys.

Thanks to Mum, Dad, Reg and my siblings. Our lives were made bearable by having each other. Without you guys I couldn't have made it through. Thanks for sharing my joy and my pain.

I know that life is full of lessons to be learned and my children will have to learn their own but I hope I have broken the cycle of shame and fear that plagued my childhood. I know their lessons won't be as hard as mine. So don't be afraid. Go out and live, laugh and love. Life is good.

I'd like to thank John Watson for being my manager, a great friend and an even better sounding board as I wrote this. You helped me make sense of my ramblings.

Thanks to Andrea McNamara for getting me started, Helen Littleton and Nicola Robinson for pointing me in the right direction, even when I didn't want to go that way, and Scott Forbes for reminding me how to speak Glaswegian.

Now that I have made some sense of this stage of my life, I truly believe that I will be better equipped to tackle my next book: the years I spent on the road making music and building a family.

There were times throughout my life when I didn't think I was going to make it. But I am so glad that I did. You have to be able to hold your head up high and say, 'Fuck it, I made some big mistakes, but everybody does. I can live with mine.'